FOREWORD

The first edition of Legislation on Coastal State Requirements for Foreign Fishing was published in 1981. A revised version, which included more information on conditions contained in access agreements, was prepared shortly after the opening for signature of the United Nations Convention on the Law of the Sea in Jamaica at the end of 1982. Developments over the course of the two years since the publication of the first revised version have been significant, if not dramatic. The period, in fact, has been one of consolidation of the developments and trends of the previous years. The United Nations Convention on the Law of the Sea closed for signature in December 1984, having by that time attracted a total of 159 signatories. The number of ratifications now stands at 25, some 35 short of the total needed to bring the Convention into force. It is, however, evidence of a broad-based consolidation of acceptance of the Convention, and a desire to achieve a balanced participation rather than pushing for the earliest date of entry into force. In the area of coastal state practice, the predominant sense is again one of consolidation of trends and practices already established. Perhaps the most significant of these trends are the strengthening of movements for the harmonization of fisheries regimes, the development of regional approaches towards the licensing and control of foreign fishing operations, and the increasing importance being accorded by coastal states to the concept of flag state responsibility for ensuring compliance by its vessels with the provisions of access agreements and coastal state laws, and the search for practical ways of implementing that concept. In this area, the South Pacific nations seem once again to be in the vanguard of developments.

These developments, plus the fact that the first two editions of Coastal State Requirements are now out of print, have led us to bring out this second revised edition. The publication includes an updated analysis of coastal state policies and requirements with respect to foreign fishing and a series of tables describing those requirements. In response to the recommendations of the FAO Expert Consultation on the Conditions of Access to the Fish Resources of the Exclusive Economic Zones in 1983 and the Fifteenth Session of the FAO Committee on Fisheries, the publication will be revised and republished periodically to provide a mirror of changing requirements.

As with the first two editions, it is hoped that the information presented here will be of use to both developing and industrialized coastal states in drawing up or revising their national policies and controls. The study may also be of interest to distant water fishing nations, whose fleets will be required to comply with these controls. In this respect, however, a word of caution should again be given. While every attempt has been made to collect reliable and up to date data, the information presented in this study is, by the very nature of the task, necessarily and inevitably incomplete and liable to error. Any fishing vessel owner or master seeking authorization to fish in waters under the jurisdiction of another state must therefore acquaint himself directly with the laws and other requirements in force in that state. It is hoped, however, that readers will comment on and provide corrections to the tables set out at the end of this volume, so that more complete and accurate information can be presented in future editions.

Acknowledgement is due to Mr. Dennis Weidner of the Division of Foreign Fisheries Analysis, US National Oceanic and Atmospheric Administration, to the South Pacific Forum Fisheries Agency and in particular the Legal Officer, Judith Swan, and to Antonio Tavares de Pinho of the FAO Legislation Branch, for their assistance in the collection of information.

Francis M. Mifsud

Chief, Legislation Branch
Legal Office

Legislative Study No. 21 Rev. 2

REMENTS
IING

e
ies Legislation Section
nch

FOOD AND AGRICULTURE ORGANIZATION OF THE UNITED NATIONS
Rome 1985

The designations employed and the presentation of material in this publication do not imply the expression of any opinion whatsoever on the part of the Food and Agriculture Organization of the United Nations concerning the legal status of any country, territory, city or area or of its authorities, or concerning the delimitation of its frontiers or boundaries.

M-40
ISBN 92-5-102359-X

TABLE OF CONTENTS

PART ONE

NATIONAL LEGISLATION RELATING TO THE LICENSING AND CONTROL OF FOREIGN FISHING OPERATIONS IN COASTAL WATERS

1. Introduction

On 10 December 1982 in Montego Bay, Jamaica, the new United Nations Convention on the Law of the Sea was signed by 119 countries 1/. The signature brought to a close almost a decade and a half of discussions and negotiations. Most of the negotiations and the drafting of the Convention itself were undertaken on the basis of a consensus amongst the participating States. It was only at the moment of adoption that a vote was called for, as a result of the problems of the United States delegation with certain of the provisions on mining and the procedures for the revision of the Convention. Despite the last minute failure to achieve consensus on the whole Convention the fishery provisions have remained largely unchanged since the time of the first Informal Single Negotiating Text in 1975. Central to these provisions is the concept of coastal state jurisdiction over all natural resources including fisheries within a so-called exclusive economic zone extending beyond the territorial sea up to a distance of 200 miles, the related responsibilities of the coastal state for fisheries management within that zone and the notion of access to living resources declared surplus to the harvesting capacity of the coastal state. Although the Convention will

---

1/ The following 117 sovereign states signed the Convention on 10 December 1982: Algeria, Angola, Australia, Austria, Bahamas, Bahrain, Banglades, Barbados, Belize, Bhutan, Brazil, Bulgaria, Burma, Burundi, Byelorussia, Cameroon, Canada, Cape Verde, Chad, Chile, China, Colombia, Congo, Costa Rica, Cuba, Cyprus, Czechoslovakia, Denmark, Djibouti, Dominican Republic, Egypt, Ethiopia, Fiji, Finland, France, Gabon, Gambia, German Dem. Rep., Ghana, Greece, Grenada, Guinea Bissau, Guyana, Haiti, Honduras, Hungary, Iceland, India, Indonesia, Iran, Iraq, Ireland, Ivory Coast, Jamaica, Kenya, Korea (Dem. Peoples Rep.), Kuwait, Lao Peoples Dem. Rep., Lesotho, Liberia, Malaysia, Maldives, Malta, Mauritania, Mauritius, Mexico, Monaco, Mongolia, Morocco, Mozambique, Nauru, Nepal, Netherlands, New Zealand, Niger, Nigeria, Norway, Pakistan, Panama, Papua New Guinea, Paraguay, Philippines, Poland, Portugal, Romania, Rwanda, S. Lucia, S. Vincent and the Grenadines, Senegal, Seychelles, Sierra Leone, Singapore, Solomon Islands, Somalia, Sri Lanka, Sudan, Suriname, Sweden, Thailand, Togo, Trinidad and Tobago, Tunisia, Tuvalu, Uganda, Ukraine, USSR, United Arab Emirates, Tanzania, Upper Volta, Uruguay, Vanuatu, Viet Nam, Yemen (Arab Rep.), Yemen (Peoples Dem. Rep.), Yugoslavia, Zambia and Zimbabwe. The Convention was also signed by the Council for Namibia and the Cook Islands. Since then the Convention has also been signed by a further 38 states: Afghanistan, Antigua and Barbuda, Argentina, Belgium, Benin, Bolivia, Botswana, Brunei Darussalam, Central African Republic, Comoros, Democratic Kampuchea, Dominica, El Salvador, Equatorial Guinea, Guatemala, Guinea, Italy, Japan, Lebanon, Libyan Arab Jamahiriya, Liechtenstein, Luxembourg, Madagascar, Malawi, Mali, Nicaragua, Oman, Qatar, Republic of Korea, St. Christopher & Nevis, Samoa, Sao Tome and Principe, Saudi Arabia, South Africa, Spain, Switzerland, and Zaire. The Convention has also been signed by the European Economic Community and Niue. As of 20 November 1985 the Convention had been ratified by the following 25 states or other entities: Bahamas, Bahrein, Belize, Cameroon, Cuba, Egypt, Fiji, Gambia, Ghana, Guinea, Iceland, Iraq, Ivory Coast, Jamaica, Mali, Mexico, Philippines, St. Lucia, Senegal, Sudan, Tanzania, Togo, Tunisia, Zambia and Namibia.

come into force only 12 months after the deposit of the sixtieth instrument of ratification or accession, a large number of coastal states have already extended their jurisdiction to 200 miles and have gained considerable experience in the implementation of schemes for the allocation and control of access by foreign fishing vessels. The objective of this analysis is to renew that experience as revealed in national legislation and bilateral agreements, bearing in mind that pending the entry into force of the Convention, and thereafter where states not party to the Convention are involved, customary international law as evidenced by state practice will be applicable. The conditions on which access is granted so far as they are known are summarized in the tables set out in the second part of this publication.

2. The extent of national jurisdiction

Part V of the Convention, which introduces the concept of 200-mile coastal state jurisdiction, provides for the establishment of exclusive economic zones beyond and adjacent to the territorial sea, within which coastal states could exercise, inter alia, sovereign rights over the exploration, exploitation and management of all natural resources including fisheries 1/.

In state practice, 200-mile coastal state jurisdiction over fisheries is now well accepted. In fact the situation has changed only slightly over the last two years. Out of 140 independent coastal states, as of 1 October 1985, some 96 states had declared jurisdiction up to 200 miles (compared with 92 states in 1983), one had legislation enacted but awaiting entry into force and a further seven states, being shelf-locked, had extended their jurisdiction up to agreed boundaries or median lines. Of the remaining 36 states, a further 4 at least are known to have draft legislation actively under consideration, 17 are located in the Mediterranean or the Black Sea, where, with the one exception of Morocco, no claims of 200-mile jurisdiction have yet been made, and two are so geographically located as to have little prospect of extending their jurisdiction substantially beyond their present claims. Two coastal states in West Africa retain intermediate claims of between 12 and 200 miles reflecting the natural configuration of the continental shelf (and hence of the main fishing grounds) in that area.

1/ In the exclusive economic zone, the coastal state has:

(a) sovereign rights for the purpose of exploring and exploiting, conserving and managing the natural resources, whether living or non-living, of the waters superjacent to the seabed and of the seabed and its subsoil, and with regard to other activities for the economic exploitation and exploration of the zone, such as the production of energy from the water, currents and winds;

(b) jurisdiction as provided for in the relevant provisions of this Convention with regard to:

(i) the establishment and use of artificial islands, installations and structures;
(ii) marine scientific research;
(iii) the protection and preservation of the marine environment;

(c) other rights and duties provided for in this Convention.

U.N. Convention on the Law of the Sea, Article 56.

The concept of the exclusive economic zone, however, although becoming increasingly popular, has not yet received universal acceptance in state practice, a number of countries having preferred, up to now, to rely instead on a combination of fishing zones and continental shelf to protect their interests in living and non-living marine resources 1/. In this respect three main groups of legislation can be seen. The first type, which is characteristic of certain countries in Latin America and Africa, consists of declarations of sovereign jurisdiction over coastal waters and the resources of these waters up to 200 nautical miles, usually under the concept of extended territorial seas. Much of this legislation, and in particular the legislation from Latin America, predates the convening of the Law of the Sea Conference 2/. There has been no change in the number of these claims over the last two years.

A second group, which includes the legislation of a number of developed countries, as well as some developing countries, and which is not restricted to any particular part of the world, provides for the extension of existing fishing zones out to the 200-mile limit without appreciably changing the legal format of the claim 3/.

The reasoning behind this approach appears to have been that the existing concepts of fishing zones and continental shelf were sufficient to protect the interests of the coastal state, at least on an interim basis pending the conclusion of the Law of the Sea Conference and in particular the fuller acceptance and definition of the concept of exclusive economic zone by the international community whether through the Convention

---

1/ Out of the 103 independent coastal states claiming limits of 200 miles or agreed boundaries or median lines, 12 claim extended territorial sea jurisdiction; 20 claim 200-mile fishing zones and 64 claim exclusive economic zones, two of these claims being in terms of both fisheries and exclusive economic zones. One claim is couched in terms of "offshore waters", but seems closer to the concept of an exclusive fishing zone than an exclusive economic zone. Two further claims are made in terms of "sovereignty and jurisdiction over the sea".

2/ Examples in Latin America are Ecuador - Civil Code, Art. 633 (1966); and Peru - Presidential Decree No. 781 of 1947. The above countries, with Chile, were signatories of the Santiago Declaration on the Maritime Zone of 1952 which sets out a common policy with respect to claims of "sole jurisdiction and sovereignty" over the sea, subsoil and seabed up to 200 nautical miles from the coast. (Note: Although Chile's claim also dates back to 1947, the claim is now described by the Government as a claim to an exclusive economic zone.) Other countries claiming 200-mile territorial seas in Latin America are Argentina - Law No. 17.094 of 1966; Brazil - Decree Law No. 1.098 of 1970; El Salvador - Political Constitution of 1950; Panama - Law No. 31 of 1967; and Uruguay - Law No. 13.833 of 1969. Claims in Africa are: Benin - Decree No. 76-92 of 1976; Congo - Ordinance No. 49/77 of 20 December 1977; Ghana - Territorial Waters and Continental Shelf (Amendment) Decree, 1977; Liberia - Act to approve Executive Order of 24 December 1976; Sierra Leone - Interpretation Act, 1971; Somalia - Law No. 37 of 1972.

3/ Examples are: Canada - Fishing Zones of Canada (Zones 4 and 5) Order, 1977, under the Territorial Sea and Fishing Zone Act, 1964-65; Denmark - Fishing Territory of the Kingdom of Denmark Act, 1976; Ireland - Maritime Jurisdiction (Exclusive Fishery Limits) Order, 1976, under the Maritime Jurisdiction Act, 1976; South Africa - Territorial Waters (Amendment) Act, 1977; U.K. - Fishery Limits Act of 1976.

or through the evolution of international customary law 1/. Many of the states that have established 200-mile fishing zones viewed them as provisional only pending the adoption of a formal Convention, and have recognized this fact explicitly in their legislation 2/. In fact a number of these states (7) have changed their claims to exclusive economic zone claims over the last two years.

In some cases, while the concept of fishing zone is used rather than exclusive economic zone, other provisions generated by the discussions at the Law of the Sea Conference are reflected in the legislation including provisions regarding access to the surplus of the allowable catch or the concept of optimum utilization of resources 3/.

The third group comprises those laws that have declared an exclusive economic zone. Of this group, a substantial number (24 States) define coastal state jurisdiction over the zone in terms based on the enumeration of rights set out in the

---

1/ The Guyana Maritime Boundaries Act, 1977 (S. 15), for example, establishes a 200-mile fishery zone with immediate effect, but empowers the President to declare an exclusive economic zone "if he considers it necessary or expedient having regard to international law and state practice...". The statement introducing the Danish draft legislation explained that "Based on the fact that the new international law concept of an "exclusive economic zone" has not yet been defined in all its aspects, the Government decided that at the present time the solution for Denmark should be an extension of the fishing territory". The Fishing Territory of the Kingdom of Denmark Bill, Explanatory Note No. 4.

2/ See e.g. Germany (Fed. Rep.) Proclamation of 22 December 1976; Japan - Law on Provisional measures relating to the Fishing Zone, 1977; U.S.S.R. - Decree of the Presidium of the Supreme Soviet of the U.S.S.R., on provisional measures to conserve living resources and regulate fishing in the sea areas adjacent to the coast of the U.S.S.R., 10 December 1976.

3/ See, e.g., Australia - Fisheries Amendment Act, 1978; Bahamas - The Fisheries Resources (Jurisdiction and Conservation) Act, 1977; The Gambia - The Fisheries Act, 1977; U.S.A. - Fishery Conservation and Management Act, 1976; U.S.S.R. - Decree of the Presidium of the Supreme Soviet on provisional measures to conserve living resources and regulate fishing in the sea areas adjacent to the coast of U.S.S.R., 1976. The issue of access to surplus will be treated in more detail in Section 3 below.

Convention and preceding Negotiating Texts 1/. A further nine states had made jurisdictional claims consistent with Part V of the Convention, though limited to natural resources and in some cases fisheries only 2/.

The claims of most of the remaining states exceed in one way or other the definition of the extent of coastal state jurisdiction over the exclusive economic zone set out on the Convention. The most common are claims of exclusive jurisdiction over the protection and preservation of the marine environment and the prevention and control of marine pollution; claims which are inconsistent with the provisions of the Convention relating to the jurisdiction of flag states 3/. In addition a number of

---

1/ Art. 56 of the Convention and Art. 44 of the Revised Single Negotiating Text, e.g. Antigua and Barbuda - Territorial Waters Act, 1982, S. 10; Cuba - Act of 24 February 1977 concerning the establishment of an economic zone, Art. 2; Dominica - Territorial Sea, Contiguous Zone, Exclusive Economic and Fishery Zones Act, 1981, S. 8; Dominican Republic - Law No. 573 of 1977, Art. 5; Guatemala - Decree No. 20-76, Art. 3; Iceland - Law No. 41 of 1 June 1979 commencing the Territorial Sea, the Economic Zone and the Continental Shelf, Art. 3; Indonesia - Declaration of 1980, para 2; Kampuchea - Declaration of 15 January 1978, para 3; Kenya - Presidential Proclamation of 28 February 1979 Schedule; Malaysia - Declaration of 1980; Mauritania - Law No. 78-043 of 28 February 1978 promulgating the Code of the Merchant Marine and Marine Fisheries, Act 185 (but note that Mauritania claims a 70-mile territorial sea); Mexico - Law implementing paragraph 8 of Article 27 of the Constitution relating to the exclusive economic zone, Art. 4; Mozambique - Decree No. 31/76 of 19 August, Art. 2 (resources only); Nigeria - Exclusive Economic Zone Decree No. 28 of 2 October 1978 (but see additional claims regarding controls over navigation in designated areas related to offshore installations); Norway - Act 17 December 1976 relating to the economic zone of Norway; Portugal - Act No. 33/77 of 1977; St. Lucia - Maritime Areas Act, 1984, S. 13; St. Vincent & the Grenadines - S. 20; Sao Tome and Principe - Decree Law No. 15/78 of 16 June 1978, Art. 4; Union of Soviet Socialist Republics - Decree on the Economic Zone of 28 February 1984 Art. 2; United Arab Emirates - Declaration by Ministry of Foreign Affairs of 1980, para 4; United States of America - Proclamation of 10 March 1983; Venezuela - Law establishing an Exclusive Economic Zone along the continental and insular coasts of Venezuela, Art. 3.

2/ Cape Verde - Decree-Law No. 126-77 of 31 December 1977; Costa Rica - Decree No. 5699 of 5 June 1975; Fiji - Marine Spaces Act, 1977; Guinea - Decree No. 366/PRG/80 of 30 July 1980; Guinea-Bissau - Law No. 3/78 of 19 May 1978; New Zealand - Territorial Sea and Exclusive Economic Zone Act, 1977; Spain - Law No. 15/1978 of 20 February 1978; Togo - Ordinance No. 24 of 16 August 1977; Western Samoa - Exclusive Economic Zone Act, 1977. Similar provisions are contained in the the Tonga Territorial Sea and Exclusive Economic Zone Act which was enacted in 1978 but has not yet been brought into force.

3/ At least 11 states claim exclusive jurisdiction with respect to the conservation of the marine environment. See Burma - Territorial Sea and Maritime Zones law, 1977, S. 18; Colombia - Decree of 25 July 1978, Art. 8; Djibouti - Law No. 52/AN/78 of 9 January 1979, Art. 13; Equatorial Guinea - Law No. 15/1984 of 12 November 1984, Art. 13; India - Territorial Waters, Continental Shelf, Exclusive Economic Zone and other Maritime Zones Act, 1976, S. 7; Mauritius - Maritime Zones Act, 1977, S. 7; Law No. 1-81 of 8 April 1981, Art. 4; Pakistan - Territorial Waters and Maritime Zones Act, 1976, S. 6; Philippines - Presidential Decree No. 1599 establishing an exclusive economic zone and for other purposes, S. 2; Seychelles - Maritime Zones Act, 1977, S. 7; Vanuatu - Maritime Zones Act, 1981, S. 10; Yemen Peoples Democratic Republic - Act No. 45 of 1977, Art. 14.

states formulate their claims to jurisdiction in wide terms such as "all rights and jurisdiction" 1/ or accord unlimited powers to take action to control pollution in the zone 2/. Differences also exist with respect to the exclusivity of jurisdiction over scientific research. As pointed out by Burke 3/, a numnber of coastal states further claim the right to exert controls over navigation in designated areas of the exclusive economic zone that could be inconsistent with the right of free navigation set out in the Convention as well as broadly drafted provisions allowing for the extension of any enactment to the EEZ, without limitation to those strictly necessary for or related to the purposes for which the zone was declared. One further small, but perhaps significant difference lies in the almost universal elimination of the reference to "duties" in the "catch-all" phrase at the end of the enumeration of coastal states' rights over the exclusive economic zone 4/.

Although the concept of the exclusive economic zone has not yet been fully applied in national legislation, as noted above, an increasing number of coastal states have been taking action since the signature of the Convention to bring their legislation into line with the new Convention. It is known that draft texts establishing exclusive economic zones are presently under consideration in a number of countries now claiming extended territorial seas or fishery zones.

3. Access to surplus

The provisions of the Convention on the Law of the Sea would oblige coastal states to manage the fisheries in their exclusive economic zones to ensure that they are not endangered by over-exploitation 5/. Subject to this, states would be required to promote the objective of optimum utilization of the living resources in the economic zone. They would be required to determine the allowable catch in their zones and their capacity to harvest these resources. Where the total allowable catch exceeds their own capacity, they would be required to give other states access to the surplus. In giving access to the fisheries of its economic zone to other states, the coastal state would be required to take into account all relevant factors, including, for example, the rights of landlocked and other geographically disadvantaged states, and traditional fishing practices 6/.

1/ Barbados - Marine Boundaries Act 1978, S. 5; Grenada - Marine Boundaries Act, 1978, S. 5.

2/ e.g. Bangladesh - Territorial Waters and Maritime Zones Act 1974, S. 8; Ivory Coast - Law No. 77.926 of 17 November 1976, Art. 6; Sri Lanka - Maritime Zone Law, 1976, S. 7.

3/ See Burke, W.T.; National Legislation on Ocean Authority Zones and the Contemporary Law of the Sea, Ocean Development and International Law Journal, 1981, Vol. 9 No. 3-4, p. 289.

4/ Only in the legislation of Antigua and Barbuda, Djibouti, Dominica and Guatemala and Kenya is the word retained. The "duties" of the coastal state in its exclusive economic zone as set out in the Convention are examined in the following section.

5/ Art. 61.

6/ Art. 62

Although the obligation to give other states access to the surplus is categorical, considerable flexibility is left under the Convention to the coastal state in its determination of what constitutes optimum utilization and in the crucial determinations of the allowable catch, the extent of the coastal state's harvesting capacity, the allocation of access and the terms and conditions under which access is granted 1/.

In reviewing state practice, it is not intended to dwell on any discussion of the management objectives adopted by various states in their legislation. In most cases, anyway, these management objectives, if formulated at all, are somewhat loosely defined 2/. Rather, accent will be placed on the expressed attitude towards allowing "access to surplus". Few cases, quite understandably, acknowledge any obligation of the coastal state to give foreign vessels access to the surplus of its fishery resources 3/. Most of the laws, in fact, are silent on issues of access to surplus, beyond the establishment of licensing systems for foreign fishing vessels. Criteria and procedures for determining surplus and its allocation are normally left to the discretion of the administration and its policy makers. In a few cases, however, references are made to the subject of access to surplus in terms reminiscent of the provisions of the Convention or Negotiating Texts 4/. In some instances, the references are general only and do not indicate procedures for establishing the size

---

1/ See generally Burke, W.T., 1982, Convention on the Law of the Sea Provisions on Conditions of Access to Fisheries subject to Extended National Jurisdiction. FAO, Rome, 1983. Paper submitted to the FAO Expert Consultation on Conditions of Access. These determinations are referred to under Article 297 of the Convention as discretionary powers of the coastal state, the exercise of which is not subject to review under the compulsary disputes settlement provisions of the Convention.

2/ See Moore G. - National Legislation for the Management of Fisheries under Extended Coastal State Jurisdiction, Journal of Maritime Law and Commerce, Vol. 11, No. 2, January 1980, pp. 163-5.

3/ National legislation by its very nature tends to be concerned more with relations between the state and individuals, whether national or foreign, and with relations among individuals rather than with inter-state relations. Legislative drafters are also traditionally cautious in using language that unnecessarily acknowledges obligations of the state under international law. The absence of any reference in national legislation to responsibilities of the coastal state under international law does not, of course, mean that such responsibilities do not exist or are not accepted by the state.

4/ See, e.g. Bahamas - The Fisheries Resources (Jurisdiction and Conservation) Act, 1977, S. 10; Cape Verde - Decree Law 126/77 of 31 December 1977, Art. 8; Cuba - Act of 24 February 1977 concerning the establishment of an economic zone, Art. 4; Fiji - Marine Spaces Act, 1977; The Gambia - Fisheries Act, 1977; Mexico - Law regulating the eighth paragraph of Art. 27 of the Constitution relating to the exclusive economic zone, 1975; New Zealand - Territorial Sea and Exclusive Economic Zone Act, 1977; Norway - Act No. 91 of 1976, S. 4; Sao Tome and Principe - Decree Law No. 15/78 of 16 June 1978, Art. 6; Tonga - The Territorial Sea and Exclusive Economic Zone Act, 1978, ss. 10-12; U.S.A. - Fishery Conservation and Management Act, 1976; Portugal - Act No. 33/77 of 1977, Art. 5; U.S.S.R. - Decree of the Presidium on provisional measures to conserve living resources and regulate fishing in the sea areas adjacent to the coast of the U.S.S.R., 1976; Vanuatu - Fisheries Act, 1982, S. 2; Venezuela - Law establishing an Exclusive Economic Zone of the continental and island coasts of the Republic of Venezuela of 3 July 1978, Art. 6.

of the surplus or allocating access to foreign vessels. Both the Portuguese and the Norwegian legislation, for example, provide for the making of regulations concerning the determination of the total allowable catch, and only general reference is made to "access by fishermen from other states to fish allotted shares of the allowable catch" (Norway) or the "catch quota allowed to aliens" (Portugal) 1/. In the Australian legislation, no express mention is made of the concept of access to surplus fish resources. However, the Act does stipulate "optimum utilization of the living resources of the Australian fishing zone" as an objective to which the Minister should have regard in the administration of the Act, and this appears to have been given an interpretation by the responsible Australian Minister akin to full utilization 2/. In his speech presenting the Bill to the House of Representative, the Minister for Primary Industry explained that, in practical terms, adherence to the objective of optimum utilization meant that Australia would be obliged to grant access to foreigners to fish for resources which Australian fishermen could not adequately exploit 3/.

The U.S.S.R. text is more explicit. The relevant decree requires the establishment of a "total allowable annual catch for each species" and the determination of "that part of the annual allowable catch ... which may be harvested by foreign fishing vessels, provided that the size of the total allowable catch of any stock of commercial species exceeds the harvesting capacity of the Soviet fishing effort" 4/.

Where procedures for determining the amount of the surplus are specified in more detail, the references to granting access to foreign nations or vessels are seldom couched in mandatory language. The Gambian legislation, for example, provides for the preparation of management plans that would, inter alia, determine the total annual catch to be allowed from each fishery and "determine the amount of resources, if any, to be made available to foreign fishing vessels on an annual basis under reciprocal fishing rights or other international arrangements, taking into account any obligations under international law, or any international convention or agreement in force" 5/. The Bahaman legislation empowers the Governor-General to determine the optimum yield of the fishery resources and the capacity of the local fishing industry, and provides that "the difference between the optimum yield and the maximum capacity of the fishing industry of the Bahamas as may be determined by the Governor-General... may be the allowable level of foreign fishing" 6/. In Fiji and New Zealand legislation the provisions are stronger. The Minister is required to determine the total allowable catch for every fishery in the zone and the portion that local vessels have the capacity to harvest. "The remaining portion shall constitute the allowable catch for that fishery for foreign fishing craft" 7/. However, in each case, the Minister is empowered rather than required to apportion the allowable catch among foreign countries. In the U.S. Magnusson Fishery Conservation and Management Act of 1976 a more complicated formula is now used to establish the total allowable level of

1/ Norway - Act No. 91 of 1976, S. 4; Portugal - Act No. 33/77 of 1977, Art. 5.
2/ Australia - Fisheries Amendment Act, 1978, S. 6
3/ Australia - House of Representatives Debates, 13 April 1978, p. 1517.
4/ U.S.S.R. - Decree of the Presidium, 1976
5/ The Gambia - The Fisheries Act, 1977 S. 4(3)(d).
6/ Bahamas - The Fisheries Resources (Jurisdiction and Conservation) Act, 1977, S. 10. See also similar provisions in the legislation of Cape Verde - Decree Law No. 126-77 of 31 December 1977, Art. 8, and Sao Tome and Principe - Decree Law No. 15/78 of 16 June 1978.
7/ Fiji - Marine Spaces Act, 1977, S. 11; New Zealand - Territorial Sea and Exclusive Economic Zone Act, 1977, S. 12.

foreign fishing 1/. Once this is established, however, the Secretary of State is required to determine its allocation among foreign nationals 2/. The provisions on access to surplus in the legislation of Cuba and Mexico are less detailed, but are worded to reflect an acknowledged obligation of the state. The Cuban Act, for example, provides that "the Republic of Cuba, through the conclusion of appropriate agreements, shall give other states access to the surplus of the allowable catch of the species concerned ..." 3/.

Even where an obligation to grant access to surplus is recognized in national legislation, the practical implications of this obligation depend ultimately on the manner in which the total allowable catch is set and the local harvesting capacity assessed. Most of the legislation is silent on these points. Where any mention is made of procedures for determining the total allowable catch, reference is often made to the concept of optimum utilization or optimum yield. The U.S. and Bahaman legislation both define optimum in this context as that which provides the greatest overall benefit to the nation and which is based on the maximum sustainable yield as modified by economic, social, or ecological factors 4/. A similar though somewhat narrower definition of total allowable catch is given in the New Zealand legislation and other laws following the New Zealand pattern 5/. The Gambian legislation also requires all relevant social and economic as well as biological factors to be taken into account in the setting of the total annual catch to be allowed from each fishery 6/. As noted above the interpretation of the term optimum utilization by the Australian Minister of Primary Industry appears to indicate a more strictly biological approach.

1/ The total allowable level of foreign fishing, if any, with respect to any United States fishery ... shall be:
(A) the level representing that portion of the optimum yield of such fishery which will not be harvested by vessels of the United States, as determined in accordance with the provisions of this Act ..., or
(B) the annual fishing level determined pursuant to paragraph (3) for the harvesting season. S. 201(d). (The procedure described in paragraph (3) is designed to allow room for and promote expansion of local fishing operations by increased reductions in the level of foreign fishing allowed). 2/ S. 201 (e)

3/ Act of 24 February 1977 concerning the establishment of an economic zone, Art. 4.

4/ Bahamas - The Fisheries Resources (Jurisdiction and Conservation) Act, 1977, S. 2; U.S.A. - Mangusson Fishery Conservatin and Management Act, Section 3 (18);

5/ Cook Islands - Territorial Sea and Exclusive Economic Zone Act 1977, S. 2; Fiji - Marine Spaces Act, 1977, S. 2; New Zealand - Territorial Sea and Exclusive Economic Zone Act 1977, S. 2; Niue - Territorial Sea and Exclusive Economic Zone Act 1978, S. 2; Tonga - Territorial Sea and Exclusive Economic Zone Act, 1978, S. 2. By omitting the general criterion of greatest overall benefit to the nation greater emphasis appears to be placed on purely biological factors, although the modifying environmental and economic factors are allowed. Note that both the U.S. and New Zealand models are more restrictive than Article 61 of the Law of the Sea Convention, in that the latter refers to maximum sustainable yield as qualified by environmental and economic factors only in connection with the taking of conservation and management measures rather than in connection with the determination of the allowable catch. Conservation and management measures are to be designed to maintain populations of harvested species at levels which can produce the qualified maximum sustainable yield, thereby providing a threshold limit on the size of the standing stock to be maintained rather than requiring any particular level of exploitation.

6/ Fisheries Act 1977, S. 4.

Few countries specify procedures for assessing the local capacity to harvest fishery resources, the other side of the equation for the declaration of surplus resources. Of note are the Gambian legislation which implies that due account will be taken of local development plans before declaring a surplus, and the new U.S. legislation which has the effect of reserving part of the surplus for future local industry expansion 1/.

Criteria for determining the apportionment of the surplus catch are provided for in the legislation of Fiji, New Zealand, preference being given to those foreign nations that have habitually fished in the area, and to those that have cooperated in research, conservation and management programmes and in enforcement 2/. Similar criteria were included in the Mangusson Fishery Conservation and Management Act of 1976. Under the amendments of 1983, however, the criteria have been revised to give precedence to considerations of market access for U.S. fish products and the extent to which the fishing nation is using the fish caught in U.S. waters to compete with U.S. products on the international market 3/. Of particular interest is the Togolese legislation in which the Government binds itself to allow land locked neighbouring states to participate in the exploitation of the living resources of its economic zone through bilateral or regional agreements 4/.

A number of bilateral agreements dealing with access take up and repeat the basic elements of Articles 61 and 62 of the Convention. The Australian Head Agreement with Japan of October 1979, for example, provides that the Government of Australia is to determine annually, in the exercise of its sovereign rights, the total allowable catch for individual stocks or complexes of stocks, the portion of the allowable catch that will be taken by fishing vessels in Australia, and allocations, as and where appropriate, for fishing vessels of Japan of parts of surpluses of such stocks. Of particular interest is the qualification that the total allowable catch is to be determined "taking into account the best available scientific evidence, the interdependence of stocks and all other relevant factors", which appears to imply a heavy reliance on objective biological factors, with no express mention of economic, social or environmental interests. The agreement also makes reference to the factors qualifying Japan for allocation of surplus, i.e. a history of fishing activities in the area and contributions to development and research. The parties are to consult periodically regarding the implementation of the agreement. Similar provisions are to be found in almost all bilateral access agreements entered into by a number of larger countries such as Canada, Mexico, New Zealand and U.S.A., and some smaller countries such as the Cook Islands 5/.

1/ American Fisheries Promotion Act, 1980.

2/ Fiji - Marine Spaces Act, 1977, S. 11; New Zealand - Territorial Sea and Exclusive Economic Zone Act, 1977, S. 12; U.S.A. - Fishery Conservation and Management Act of 1976, S. 201 (e); S. 10 of the Bahamas Fisheries Resources (Jurisdiction and Conservation) Act, 1977 also provides for traditional fishing practices to be taken into account in allocating access to surplus.

3/ U.S. Public Law 97-453 of January 12, 1983.

4/ Togo - Ordinance No. 24 of 16 August 1977, Art. 4. Similar provisions are to be found in the new Moroccan legislation.

5/ Where the agreements deal with highly migratory species, as in the case of the Cook Islands and partly New Zealand, they reflect the spirit of cooperation embodied in Article 64 of the Convention. However in the case of small countries having only limited scientific information on the resources such provisions could be viewed as giving the foreign fishing partners in practice an excessive say in the determination of the allowable catch and consequently the fishing policies of the coastal state.

4. Coastal state conditions for foreign fishing

Article 62.4 of the Convention on the Law of the Sea provides that foreign nationals are to comply with conservation measures and "other terms and conditions established in the regulations of the coastal state". These may include licensing and payment of fees (in the case of developing coastal states they may consist of "compensation in the field of financing, equipment and technology relating to the fishing industry), management measures including regulation of catch effort, and conditions relating to reporting, the placing of observers and trainees on board vessels, the conduct of specified research programmes, the landing of catch in the coastal state, joint ventures and other cooperative arrangements, the training of personnel and transfer of technology and enforcement procedures 1/. The list of examples is not exhaustive.

Almost all countries that have extended their jurisdiction to 200 miles make provision for foreign fishing in those waters 2/, and establish the conditions for

---

1/ "(a) licensing of fishermen, fishing vessels and equipment, including payment of fees and other forms of remuneration, which in the case of developing coastal states, may consist of adequate compensation in the field of financing, equipment and technology relating to the fishing industry;
(b) determining the species which may be caught, and fixing quotas of catch, whether in relation to particular stocks or groups of stocks or catch per vessel over a period of time or to the catch by nationals of any State during a specified period;
(c) regulating seasons and areas of fishing, the types, sizes and amount of gear, and the numbers, sizes and types of fishing vessels that may be used;
(d) fixing the age and size of fish and other species that may be caught;
(e) specifying information required of fishing vessels, including catch and effort statistics and vessel position reports;
(f) requiring, under the authorization and control of the coastal state, the conduct of specified fisheries research programmes and regulating the conduct of such research, including the sampling of catches, disposition of samples and reporting of associated scientific data;
(g) the placing of observers or trainees on board such vessels by the coastal state;
(h) the landing of all or any part of the catch by such vessels in the ports of the coastal state;
(i) terms and conditions relating to joint ventures or other cooperative arrangements;
(j) requirements for training personnel and transfer of fisheries technology, including enlargement of the coastal state's capability of undertaking fisheries research;
(k) enforcement procedures".

2/ The Maldives is one exception. In a number of countries the possibility of foreign fishing may be provided for but not allowed in practice, as, e.g., in the Republic of Korea.
The provisions concerning foreign fishing are sometimes set out in the legislation establishing the extended jurisdiction (e.g. in New Zealand, Fiji, Cook Islands, Bahamas, USA, and Barbados) and sometimes in the general fisheries legislation. In many of those countries that have followed the New Zealand model, there does seem to be a certain amount of rethinking of this approach. A number of these countries are now considering revisions that would have the effect of excising the foreign fishing provisions from the legislation establishing the maritime zones and incorporating them into new comprehensive fisheries legislation.

such fishing, whether in general fisheries legislation or regulations, in EEZ legislation or regulations or in access agreements. In general many of these conditions cover, at least in part, the same ground as the examples set out in Article 62.4 of the Convention of the Law of the Sea. Conditions concerning management are of course contained in general fisheries legislation as well as that applying specifically to foreign fishing. Some laws give a list of the type of conditions to which foreign fishing licences may be subject. This is the case, for example, in the legislation of Fiji and New Zealand and other countries following the New Zealand model 1/. In most cases a distinction is made between general conditions, which are set out in the law and regulations, and particular conditions which may change from vessel to vessel and which are usually set out in the licence itself 2/.

(a) Licensing, nationality criteria and payment of fees

In some countries foreign fishing operations are subject to the same general requirements and system of licensing as national fishing operations. In Pakistan, for example, the Territorial Waters and Maritime Zones Act, 1976, provides that fishing operations in the exclusive economic zone are to be regulated by the provisions of the Exclusive Fishing Zone (Regulation of Fishing) Act, 1975, which apply alike to national and foreign craft 3/.

In most cases where countries claim extended jurisdiction, however, a distinction is made between national and foreign fishing operations from an administrative point of view. Separate licensing systems are established for foreign fishing operations accompanied by separate criteria for issuing licences and conditions attaching to the licences. Under the new Vanuatu legislation, for example, local fishing licences issue as of right except in certain specified cases and subject to fisheries management considerations; foreign fishing licences are granted at the discretion of the Minister and may not be issued except under a bilateral access agreement unless the foreign vessel is locally based 4/. Whether or not separate criteria are specified, provision is very often made for decisions to be taken at a higher level where licensing of foreign fishing operations is concerned. The Mauritius Maritime Zone Act, 1977, for example, requires that fishing operations by foreign vessels are to be authorized only by licences issued under the authority of the Prime Minister 5/.

1/ Cook Islands - Territorial Sea and Exclusive Economic Zone Act, 1977, S. 13; Fiji - Marine Spaces Act, 1977, S. 12; New Zealand - Territorial Sea and Exclusive Economic Zone Act, 1977, S. 15; Tonga - Territorial Sea and Exclusive Economic Zone Act 1978, S. 14; U.S.A. - Fishery Management and Conservation Act of 1976 and NOAA Regulations on Conditions and Restrictions concerning Foreign Fishing off the Coasts of the U.S.A., 1978; Western Samoa - Exclusive Economic Zone Act 1977, S. 5. See also Kenya - Proclamation of 28 February 1979.

2/ As e.g. in Canada - Coastal Fisheries Protection Regulations, 1976; Fiji - Marine Spaces Act, 1977; The Gambia - Fisheries Act and Regulations, 1977; New Zealand - Territorial Sea and Exclusive Economic Zone Act, 1977, and Exclusive Economic Zone (Foreign Fishing Craft) Regulations, 1978; Vanuatu - Fisheries Act, 1982.

3/ Many countries that have not yet extended their jurisdiction also make no distinction between local and foreign vessels under their licensing systems. This is the case, for example, in Iraq, Kenya and Sudan. Kenya has recently proclaimed jurisdiction over a 200-mile exclusive economic zone, but has not as yet adopted implementing legislation or revised its basic fisheries legislation.

4/ Fisheries Act, 1982.

5/ Provisions requiring a higher level of decision making are to be found also in Brazil, Burma, Fiji, India, New Zealand, The Gambia and Vanuatu (the power to issue local licences may be delegated by the Minister to the Director; the power to issue foreign fishing licences may not.)

The establishment of separate licensing systems for foreign fishing vessels necessitates decisions, first as to the definition of what constitutes a national or foreign vessel, and secondly as to what should be covered by the term fishing vessel.

Differences over nationality criteria have on occasion been the cause of substantial misunderstandings between countries interested in negotiating reciprocal fishing agreements. Until recently nationality criteria for fishing vessels have tended naturally to follow the nationality criteria applicable to merchant vessels. Traditionally two main groups may be identified. Those countries following the French law tradition tend to adopt a standard formula requiring national vessels to be at least half owned by nationals or national companies. In order to qualify as a national company, however, further conditions are stipulated. The registered office must be located in the country, the chairman, the general manager or managers and a majority of the Board of Directors, or supervisory board, must all be nationals, and at least 50 percent of the share capital must be held by nationals 1/. The standard rule in countries with common law tradition, on the other hand, has been not to go behind the "veil of incorporation" to ascertain the ownership of company shares, but to treat any company incorporated under the local law as a local company 2/. In recent years, however, governments have begun to recognize that the concerns underlying the according of local status to fishing vessels are substantially different from those underlying the right to fly their flags. According local status to fishing vessels is substantially an allocation of preferred access to resources; according the right to fly a country's flag on the other hand raises issues of jurisdiction, control and revenue. More Governments are consequently separating the two types of nationality criteria and designing those applied to fishing vessels to accord with their general fisheries policies. A number of common law countries, for example, have now introduced more stringent criteria that would require majority shareholding or control by nationals before a locally incorporated company can claim local status for its vessels, in order to restrict the number of vessels that can claim preferential access to fishery resources. Such restricted criteria may be particularly important in the case of the so-called "flag of convenience" countries. The Liberian Revised Rules and Regulations on Fisheries, for example, now define national vessels as those owned by Liberians or by companies in which a controlling interest is held by Liberians. Similar criteria have recently been adopted in Antigua & Barbuda, Bangladesh, Mauritius, Seychelles, The Gambia, Sri Lanka, Malaysia, St. Christopher & Nevis, St. Lucia, 3/, and are contemplated in a number of other countries. In the Bahamas and Ghana, the law requires that vessels be wholly owned by local citizens or by companies, all of whose shares are owned by nationals, before they can be accorded local fishing rights. In other cases more liberal criteria have

---

1/ This type of criteria is to be found in Cameroun, Congo, Gabon, Madagascar, Mauritania and Senegal. Similar requirements are set out in the definition of national vessels in the Lomé Convention between the EEC and the ACP countries.

2/ As, e.g., in Bangladesh, Canada, Fiji, India, Pakistan, Papua New Guinea, Solomon Islands, Sri Lanka, U.K. and U.S.A.

3/ Antigua & Barbuda - Fisheries Act 1983, S. 2; Liberia - Revised Rules and Regulations on Fisheries; Mauritius - Maritime Zones (Fishing Licences) Regulations, 1978; Seychelles - Control of Foreign Fishing Vessels Decree, 1979, S.2; The Gambia - The Fisheries Act, 1977, S.2; Sri Lanka - Fisheries (Regulation of Foreign Fishing Boats) Act, No. 59 of 1979, S. 28; Malaysia - Fisheries Act 1984, S. 2; St. Christopher & Nevis - Fisheries Act, 1984 S. 2; St. Lucia - Fisheries Act 1984 S. 2. El Salvador and Guatemala also require that the company be locally controlled.

been consciously adopted in order to encourage the development of locally based fishing industries. The recent Vanuatu legislation, for example, creates three categories of vessels, local vessels, which include any vessels owned by locally incorporated companies, whatever their shareholding, locally based foreign vessels, which enjoy some of the advantages accorded to local vessels, and other foreign vessels. As Vanuatu is a flag of convenience country, controls over allocation of preferential access to fish resources are retained through a provision requiring approval for all foreign investments in fisheries. Without this approval local fishing licences may be withheld 1/. Fiji similarly adopts broadly worded criteria that allow locally based vessels under charter to local companies to be classified as local in order to encourage landings to the Levuka transhipment and processing base 2/. Under the Australian Fisheries Act, a degree of flexibility is obtained by allowing the Minister in his discretion to treat foreign vessels imported for limited periods of time under joint venture arrangements as Australian vessels 3/. Similar discretionary powers are provided for under the Pakistan Exclusive Fishing Zone (Regulation of Fishing) Act, 1975.

As noted above the possibilities for misunderstandings over nationality criteria are greatest in the context of bilateral or regional agreements providing for reciprocal or preferential fishing rights for vessels belonging to the other party or parties. Nationality criteria to be adopted for this purpose are thus sometimes included in such agreements 4/. Indeed there is no reason why the national criteria agreed upon for this purpose should be the same as that in force in the national legislation of either party to the agreement.

So far as the definition of fishing vessels is concerned, the trend seems now to be to include fishery support vessels, such as motherships, transport ships or even refuelling ships, as well as vessels actually engaged in fishing operations 5/. The inclusion has the advantage of facilitating controls over both licenced and unlicensed fishing operations and over activities not actually involving fishing such as "over-the-side" sales.

In establishing licence fees and other payments for fishing rights, coastal states are faced with a basic choice between royalty fees based on the actual catch, fees based on the fishing capacity of the vessel, and lump sum payments. Royalty payments may present a more accurate and, in a sense, more equitable method of revenue sharing between foreign vessels and coastal states, and they avoid the danger of encouraging over-intensive fishing methods. They also place least risk on the foreign fishing fleet, which has to pay only for the fish actually caught. At the same time the effective collection of royalty payments requires a reliable system of reporting

---

1/ Fisheries Act, 1982.

2/ Fiji - Marine Spaces Act, 1977, S. 2.

3/ Fisheries Amendment Act, 1980, S. 3.

4/ As, for example, in the reciprocal fishing agreement between Senegal and Gambia of 1982 and the agreement between Equatorial Guinea and Nigeria of 27 November 1981.

5/ See, e.g., Bahamas - Fisheries Resources (Jurisdiction and Conservation) Act, 1977, S. 2; Canada - Coastal Fisheries Protection Act, 1952-53; Fiji - Marine Spaces Act, 1977, S.2; New Zealand - Territorial Sea and Exclusive Zone Act, 1977, S. 2; The Gambia - Fisheries Act, 1977, S.2; U.S.A. - Fisheries Conservation and Management Act of 1976, S. 3; Vanuatu - Fisheries Act, 1982, S. 2; Malaysia - Fisheries Act 1984, S. 2; St. Christopher & Nevis - Fisheries Act, 1984 S. 2; St. Lucia - Fisheries Act 1984 S. 2.

and compliance control. At the other end of the scale, lump sum payments place the least administrative burden on the coastal state. They also place the maximum risk on the foreign fleet, a factor which should, at least theoretically, be reflected in the level of the fees paid. In the middle are fees based on the number, size, power or capacity of the vessel licenced to fish.

The methods of calculation and amounts of licence fees and other payments vary very considerably from country to country and it is not easy to make generalizations. However certain regional tendencies are discernible. In the Western Pacific, for example, given the difficulties of compliance control, the lump sum payment method has been traditionally favoured by the coastal states, with an expressed target of 5 percent of the landed price but with actual returns being somewhat lower 1/. Recently, however, there has been a movement towards the calculation of fees on a vessel capacity/trip basis, with an allowance for market price fluctuations, partly because of a desire for higher returns and partly due to resistance to lump sum fees on the part of foreign fishing operators. In Latin America the tendency has been to favour fees based on vessel capacity (expressed in net register tonnage) per trip. West African and Indian Ocean countries seem traditionally to have charged fees on vessel size (expressed in gross tonnage) 2/ and on an annual basis, with Mauritania leading the field with rates of up to US$1,000 per gross ton per year for some fisheries although there does seem a tendency now towards payments based on a percentage of the landed value of the catch 3/. A number of countries in West Africa, including Maritania, structure their fee systems in such a way as to encourage local landing and processing. The Senegalese system is of particular note. Fees for sardine boats are based on a fixed annual fee (CFA 500 000 to CFA 1 500 000) and for trawlers on a fee per gross ton (CFA 7 500 to CFA 25 000). The level of the fees, however, depends on whether the vessel is local or operates under a bilateral agreement, or without such an agreement 4/. For tuna boats licence fees are calculated on a royalty basis on the weight of fish landed. Where the vessel is not linked with a Senegalese processing company, the fee is doubled, and if the vessel operates outside a bilateral agreement, the fee is trebled.

In Europe, no fees at all are charged by the EEC for licences, which are issued on a reciprocal basis. In North America, Canada now charges a modest though increasing fee based on the size of the vessel and time spent on the fishing grounds, while the U.S.A. operates a fee system based on a poundage fee expressed in dollars per metric ton for listed species. Under section 204 (B) (L) of the U.S. Mangusson

---

1/ Both Fiji and Papua New Guinea provide for the figure of 5 percent in their regulations, though Fiji does not at the moment licence foreign vessels not operating to the local shore-based industry. Most countries provide for the main payments to be collected under access agreements. In some cases, even where fees are expressed in terms of lump sum payments, it is indicated that the level of the payments has been calculated on the basis of 5 percent of the landed value of the catch.

2/ The difference between the use of gross tonnage as a measure in West Africa and net tonnage in Latin America reflects the different types of fishing. Net tonnage, which represents the hold capacity would seem a more useful measure for tuna purseiners, while gross tonnage or horse power measurements may be more appropriate for trawl fisheries.

3/ As in Mauritania and Sao Tome and Principe.

4/ Senegal - Marine Fisheries Code, 1976, and Decree No. 76-836 of 1976 establishing the conditions for issuing fishing licences and the level of fees.

Fishery Conservation and Management Act of 1976, "reasonable fees" are to be established by the Secretary of Commerce in consultation with the Secretary of State, taking into account the cost of implementation of the Act. Poundage fees now amount to 24.2 percent of the landed value of the catch.

It is not easy to compare levels of fees and other payments charged or even calculate their precise levels in view of the different forms that such payments may take, including, for example, development aid, construction projects, training and joint venture development. A number of countries including Canada, Australia, New Zealand and U.S.A. also link access to trade concessions such as market access for fish and other export products.

The present level of fees and other payments charged, so far as they are known, are set out in Table B.

(b) Management measures

Most, if not all, coastal states that licence foreign fishing operations provide, at least in theory, for the taking of management measures of some sort or other as a condition of the lincences. General management measures such as minimum mesh or species sizes are normally contained in the basic fisheries law and regulations, and are usually incorporated by reference as conditions of the foreign fishing vessel licence 1/.

Fairly strict management controls specifically over foreign fishing operations are included in the legislation of a few countries. In the Canadian and U.S. legislation, for example, licences for foreign fishing are made subject to strict quota limitations, and a whole array of control mechanisms are set up for monitoring and cutting off fishing once those quotas have been reached. This in fact reflects the main policy interest of the coastal states concerned, which is in the proper management of the fisheries for the primary benefit of the local industry, rather than in revenue collection. In most cases, however, and particularly where greater emphasis is placed on revenue collection, management measures tend to be based not on quota systems, but on a limitation of the number and size of vessels allowed to fish.

In a number of cases, restrictions are also placed on the areas within which foreign fishing operations are allowed. These restrictions may be based on conservation principles, or even on compliance control considerations, particularly where the devices of so-called "windows" and "boxes" are concerned. On the other hand "zoning" of fishery operations tends more commonly to be based on policies of protecting local fisheries and, in particular, local artisanal fisheries from competition with foreign fleets. Examples of simple zoning provisions exist in Brazil (fishing areas up to 100 miles from the coast reserved for local fisheries), Ecuador (40 miles from the coast) and El Salvador and Uruguay (12 miles) 2/. The new Sri Lanka regulations, on the other hand, set up a slightly more complicated zoning system. Waters up to 24 nautical miles are reserved for local artisanal fisheries. Joint venture enterprises are allowed to operate in the 24 to 50 mile zone and other licenced foreign vessels only beyond that limit. The Senegalese Marine Fisheries Code

1/ As, e.g. in The Gambia - The Fisheries Regulations, 1978.

2/ Brazil - Decree No. 68.459 of 1971; El Salvador - Order No. 12263 of 1974 and Uruguay - Law No. 13.833 of 1969.

of 1976 provides for an even more complicated zoning based on the nationality of the vessel, the type of fishing operation and whether or not an intergovernmental agreement is in force 1/. In many other countries authorized and reserved or prohibited fishing areas are designated by administrative act and/or intergovernmental fishing agreement 2/. In order to make such provisions more effective, a number of countries require fishing gear to be stowed away while the vessel is in a prohibited fishing area 3/. While zoning for local and foreign fisheries is still the more prevalent practice, some states, such as Brazil 4/ and Mexico 5/ expressly reserve certain types of fishery, such as the high-value lobster and shrimp fisheries, for national fleets.

(c) Reporting requirements and observers

The critical points at which reporting is required, as specified in coastal state legislation or access agreements, tend to be entry into the fishery zone and departure from the zone. In addition, many countries require periodical radioed position and catch and effort reports 6/. These are usually required on a weekly or daily basis. During the period of fishing operations, foreign vessels are now normally required to maintain on a daily basis logbooks of position, effort, catch and other relevant data, such as records of any transhipment of catches 7/. These logbooks or records are usually to be turned into the coastal state authorities at the end of fishing operations or within a specified period after the end of such operations. With respect to both log books and timely reporting of position and catch, there are quite clear regional disparities in state practice. In the South Pacific, for example, the requirements for both log books and reports are almost universal and uniform. In West Africa, on the other hand, few countries have yet insisted on such requirements. The Indian Ocean region and the Americas fall somewhere in between. Several countries also make provision for observers to be placed on board foreign vessels, very often at the expense of the foreign vessel, and to be given food, accommodation and the necessary access to vessels and facilities, such as radio communications equipment, to carry out their functions 8/. The system of observers seems to be most productive where large foreign fishing vessels are involved and where adequately trained observers are available.

(d) Research

A few countries make reference in their foreign fishing licence conditions to the carrying out of agreed programmes of research and sampling. The Canadian legislation, for example, makes it a condition of any licence issued in respect of a foreign fishing vessel that the master of the vessel should comply with instructions given to him by authorized officials of the flag state in respect of any programme of sampling,

---

1/ Senegal - Code de la Pêche Maritime, 1976, Arts. 18 and 20.
2/ As, e.g. in Cameroun, Canada, Congo, Liberia, Sierra Leone and U.S.A.
3/ As, e.g. Canada - Coastal Fisheries Protection Regulations, 1976; or Iceland - Regulations concerning the Fishery Limits Off Iceland, 1975, Art. 4.
4/ Brazil - Decree No. 68.459 of 1971.
5/ Mexico - Decree amending Art. 37 of the Federal Law on Fisheries Development, 1976.
6/ As, e.g., in Brazil, Canada, New Zealand, Norway, Sweden, U.S.A. and Uruguay. The European Community licence conditions for foreign fishing in Community waters require daily radio reports on position and catch for some fleets and reports every three days or weekly for other fleets and specified target species.
7/ As, e.g. in Brazil, Canada, Guatemala, New Zealand, Sri Lanka, Sweden and U.S.A.
8/ As, e.g., in Canada, New Zealand and U.S.A.

observation or research requested of the flag state by the Minister 1/. An obligation to conduct specified programmes of fisheries research is also one of the possible conditions of foreign fishing vessel licences provided for under both the Fiji and New Zealand legislation 2/. General provisions relating to fisheries research are to be found in much of the legislation establishing or managing extended fisheries jurisdiction normally with the aim of establishing in some way the control of the coastal state over fisheries research in its zone. This control may take the form of a requirement that fisheries research vessels as well as commercial vessels hold formal licences 3/, or, more often, that research operations be authorized in some less formal way but still be subject to any conditions imposed by the coastal state authorities 4/. In some cases, however, scientific research operations are specifically excluded from the purview of the legislation 5/.

(e) Landing of catches and other requirements

Reference has already been made to the use of nationality criteria for encouraging local landings and the development of shore based processing industries. A number of countries also provide for conditions concerning the landing and processing of catch to be attached to foreign fishing licences. Some, such as Mauritania, Ghana, directly require that the catch be landed and/or processed locally. In Senegal and Guatemala, encouragement is given to local landings and processing through the level of licence fees and royalty payments, while in El Salvador the legislation provides that priority in sale of catch must be given to supplying the needs of the local market. Other countries, such as Fiji, Mauritius and Uruguay merely indicate that requirements concerning local landings and processing may be made a condition of the fishing licence. Whether local landings are to be encouraged or not depends, of course, on the state of the local fishing effort and market, and the needs of the processing industry sector; in some cases a glut of landings would merely depress the local market prices to the disadvantage of local fishermen. For this reason, Brazil, Mexico, New Zealand and Uruguay prohibit local landings by foreign vessels unless specifically authorized.

(f) Joint ventures

With the general extension of national jurisdiction, a number of coastal countries have recently embarked on general reviews of their national policies towards joint ventures in fisheries 6/. In some cases, policies have been adopted requiring all access to be in the form of joint ventures, whether or not this policy is actually embodied in legislation. Examples are Mauritania, Angola, Argentina, Brazil, Ghana and the Philippines. In Sri Lanka access to the 24-35 mile zone is reserved for joint

1/ Coastal Fisheries Protection Regulations, 1976, Reg. 11 (m). The regulation tries to ensure that obligations undertaken at an intergovernmental level are passed down to the practical level of implementation.

2/ Fiji - Marine Spaces Act, 1977, S. 12 (3) (i) or (j); New Zealand - Territorial Sea and Exclusive Economic Zone Act, 1977, S. 15 (j).

3/ e.g., Canada - Coastal Fisheries Protection Regulations, Reg. 5(a)

4/ e.g., The Gambia - The Fisheries Act, 1977, S. 50; Fiji - Marine Spaces Act, 1977, S. 21; Japan - Law No. 31 of 2 May, 1977, on Provisional Measures Relating to the Fishing Zone, Art. 9; New Zealand - Territorial Sea and Exclusive Economic Zone Act, 1977, S. 23.

5/ e.g., U.S.A. - Fishery Conservation and Management Act of 1976, S.3 (10).

6/ As, for example, in Australia, Canada, India and the Philippines.

ventures in specified fisheries 1/. In other cases, criteria are set down for joint venture operations, usually with a requirement for majority shareholding by nationals 2/. A legal requirement for all access to be in the form of joint ventures does not of course automatically lead to the establishment of genuine joint venture industries of the desired sort. In many cases such policies have led to the setting up of fake joint ventures with little if any development or revenue benefit to the coastal state.

(g) Regional cooperation

Disparities in access conditions, particularly with respect to identification of vessels, and reporting and logbook requirements, can cause difficulties for both coastal states and foreign fishing fleet operators where fishing operations tend to move across several coastal state jurisdictions as in the case of the tuna fisheries of the Western Pacific. To circumvent some of these difficulties coastal countries of the Western Pacific have been moving recently towards the harmonization of access regimes and conditions. The member countries of the so-called Nauru Group 3/ have embodied this harmonization in an international agreement and implementing arrangement 4/. On a wider geographical basis the member countries of the South Pacific Forum meeting in Rotorua in August 1982 agreed on a series of harmonized minimum access conditions, dealing with identification of foreign vessels, reporting requirements, logbooks and observers, as well as the establishment of a regional register of foreign fishing vessels. Although the Western Pacific movement is the most advanced, similar movements towards harmonization of access regimes are underway in other regions. In the Caribbean the member countries of the Organization of Eastern Caribbean States (OECS), working with the FAO Fisheries Law Advisory Programme, have drawn up harmonized fisheries legislation and regulations for each of their countries 5/. As foreign fishing activities are far less important in the OECS region than in the South Pacific, the legislation concentrates mainly on the national regulation of fisheries and the harmonization of management regimes and planning. The legislation, however, also provides for the possibility of joint licensing schemes for foreign fishing and regional cooperation in the control of those operations, including the possibility of establishing a regional register of fishing vessels. The regulations would provide for harmonized terms and conditions of access. The legislation has now been enacted in three of the member countries, 6/ and is in various stages of approval in the remainder. In West Africa, harmonization of fishery regimes, with particular though not exclsuive reference to foreign fishing, has been the expressed objective of a number of regional and subregional groupings 7/, though no positive action has yet been taken.

1/ Foreign Fishing Boat Regulations, 1981, Reg. 6.

2/ In this context it should be noted that majority shareholding does not necessarily and often does not confer control over the operations of the joint venture enterprise. See generally, Crutchfield, Hamlisch, Moore and Walker, Joint Ventures in Fisheries, IOFC/DEV/75/37.

3/ Nauru, Papua New Guinea, F.S.M., Kiribati, Palau, Marshall Islands and Solomon Islands.

4/ The Nauru Agreement has now been ratified by all participating countries. The implementing arrangement is not yet in force.

5/ A series of three workshops was held in Castries, St. Lucia, in 1983; in St. John's, Antigua again in 1983; and in Castries, St. Lucia in 1984.

6/ Antigua & Barbuda - Fisheries Act 1983; St. Christopher & Nevis - Fisheries Act, 1984; St. Lucia - Fisheries Act 1984.

7/ E.g. the ECOWAS Conference on Fisheries, Dakar, Senegal, 25 - 29 March 1985; The Sub-regional Conference of Fsiheries Ministers from Cape Verde, Gambia, Guinea-Biassau, Mauritania and Senegal; and the Convention on the Regional Development of Fisheries in the Gulf of Guinea, 21 June 1984.

(h) Other conditions

In general, most of the conditions for foreign fishing contained in national legislation are covered by the examples cited in Article 62.4 of the Convention. Additional conditions, such as marking of vessels, the carrying of transponders and the carrying of other position fixing or identification equipment are normally concerned with details of compliance control, and thus covered by the general expression in the Convention Article 62.4 of "enforcement procedures". Not covered by the list of examples and of particular interest is the requirement in the Bahamas legislation that licence allocations can only be made to foreign states under a bilateral agreement which specifies, inter alia, that access to the markets of that foreign state shall be granted for the fishery resources and fishery products harvested by the fishermen of the Bahamas in the exclusive fishery zone 1/. As noted above, similar policies have been adopted in U.S.A., Canada, New Zealand and Australia 2/. In the latter two cases, access to export markets have been sought for products other than fish.

5. Enforcement

Article 73 of the Convention on the Law of the Sea recognizes the right of coastal states to take such measures in the exclusive economic zone, including boarding, inspection, arrest and judical proceedings, as may be necessary to ensure compliance with its laws and regulations. Arrested vessels and their crews are to be released promptly on posting of reasonable bond or other security. Penalties are not to include imprisonment in the absence of agreement to the contrary with the states concerned, or other form of corporal punishment. Where foreign vessels are arrested or detained, the coastal state is to notify the flag state of the action taken and penalties imposed.

Many countries authorize the use of defence forces for surveillance and enforcement operations as well as civilian protection services 3/. Broadly similar powers of stopping, boarding, inspection, seizure and arrest in the event of suspected contraventions are normally provided for. In a few countries, and particularly those with a French law tradition, detailed procedures for the reporting of offences and for arresting vessels are set out in the legislation. The Moroccan law, for example, authorizes a standard procedure for stopping and detaining offending vessels, including opening fire in cases of refusal to stop, while the Senegalese Marine Fisheries Code provides for three different procedures for reporting offences and arresting vessels, depending on the conditions and reaction of the target vessels. The Senegalese procedures also authorize pursuit of offenders over jurisdictional boundaries, provided that such pursuits and incursions are allowed under agreements with bordering countries. This provision is of particular interest given the new trend towards regional or subregional cooperation in surveillance and enforcement 4/.

1/ Bahamas - The Fisheries Resources (Jurisdiction and Conservation) Act, 1977, S. 10(4).

2/ See, e.g. Exchange of Letters between Canada and EEC dated 30 December 1980. U.S.A. Mangusson Fishery Conservation and Management Act S. 201 (e).

3/ As, e.g., in Brazil, Fiji, The Gambia, New Zealand, U.S.A. On the use of defence forces for fisheries protection, see generally Fidell, E.R., Fisheries Legislation: Naval Enforcement, Journal of Maritime Law and Commerce, Vol. 7, No. 2, January 1976, pp. 351-366.

4/ Movements towards subregional cooperation can be seen in West Africa, among the states of Cape Verde, The Gambia, Guinea-Bissau, Mauritania and Senegal, and among the island states of the South Pacific and the Caribbean.

It also raises the interesting thought that whereas "hot pursuit" under traditional international law has almost always been from the territorial sea (or exclusive fishery zone) on to the high seas, with the extension of jurisdiction over fisheries to 200 miles, the most convenient "escape routes" for illegal foreign fishing vessels will often be across national boundaries into the jurisdictional waters of neighbouring states 1/.

The level of fines imposed for illegal foreign fishing ranges from a low of about US$6 in Dominican Republic 2/ to over almost US$2 million in Mauritania 3/. In addition to fines, the vast majority of countries empower the courts to order forfeiture of catch, fishing gear and boats 4/. In a few cases, forfeiture of vessels is automatic, even on the first offence 5/. Despite the provisions of the Convention, imprisonment is provided for as a possible penalty for illegal unlicensed fishing in 32 countries that have extended jurisdiction over fisheries to 200 miles 6/, although the more recent trend seems to be to limit penalties to fines and forfeiture of catch, gear and vessels 7/. In the imposition of fines, there seems to be a tendency towards the use of administrative proceedings, in order to allow for speedier settlement of cases. The U.S. legislation, for example, provides for four categories of penalty for violations. These are, in ascending order of severity: citations (administrative notices of violations not entailing monetary penalties); assessment of civil monetary penalties; judicial forfeiture of vessel and catch, and, finally, criminal prosecution 8/. Canada also now provides for a system of civil monetary penalties along the lines

---

1/ The Geneva Convention of the High Seas of 1958 and the Information Composite Negotiating Text provide that the right of hot pursuit ceases only where the ship pursued enters into its own territorial sea or that of a third state. No general account of state practice on the subject is known. Instructions to U.K. fishery protection vessels, however, authorize them to maintain hot pursuit in appropriate cases into other countries' fishery zones up to the limits of their territorial seas. See The Fishing Industry: Government Observations on the Fifth Report from the Expenditure Committee, Session 1977-78, H.C. 356, Cmnd 7434 para. 57. See, however, the Fifth Report from the Expenditure Committee, Session 1977-78 itself (House of Commons publication No. 356, 1978) which indicates at paragraph 222 that in practice fishing vessels are not usually pursued into the fishery zones of other states.

2/ Dominica Republic - Law No. 5914 of 22 May 1962, Art. 47 and 49.

3/ Mauritania - Code of Merchant Shipping, Act No. 78-043 of 28 February 1978, Art. 206 as amended.

4/ As, e.g., in Brazil, Burma, Canada, El Salvador, The Gambia, Ghana, Guyana, Japan, Madagascar, Mauritius, New Zealand, Nigeria, Norway, Papua New Guinea, Portugal, Senegal, Seychelles, Sri Lanka and U.S.A.

5/ As, e.g. in Papua New Guinea, Malta, New Zealand, Cook Islands, Niue and Sri Lanka. This type of provision, by limiting the freedom of the courts, can on occasion prove embarassing to the government concerned.

6/ Bahamas, Bangladesh, Barbados, Benin, Burma, Cape Verde, Chile, Congo, Gabon, Gambia, Ghana, Grenada, Guinea-Bissau, Haiti, Kenya, Maldives, Mauritius, Morocco, Nauru, Niue, Nigeria, Papua New Guinea, Philippines, Senegal, Sierra Leone, Somalia, South Africa, Suriname, Togo, Tonga, Western Samoa, Yemen (PDR).

7/ As, e.g., in Angola, Argentina, Australia, Belgium, Brazil, Cameroon, Colombia, Denmark, Ecuador, El Salvador, Fiji, Germany (Dem. Rep.), Guatemala, Guyana, Honduras, Iceland, India, Ireland, Ivory Coast, Japan, Kiribati, Liberia, Mauritania, Mexico Mozambique, New Zealand, Norway, Panama, Peru, Portugal, Sao Tome and Principe, Seychelles, Solomon Islands, Spain, Sri Lanka, U.K., U.S.S.R., Uruguay and Vanuatu.

8/ U.S.A.: NOAA Interim Regulations on civil procedures to be applied with regard to violations under the Fishery Conservation and Management Act.

of traffic "tickets" 1/. In some cases the institution of administrative penalties and procedures has raised constitutional objections related to the concept of the separation of powers. To overcome these objections, a number of countries have turned to the old common-law concept of compounding of offences 2/. Under these procedures a Minister or official may be given powers to drop criminal charges and release seized property against payment of a substantial sum of money. The concept offers a considerable degree of flexibility in dealing with foreign fishing violations, including the added attraction of avoiding the limitations inherent in the service of criminal process outside the coastal state jurisdiction. So far as criminal liability is concerned, primary responsibility is usually placed on the master of the vessel. Many countries, however, now provide that vessel owners and local representatives are also to be liable for the payment of fines 3/.

Following the provisions of the Convention, a number of countries now allow for the release of seized vessels on the posting of a satisfactory bond or other form of security 4/, although the procedure is far from universal. The bond or the vessel itself is normally held as security for the full payment of any fine or other penalty ordered by the court.

While the effectiveness of surveillance and enforcement operations depends ultimately on the physical and financial means available, a number of coastal states have sought to lessen the burden by the adoption of provisions in their national legislation aimed at facilitating enforcement. One example is the tendency to place more responsibility on the foreign flag state for ensuring compliance by its vessels with the agreed terms and conditions of authorized fishing operations. The U.S. legislation, for example, requires "governing international fishery agreements" to be entered into by foreign flag states wishing to fish within the U.S. fishery conservation zone. Under such an agreement, the foreign flag state must take on a binding commitment, both on its own behalf and on behalf of its vessels, to comply with the conditions applicable to foreign fishing operations 5/. Similar provisions are contained in the legislation of Bahamas, Federated States of Micronesia, Marshall Islands and Palau 6/. A number of states also specify past cooperation in enforcement as a criterion for allocating licences to a foreign state 7/ as well as in an increasing number of bilateral agreements themselves. The Australia-Japan Head Agreement of 1979, for example, provides that the Government of Japan is to take measures to ensure that both licenced and unlicensed vessels flying its flag comply with the terms of the agreement. Other countries require that flag state authorities should assume responsibility for compliance with certain aspects of coastal state controls, such as ensuring that proper reports are given on authorized fishing

---

1/ Similar procedures for assessing administrative fines are found in several other countries, e.g., in Brazil and U.S.S.R..

2/ e.g., Antigua & Barbuda, Cameroun,Gabon, Guinea, Malaysia, Mauritania, Morocco, Norway, Senegal, St. Christopher & Nevis, St. Lucia and Vanuatu

3/ As, e.g., in Ecuador, Fiji, Guatemala, Guyana, Japan, New Zealand, Senegal, Seychelles and U.S.A.

4/ As, e.g., in Canada, Fiji, The Gambia, Mauritania, New Zealand, Senegal, Sri Lanka, U.S.A. and Vanuatu.

5/ U.S.A.: Mangusson Fishery Conservation and Management Act, 1976, S. 201.

6/ The Bahamas: The Fisheries Resources (Jurisdiction and Conservation) Act, 1977, S. 10(4)(c).

7/ Fiji - Marine Spaces Act, 1977, S. 11(4)(c); New Zealand - Territorial Sea and Exclusive Economic Zone Act 1977, S. 13(2)(c); U.S.A. - Fishery Conservation and Management Act, 1976, S 201(e)(3).

operations 1/. While the concept of flag state responsibility for compliance control can be said to be well accepted in state practice 2/, coastal states now seem to be searching out practical ways of giving effect to the general commitments already made. This movement is particularly evident in the South Pacific region. A number of access agreements in that region, for example, provide for Association guarantees for the satisfaction of judgment orders entered against members vessels 3/, while one recent agreement actually provides for the extradition of flag state violators to the coastal state. Flag state compliance control and procedures for investigation, reporting and sanctioning of offending vessels by the flag state, are figuring predominantly in new access negotiations in the region.

On the other side of the fence, as it were, a number of flag states are now adopting administrative measures to control the activities of their vessels while operating outside flag state waters. Spain, for example, now requires any vessel operating in another state's waters to hold a licence issued by Spain. One of the conditions for the issue of such licences, is that the vessel holds a valid licence or other fishing authorization from the coastal state in whose waters it is to fish 4/.

In an effort to ensure that foreign fishing operations are subject to coastal state jurisdiction in a real as well as a formal sense, some states now require that licenced vessels must maintain local agents or representatives who can assume legal and financial responsibility for the conduct of the fishing operations 5/. Under the Senegalese legislation, foreign fishing vessels not operating under a bilateral fishing agreement, are required to post a bond with the government guaranteeing performance of the conditions of the fishing licence 6/. Almost all legislation requires foreign fishing vessels to bear distinctive markings as an aid to enforcement, though there is great disparity in the standards imposed. The desirability of harmonizing on a single marking standard was recognized at the FAO World Conference on Fisheries Management and Development. As a follow-up to the Conference an Expert Consultation on the Marking of Fishing Vessels was held in Halifax, Nova Scotia, Canada in March 1985, which recommended standardization on the international radio call sign, marked in characters at least 1 metre high. The recommended standard in fact coincides with the standards already enforced in a number of coastal states, as well as those recommended as a regional standard in the Western Pacific by the Forum Fisheries Agency. Again there are regional disparities in the requirements actually applied, with West Africa and the Caribbean lagging somewhat behind the South Pacific and the Indian Ocean regions.

1/ e.g., Canada - Coastal Fisheries Protection Regulations, 1977; EEC - Council Regulation laying down certain measures for the conservation and management of fishery resources applicable to vessels registered in the Faroe Islands, 1978; U.S.A. - NOAA Regulations on Conditions and Restrictions Concerning Foreign Fishing Off the Coasts of the United States, 1977.

2/ See the examples noted above and the other examples noted in the annexed tables C and D. The concept of flag state responsibility has received specific acknowledgement in the Strategy adopted by the recent FAO World Conference on Fisheries Management and Development. See Report of the Conference, Strategy III (xvii) p. 20.

3/ See e.g. Agreement between Palau and the Fisheries Associations of Japan, 1983; Agreement between Marshall Islands and Japan, 1983; Agreement between the Federated States of Micronesia and the Japanese Fishing Associations, 1984.

4/ Spain - Order of 2 March 1982.

5/ As, e.g., in Brazil - Decree Law No. 221 of 1967; Canada - Coastal Fisheries Protection Regulations, 1977; U.S.A. - Fisheries Conservation and Management Act, 1976, S. 201.

6/ Senegal: Marine Fisheries Code, 1976. It is understood that this requirement is not applied in practice.

Several laws also refer to a possible requirement of installing transponders or other position-fixing equipment on board the licenced vessel, although, as far as it is known, no transponder scheme has yet been adopted 1/. A condition requiring acceptance of observers on board a licenced vessel is also often used as a means of facilitating surveillance and monitoring of operations 2/, as well as requirements concerning the reporting of entry into, or departure from, zones under coastal state jurisdiction, and periodic position reporting by radio 3/.

In addition to physical aids to enforcement, most states make some use of presumptions in order to ease evidentiary problems. These may take the form of legal presumptions, for example, that all fish found on board a fishing vessel that has been discovered committing an offence in waters under the jurisdiction of the coastal state, shall be presumed to have been caught in those waters during the commission of the offence, until the contrary is proved 4/. The presumption avoids the evidentiary difficulties of proving the origin of fish caught over a period of time and perhaps mixed in cold storage with fish caught elsewhere.

6. Controls over transit of unlicenced fishing boats

Article 58 of the Law of the Sea Convention safeguards the rights of all states to freedom of navigation through the exclusive economic zone, "subject to the relevant provisions of (the) Convention". At the same time Article 73 empowers the coastal state to take measures to ensure compliance with its laws and regulations adopted in the exercise of its sovereign rights over the living resources of the zone. One area in which the balancing of these rights is most sensitive is in the adoption by the coastal state of controls over unlicensed fishing vessels transitting its zone.

The situation on this point is not clear either under customary international law or under the Convention itself 5/. In general it would appear that controls requiring the stowage of gear would be acceptable, provided that methods of stowage are specified that would not cause excessive inconvenience to transitting vessels. Other controls, including requirements for vessels to report entry into the zone would appear to raise more difficult questions, given the sensitivity over the issue of reporting by warships when exercising innocent passage through the territorial seas. Such requirements present a borderline case, the legality of which may well be determined only over a period of time through state practice.

1/ e.g., Canada - Coastal Fisheries Protection Regulations, 1977; Fiji - Marine Spaces Act, 1977, S. 12(3)(p); New Zealand - Territorial Sea and Exclusive Economic Zone Act, 1977, S. 15(3)(p); U.S.A. - Fishery Conservation and Management Act, 1976, S. 201 (c)(2)(c). In the U.K., the possible use of transponders is being studied. To-date their use has been precluded because of cost and relative lack of specificity and security of equipment. See U.K. Report from the Expenditure Committee, Session 1977-78; The Fishing Industry, House of Commons, publication No. 356, 1978, p. 76.

2/ As, e.g. in Canada, Fiji, New Zealand, U.S.A.

3/ As, e.g. in Canada, EEC, New Zealand and U.S.A.

4/ Such rebuttable presumptions are to be found, for example, in the legislation of the Papua New Guinea (Fisheries Act, 1974, S.21); The Gambia (Fisheries Act, 1974); Seychelles (Fishery Limits Ordinance, 1977) and U.S.A. (Fishery Conservation and Management Act, 1976, S. 310(e)).

5/ See Burke, W.T.: Fisheries Regulations under extended jurisdiction and international law, FIPP/T223, FAO, Rome, 1982.

In practice, a large number of coastal states do require unlicensed transitting fishing vessels to comply with coastal state regulations concerning stowage of gear 1/. Three coastal states require unlicensed fishing vessels to obtain permission before exercising their rights of free navigation through the zone 2/; Costa Rica also requires unlicensed vessels to maintain a radio watch on a specified frequency while transitting the zone, while Australia requires transitting vessels to take the shortest practicable route. A similar requirement is in practice provided for in the legislation of a number of other countries through the definition of the activity of fishing. In Mozambique, for example, both fishing and "preparing to fish" by unlicensed vessels are prohibited. Preparing to fish is defined as including activities such as stopping or following a zig-zag course, presumably while searching for fish 3/. A similar definition of fishing, is given in the new harmonized fisheries legislation adopted by the member countries of the Organization of Eastern Caribbean States and in the U.S. Foreign Fishing Regulations; the latter specifies that the notion of preparing to fish is to include scouting or exploring for the presence of fish by visual or acoustic or other means 4/. In a number of other countries, controls are exerted through the device of presumptions. In India and Bahamas, for example, all fish found on board a vessel inside the zone, is presumed to have been caught in the zone, without any requirement that a separate identifiable offence has been committed. Similarly the new Suriname legislation provides that any unlicensed foreign vessel found in the zone is committing an offence unless proved to be in direct transit or there for some other purpose related to navigation or communication recognized by international law. The Australian legislation obtains the same effect by stipulating a wide-ranging offence of possessing a foreign fishing vessel in the zone and then providing for a number of defenses, one of which is that the vessel was in fact transitting the zone. In Seychelles, a presumption similar to that provided for in Bahamas is included in the legislation, with the proviso, however, that the presumption may be rebutted by reporting entry into the zone in a prescribed format. The same rebuttable presumption is contained in the new Malaysian legislation, coupled with a positive requirement for vessels intending to enter Malaysian fisheries waters for the purpose of "innocent passage" to notify the Malaysian authorities by radio, giving details of the route to be followed and the amount of fish on board. 5/

7. Regional cooperation

In an effort to alleviate some of the difficulties of compliance control in an area characterized by vast expanses of ocean and few means of surveillance and enforcement, the member countries of the South Pacific Forum and the two observer countries of the Forum Fisheries Agency, have established a regional register of

---

1/ As, e.g. in Australia, Canada, Guyana, The Gambia, Maldives, New Zealand, Solomon Islands, Spain, U.K., Vanuatu, although not always are the methods of stowage specified in detail.

2/ El Salvador - General Law on Fisheries Activities, Decree No. 799 of 14 September 1981; Costa Rica - Law No. 6267 of 1978, Art. 7 (in both cases vessels have 48 hours to transit through the zone); and Maldives.

3/ Mozambique - Law No. 8/78 of 22 April 1978, Art. 1.

4/ Antigua & Barbuda - Fisheries Act 1983, S. 2; St. Christopher & Nevis - Fisheries Act, 1984 S. 2; St. Lucia - Fisheries Act 1984 S. 2; U.S.A. - CFR S. 611.2.

5/ Malaysia - Fisheries Act, 1984, S. 16 & 56

foreign fishing vessels. The regional register, which is located in Honiara, Solomon Islands, has been operative since 1 September 1983, and FFA member and observer states have agreed that only those foreign fishing vessels listed in good standing on the regional register may be granted licences to fish in the region. The register performs two main functions. Firstly, it provides a central computerized source of information on all foreign fishing vessels licenced to operate in the region which can be drawn upon for licensing decisions and procedures and as an aid in surveillance operations. Secondly, it provides a basis for alternative systems of compliance control to be taken on a regional basis, that reduce the need for reliance on costly surface enforcement operations. Although the regional register has only been functioning for a matter of two years, it has already proved effective in the realization of its objectives. Removing a vessel from good standing on the register, which has not yet proved necessary, is a serious event and can only be done with the full agreement of all participating FFA coastal countries. The main reason for requesting removal from good standing is refusal by a vessel to submit to the jurisdiction of the coastal state to answer a prima facie charge of violating the fishery laws of that coastal state. So far the regional register is unique to the FFA region. The possibility of establishing similar registers has, however, been discussed in a number of other regions, and reference is made to the concept in the harmonized fisheries legislation recently adopted in the Lesser Antilles region by the member countries of the Organization of Eastern Caribbean States (OECS). 1/

1/ See Antigua & Barbuda - Fisheries Act 1983, S. 6; St. Christopher & Nevis - Fisheries Act, 1984 S. 6; St. Lucia - Fisheries Act 1984 S. 6.

PART TWO

TABLES

TABLE A

LIMITS OF TERRITORIAL SEAS, FISHING ZONES AND EXCLUSIVE ECONOMIC ZONES

STATE	TERRITORIAL SEA	FISHING ZONE	ECONOMIC ZONE	OTHER
Albania	15 mi (1976)			
* Algeria	12 mi (1963)			
* Angola	20 mi (1975)	200 mi (1975)		
* Antigua & Barbuda	12 mi (1982)	200 mi (1982)	200 mi (1982)	
* Argentina	200 mi (1967)			
* Australia	3 mi (1973)	200 mi (1979)		
**Bahamas (The)	3 mi (1878)	200 mi (1977)		
**Bahrain	3 mi			
* Bangladesh	12 mi (1974)		200 mi (1974)	
* Barbados	12 mi (1979)		200 mi (1979)	
* Belgium	3 mi (1958)	Up to median line (1978)		
**Belize	3 mi (1878)			
* Benin	200 mi (1976)			
* Brazil	200 mi (1970)			
* Brunei Darussalam	12 mi (1983)	200 mi or median line (1983)		
* Bulgaria	12 mi (1951)			
* Burma	12 mi (1968-1977)		200 mi (1977)	
**Cameroon	50 mi (1974)			
* Canada	12 mi (1970)	200 mi (1977)		
* Cape Verde	12 mi (1977)		200 mi (1977)	
* Chile	3 mi		200 mi (1947-52)	
* China	12 mi (1958)			
* Colombia	12 mi (1970-78)		200 mi (1978)	
* Comoro Islands	12 mi (1976-82)		200 mi (1976-82)	
* Congo (People's Republic)	200 mi (1977)			
* Costa Rica	12 mi (1972-75)		200 mi (1975)	
**Cuba	12 mi (1977)		200 mi (1977)	
* Cyprus	12 mi (1964)			
* Denmark	3 mi (1966)	200 mi (1977)		
* Djibouti (Rep. of)	12 mi (1971-79)		200 mi (1979)	
* Dominica	12 mi (1981)	200 mi (1981)	200 mi (1981)	
* Dominican Rep.	6 mi (1967)		200 mi (1977)	
Ecuador	200 mi (1966)			
**Egypt, Arab Rep.	12 mi (1958)			
* El Salvador	200 mi (1950-83)			
* Equatorial Guinea	12 mi (1970-84)		200 mi (1984)	
* Ethiopia	12 mi (1953)			
**Fiji	12 mi (1978)		200 mi (1981)	
* Finland	4 mi (1956)	12 mi (1975) or agreed boundary		
* France	12 mi (1971)		200 mi (1977) (Except Mediterranean)	
French Dependent Territories	12 mi (1971)		200 mi (1978)	

* Country is a signatory to the UN Law of the Sea Convention
**Country has ratified the UN Law of the Sea Convention

TABLE A

LIMITS OF TERRITORIAL SEAS, FISHING ZONES AND EXCLUSIVE ECONOMIC ZONES

STATE	TERRITORIAL SEA	FISHING ZONE	ECONOMIC ZONE	OTHER
* Gabon	100 mi (1972)			
**Gambia (The)	12 mi (1969)	200 mi (1978)		
* German Dem. Rep.	12 mi (1985)	Up to median line (1978)		
Germany, Fed. Rep.	3 mi ***	200 mi (1977)		
**Ghana	200 mi (1977)			
* Greece	6 mi (1936)			
* Grenada	12 mi (1978)		200 mi (1978)	
* Guatemala	12 mi (1934-76)		200 mi (1976)	
**Guinea	12 mi (1980)		200 mi (1980)	
* Guinea-Bissau	12 mi (1978)		200 mi (1978)	
* Guyana	12 mi (1977)	200 mi (1977)	****	
* Haiti	12 mi (1972)		200 mi (1977)	
* Honduras	12 mi (1965)		200 mi (1951-80)	
**Iceland	12 mi (1979)		200 mi (1979)	
* India	12 mi (1967-76)		200 mi (1977)	
* Indonesia	12 mi (1957-60) straight baselines surrounding archipelago		200 mi (1980)	
* Iran	12 mi (1959)	Outer limits of the superajacent waters of the continental shelf. median line in the Sea of Oman (1973-7).		
**Iraq	12 mi (1958)			
* Ireland	3 mi (1959)	200 mi (1977)		
Israel	6 mi (1956)			
* Italy	12 mi (1974)			
**Ivory Coast	12 mi (1977)		200 mi (1977)	
**Jamaica	12 mi (1971)			
* Japan	12 mi (1977)	200 mi (1977) Provisional		
Jordan	3 mi (1943)			
* Kampuchea	12 mi (1969)		200 mi (1979)	
* Kenya	12 mi (1969-72)		200 mi (1979)	

* Country is a signatory to the UN Law of the Sea Convention
** Country has ratified the UN Law of the Sea Convention
*** Limits extended off parts of North Sea coast up to approx. 16 miles in order to deal with oil tanker casualties (1984) (Areas defined by geographical coordinates)
**** The Guyana Maritime Boundaries Act 1977 empowers the President to declare a 200 mile exclusive economic zone. To date no such zone has been declared.

TABLE A

LIMITS OF TERRITORIAL SEAS, FISHING ZONES AND EXCLUSIVE ECONOMIC ZONES

STATE	TERRITORIAL SEA	FISHING ZONE	ECONOMIC ZONE	OTHER
Kiribati	12 mi (1983)		200 mi (1983)	
* Korea, Dem. People's Rep.	12 mi		200 mi (1977)	
* Korea, Rep. of	12 mi (1978)	12 mi		
* Kuwait	12 mi (1967)			
* Lebanon	12 mi (1983)			
* Liberia	200 mi (1976)			
* Libya	12 mi (1959)			
* Madagascar	12 mi (1985)		200 mi (1985)	
* Malaysia	12 mi (1969)		200 mi (1980-84)	
* Maldives Islands	12 mi (1975)		Areas defined by geographical coordinates (1976)	
* Malta	12 mi (1978)	25 mi (1978)		
* Mauritania	70 mi (1978)		200 mi (1978)	
* Mauritius	12 mi (1970-77)		200 mi (1977)	
**Mexico	12 mi (1969-72)		200 mi (1976)	
* Monaco	12 mi (1973)			
* Morocco	12 mi (1973)		200 mi (1981)	
* Mozambique	12 mi (1976)		200 mi (1976)	
**Namibia	6 mi (1963)	12 mi (1963)		
* Nauru	12 mi (1971)	200 mi (1978)		
* Netherlands	12 mi (1985)	200 mi (1977)		
* New Zealand	12 mi (1977)		200 mi (1978)	
New Zealand				
-Dependent Territ.				
Tokelau	12 mi (1977)		200 mi (1977)	
-Associated States				
* Cook Islands	12 mi (1977)		200 mi (1977)	
Niue	12 mi (1978)		200 mi (1978)	
* Nicaragua				200 mi (1979) Sovereignty and jurisdiction over the sea adjacent to its coasts up to 200 mi.
* Nigeria	30 mi (1971)		200 mi (1978)	

* Country is a signatory to the UN Law of the Sea Convention
**Country has ratified the UN Law of the Sea Convention

TABLE A

LIMITS OF TERRITORIAL SEAS, FISHING ZONES AND EXCLUSIVE ECONOMIC ZONES

STATE	TERRITORIAL SEA	FISHING ZONE	ECONOMIC ZONE	OTHER
* Norway	4 mi (1812)		200 mi (1977) (Economic Zone)	
* Oman	12 mi (1977-81)		200 mi (1981)	
* Pakistan	12 mi (1966-76)		200 mi (1976)	
* Panama	200 mi (1967)			
* Papua New Guinea	12 mi (1978)			200 mi (1978) (offshore waters)
Peru				200 mi (1947) Sovereignty and jurisdiction over the sea, its soil and subsoil up to 200 mi (1947)
**Philippines	In accordance with treaties of 1898, 1900 and 1930. Straight baselines surrounding archipelago (1961)		200 mi (1978)	
* Poland	12 mi (1978)	Up to median line (1978)		
* Portugal	12 mi (1977)		200 mi (1977)	
* Qatar	3 mi	Outer limits of the superjacent waters of the continental shelf (1974)		
* Romania	12 mi (1951-56)			
* St. Christopher & Nevis	12 mi (1984)		200 mi (1984)	
**St. Lucia	12 mi (1984)		200 mi (1984)	
* St. Vincent & the Grenadines	12 mi (1983)		200 mi (1983)	
* Sao Tome & Principe	12 mi (1978)		200 mi (1978)	
* Saudi Arabia	12 mi (1958)	Outer limits of the superjacent waters of the continental shelf (1974)		
**Senegal	12 mi (1985)		200 mi (1985)	
* Seychelles	12 mi (1977)		200 mi (1977)	
* Sierra Leone	200 mi (1971)			

* Country is a signatory to the UN Law of the Sea Convention
**Country has ratified the UN Law of the Sea Convention

TABLE A

LIMITS OF TERRITORIAL SEAS, FISHING ZONES AND EXCLUSIVE ECONOMIC ZONES

STATE	TERRITORIAL SEA	FISHING ZONE	ECONOMIC ZONE	OTHER
* Singapore	3 mi (1878)			
* Solomon Islands	12 mi (1978)	200 mi (1978)	(200 mi)***	
* Somali Dem.Rep.	200 mi (1972)			
* South Africa	12 mi (1977)	200 mi (1977)		
* Spain	12 mi (1977)		200 mi (1978) (Except Mediterranean)	
* Sri Lanka	12 mi (1971-77)		200 mi (1977)	
**Sudan, The	12 mi (1960-70)			
* Suriname	12 mi (1978)		200 mi (1978)	
* Sweden	12 mi (1980)	200 mi (1978)		
Syrian Arab Rep.	35 mi (1981)			
**Tanzania	50 mi (1973)			
* Thailand	12 mi (1966)		200 mi (1982)	
**Togo	30 mi (1977)		200 mi (1977)	
Tonga	Territorial limits defined by geographical coordinates 173°-177W and 15°-23°30'S (1887) (12 mi)***		(200 mi)***	
* Trinidad and Tobago	12 mi (1969)			
**Tunisia	12 mi (1973)			
Turkey	6 mi (1964) in Aegean only 12 mi in Mediterranean and Black Sea (1982)	12 mi (1964)		
* Tuvalu	12 mi (1984)		200 mi (1984)	
* U.S.S.R.	12 mi ((1909-82)		200 mi (1984)	
* United Arab Emirates	3 mi (12 mi in the case of Sharga (1970))		Limits to be defined by agreement failing which median line (1980)	
United Kingdom	3 mi (1878)	200 mi (1977)		

* Country is a signatory to the UN Law of the Sea Convention
** Country has ratified the UN Law of the Sea Convention
*** Legislation enacted but not yet in force

TABLE A

LIMITS OF TERRITORIAL SEAS, FISHING ZONES AND EXCLUSIVE ECONOMIC ZONES

STATE	TERRITORIAL SEA	FISHING ZONE	ECONOMIC ZONE	OTHER
U.K. Dependent Territories				
- Ascension	3 mi (1878)	200 mi (1978)		
- Bermuda	3 mi (1878)	200 mi (1977)		
- British Virgin Islands	3 mi (1878)	200 mi (1977)		
- Cayman Islands	3 mi (1878)	200 mi (1977)		
- Montserrat	3 mi (1878)	200 mi (1983)		
- Pitcairn, Henderson, Ducie & Oeno Islands	3 mi (1878)	200 mi (1980)		
- St. Helena	3 mi (1878)	200 mi (1977)		
- Tristan da Cunha	3 mi (1878)	200 mi (1977)		
- Turks and Caicos	3 mi (1878)	200 mi (1978)		
- Others	3 mi (1878)			
United States of America	3 mi (1793-1972)	200 mi (1977)	200 mi (1983)	
US Trust Territories				
- Federated States of Micronesia	3 mi	200 mi (1979)		
- Marshall Islands	12 mi (1984)	200 mi (1979)		
- Northern Marianas	3 mi	200 mi (1978)	200 mi (1983)	
- Palau	3 mi	200 mi (1979)		
* Uruguay	200 mi (1969)			
* Vanuatu	12 mi (1978/82)		200 mi (1978/82)	
Venezuela	12 mi (1956)		200 mi (1978)	
* Viet Nam	12 (1977)		200 mi (1977)	
* Western Samoa	12 mi (1971)		200 mi (1980)	
* Yemen Arab Rep.	12 mi (1967)			
* Yemen People's Dem. Republic	12 mi (1970-78)		200 mi (1978)	
* Yugoslavia	12 mi (1979)			
* Zaire	12 mi (1974)			

* Country is a signatory to the UN Law of the Sea Convention
** Country has ratified the UN Law of the Sea Convention

TABLE B

LICENCE FEES, BILATERAL AGREEMENT OR JOINT VENTURE REQUIREMENTS AND NATIONALITY CRITERIA

STATE	Licence fees, royalties and other payments		Requirements concerning bilateral framework agreements or joint venture participation	Nationality criteria for fishing vessels
	Local currency	US$ Equiv.		
ALBANIA	NO INFORMATION			
ALGERIA	LEGISLATION Commercial fishing by foreign vessels forbidden in territorial waters. (Ordinance No. 76-84, 1976, art. 6)			
ANGOLA	LEGISLATION Foreign vessels authorized to fish in Angolan waters required to respect such conditions as fixed in licence. No direct reference to fees. (Decree on Protection of Marine Resources No.12-A/80 Art 6.) AGREEMENTS *Agreement with USSR -Information on revenues from joint Soviet/Angolan operations not available. *Agreement with Cape Verde, 1981 allows fishing vessels of Cape Verde to fish in Angolan waters from Oct to May when there is shortage of tuna in Cape Verde's waters. *Agreement with Nigeria 23 Feb 1982 Experimental fishing for 90 days 50% of catch delivered to Angola Angolan contribution to include fuel and salary of Angolan crew.		LEGISLATION Foreign fishing authorizations may be granted within framework of negotiations, agreements and contracts concluded by members of the Government. (Decree on Protection of Marine Resources No.12-A/80 Art 5 para 1.)	

TABLE B

LICENCE FEES, BILATERAL AGREEMENT OR JOINT VENTURE REQUIREMENTS AND NATIONALITY CRITERIA

STATE	Licence fees, royalties and other payments: Local currency	Licence fees, royalties and other payments: US$ Equiv.	Requirements concerning bilateral framework agreements or joint venture participation	Nationality criteria for fishing vessels
ANGOLA (Cont'd)	*Agreement with Spain signed end 1984 For crustaceans: - Spanish vessels authorized to catch 10 000 tonnes of crustaceans against payment in kind of 2.1 tonnes of mixed species fish for each tonne of crustaceans + lump sum of US$300 00 payable in quarterly instalments. For finfish: For first 700 tonnes lump sum payment of US$40 000 per year. For catches over 700 tonnes, for each 10% of the additional catch, fees for 95% of the excess catch set at US$530 per tonne and remaining 5% at US$930 per tonne. Spanish vessels also to hand over by-catch from shrimp operations. Spain to provide 40 scholarships (ENTRY VERIFIED - OCTOBER 1985)			
ANTIGUA & BARBUDA	LEGISLATION Such fees as may be prescribed plus such royalties or other charges as the Minister may determine. (S. 14) (The Fisheries Act No 14 of 1983) Fisheries Regulations not yet promulgated. (ENTRY VERIFIED - OCTOBER 1985)		LEGISLATION No foreign fishing vessel licence to be issued unless there is in force an access agreement with the flag state or association representing the owners. Flag state includes regional organization with delegated power to make agreements. Requirement does not apply to licences issued for test	LEGISLATION Local fishing vessel defined as any fishing vessel (a) wholly owned by the Govt. of Antigua & Barbuda or any public corporation established by or under any law; or (b) wholly owned by one or more persons who are citizens of Antigua & Barbuda: or (c) wholly owned by any company, society or other association of persons incorporated or established in Antigua & Barbuda of which at least

TABLE B

LICENCE FEES, BILATERAL AGREEMENT OR JOINT VENTURE REQUIREMENTS AND NATIONALITY CRITERIA

STATE	Licence fees, royalties and other payments		Requirements concerning bilateral framework agreements or joint venture participation	Nationality criteria for fishing vessels
	Local currency	US$ Equiv.		
ANTIGUA & BARBUDA (Cont'd)			fishing operations or locally based fishing operations. (The Fisheries Act No 14 of 1983 S. 8)	51% of the voting shares are held by citizens locally based foreign fishing vessel defined as one based in Antigua & Barbuda which lands all its catch there (The Fisheries Act No 14 of 1983 S. 2)
ARGENTINA	LEGISLATION Fishing by foreign flag vessels prohibited in territorial sea. (Act No. 17.500 of 1967 (as amended by Act No. 20.136 of 1973) (Art. 2)	-	LEGISLATION -Joint ventures normally required. AGREEMENTS Under arrangements with certain enterprises in Japan, (January 1978), Germany(FDR) (April 1978) and USSR (June 1981) - experimental fishing by foreign vessels allowed for one year at end of which **feasibility studies and proposals for future joint venture fishing operations to be submitted.**	LEGISLATION Argentine vessel (enrolled on national register) = owner (or majority of co-owners owning over 50% of vessel) must be domiciled in Argentina. Where vessel is owned by a company, this must be constituted in accordance with the laws of Argentina or if in-rated abroad, and have a branch office or other permanent representation in Argentina. (Law No. 20.094, 1973 Art.52)

TABLE B

LICENCE FEES, BILATERAL AGREEMENT OR JOINT VENTURE REQUIREMENTS AND NATIONALITY CRITERIA

STATE	Licence fees, royalties and other payments		Requirements concerning bilateral framework agreements or joint venture participation	Nationality criteria for fishing vessels
	Local currency	US$ Equiv.		
AUSTRALIA	LEGISLATION - licence to engage in fisheries = A$ 20	US$ 13	LEGISLATION - Licences may be issued only where a bilateral agreement is in force, or for feasibility fishing operations or under commercial joint ventures. Source: [Australian Fishing Zone (AFZ) Information Bulletin N° 1, January 1980]	LEGISLATION "Australian Boat" means a boat the operations of which are based on a place in Australia or an external Territory and that is wholly owned by a natural person who is a resident of, or by a company incorporated in, Australia or an external Territory, being a boat that - (a) was built in Australia or an external Territory, (b) has been lawfully imported into Australia, otherwise than for a limited period, or into an external Territory; or (c) has been sold, or otherwise disposed of, in Australia or an external Territory after having been forfeited or distrained under this or any other Act or under a law of a State or Territory;- Fisheries Act 1952, S. 4 (1) -Where a boat has been lawfully imported into Australia for a limited period and the Minister is satisfied that the extent of participation by citizens or residents of Australia, either directly or through the holding of shares in a company or otherwise indirectly, in the control of the operations of the boat in proclaimed waters during that period, and the nature of those operations, will be such as to justify him in so
	- licence for fishing boat = A$ 35 per metre overall length	US$ 23		
	- additional fees for authority to carry fish taken by another boat = A$ 80, or to process = A$ 100	US$53 or US$66		
	- Fees for authority to carry or process fish taken by another boat where no licence to fish Carrying = A$80 + A$35 per metre	US$ 53 +US$ 23		
	Processing=A$100 + A$35 " "	US$ 66 +US$ 23		
	(Fisheries Regulations Sched. 1 & Torres Strait Fisheries Regs Sch.1)			
	AGREEMENTS *Australia/Japan Agreement on Tuna Longlining - Oct. 1983 valid through end Oct. 1984- $A 2 275 000 for up to 290 Japanese longliners	US$ 1 496 711		
	*New Agreement with Japan signed 30 Oct. 1984 valid thru' end Oct. 1985 new level of fees unknown. (Source AFZ Bulletin No.28 Oct 84)			
	*Australia/KKFC Pty Ltd. Agreement Aug.1984 valid thru' end July 1985. $A 1 447 985 lump sum access fee for up to 30 gillnetters (quota of 5 000 tonnes of pelagic fish), and 120 pair trawlers (quota of 27 500 tonnes of demersal finfish)	US$ 952 623		

TABLE B

LICENCE FEES, BILATERAL AGREEMENT OR JOINT VENTURE REQUIREMENTS AND NATIONALITY CRITERIA

STATE	Licence fees, royalties and other payments		Requirements concerning bilateral framework agreements or joint venture participation	Nationality criteria for fishing vessels
	Local currency	US$ Equiv.		
AUSTRALIA (Cont'd)	Note: Fee increased from 1983/4 fee of A$1 236 000and quota for finfish increased by 7 500 tonnes 1983/4 fee based on 6% of estimated landed value of the catch. *Australia/Rep. of Korea-Agreement on Squid Fishing - renewed 16 Oct. 1984 valid thru' 15 Oct 1985 -Up to 12 Korean vessels permitted to fish for squid in designated area off Tasmania, Victoria & South Australia. Access fee of A$189 000 to be paid for initial quota of 1 800 tonnes. Further quota of 2 200 tonnes available if required to be paid for at same rate. (Source: AFZ Bulletin No 27, May/July 1984) (ENTRY VERIFIED - OCTOBER 1985)	US$124 342		doing, he may, in his discretion, by instrument published in the Gazette, declare that, during that period, the boat is to be deemed to be an Australian boat for the purpose of this Act and, while such an instrument is in force in respect of a boat, the boat shall be deemed to be an Australian boat for the purposes of this Act. (Fisheries Act 1952, S. 4 (2))
BAHAMAS	LEGISLATION To be prescribed by the Minister. (Fisheries Resources (Jurisdiction and Conservation) Act 1977 S. 18) Note: No foreign fishing for commercial purposes at present. (ENTRY VERIFIED - OCTOBER 1985)		LEGISLATION Foreign fishing other than for research or sport authorized only under bilateral agreement and licence (S. 7) Licence may not be granted to any vessel the owner or operator of which is not a national of the foreign state which is a party to the fishery treaty. (S.9)	LEGISLATION Local fishing vessel defined as a fishing vessel that is owned by a citizen resident or a company registered in the Bahamas in which all the shares are owned by citizens of the Bahamas resident in the Bahamas. [Fisheries Resources (Jurisdiction and Conservation Act, 1977 (S.2)

TABLE B

LICENCE FEES, BILATERAL AGREEMENT OR JOINT VENTURE REQUIREMENTS AND NATIONALITY CRITERIA

STATE	Licence fees, royalties and other payments: Local currency	Licence fees, royalties and other payments: US$ Equiv.	Requirements concerning bilateral framework agreements or joint venture participation	Nationality criteria for fishing vessels
BAHAMAS (Cont'd)			(Fisheries Resources Jurisdiction and Conservation) Act, 1977 No agreement granting access rights yet concluded.	
BAHREIN	LEGISLATION Fees to be determined by Minister of Commerce and Agriculture with approval of Council of Ministers (Decree Promulgating Law No 5 of 1981 on Fishing Regulation Art. 9) (ENTRY VERIFIED - OCTOBER 1985)			LEGISLATION Local vessel defined as any vessel or boat registered in State of Bahrain for catching fish. (Decree Promulgating Law No 5 of 1981 on Fishing Regulation Art. 1)
BANGLADESH	LEGISLATION For carrying capacity of vessel: -up to 250 tons = T. 750 250 t. up to 350 t. = T. 1 000 350 t. up to 450 t. = T. 2 000 450 t. up to 600 t. = T. 5 000 -over 600 tons = T.10 000 (Marine Fisheries Rules, 1983 R. 6) (ENTRY VERIFIED - OCTOBER 1983)	 US$ 29 US$ 38 US$ 76 US$ 191 US$ 382		LEGISLATION Local fishing vessel defined as any fishing vessel (i) wholly owned by one or more persons who are citizens of Bangladesh; or (ii) wholly owned by any company, society or other association of persons established under the law of Bangladesh of which at least 51% of the shares are held by citizens of Bangladesh and includes any fishing vessels registered in Bangladesh and operating under Bangladesh flag under joint venture or any other approved arrangements; or (iii) wholly owned by the Government or by a statutory corporation established under a law of Bangladesh. (Marine Fisheries Ordinance 1983 S. 2)

TABLE B

LICENCE FEES, BILATERAL AGREEMENT OR JOINT VENTURE REQUIREMENTS AND NATIONALITY CRITERIA

STATE	Licence fees, royalties and other payments: Local currency	Licence fees, royalties and other payments: US$ Equiv.	Requirements concerning bilateral framework agreements or joint venture participation	Nationality criteria for fishing vessels
BARBADOS	LEGISLATION Fees and charges to be set and approved by cabinet. (Marine Boundaries and Jurisdiction Act, 1978, S. 12) Note: No foreign fishing at present (ENTRY VERIFIED - OCTOBER 1985)	-		LEGISLATION Local fishing vessel- (a) Wholly owned by a citizen of Barbados or by a body corporate whose members or, if that body corporate is a company, whose share-holders, as the case may be, are all citizens of Barbados, or, (b) certified in writing by the Cabinet as having such substantial economic connections with Barbados in relation to its ownership as to be deemed, for the purposes of this Act to be a Barbados vessel . (Marine Boundaries and Jurisdiction Act, 1978, S.2)
BELGIUM	Licences issued by E.E.C. within the common fishing zone. No fees. See entry under European Community (ENTRY VERIFIED - OCTOBER 1985)	-	Access to common fishing zone of E.E.C. governed by bilateral agreements with third countries on a reciprocal basis.	Local fishing vessel defined as fishing vessel owned more than 50% by nationals resident in Belgium or by companies of which main office is located in the country.
BELIZE	LEGISLATION Minister may make regulations prescribing level of fees to be paid for licences to fish (Fisheries Ordinance, CAP 174 S.13) Note: No licensed foreign fishing at present. (ENTRY VERIFIED - OCTOBER 1985)			LEGISLATION No distinction made between local and foreign fishing boats in present law (Fisheries Ordinance, CAP 174)

TABLE B

LICENCE FEES, BILATERAL AGREEMENT OR JOINT VENTURE REQUIREMENTS AND NATIONALITY CRITERIA

STATE	Licence fees, royalties and other payments: Local currency	Licence fees, royalties and other payments: US$ Equiv.	Requirements concerning bilateral framework agreements or joint venture participation	Nationality criteria for fishing vessels
BENIN	LEGISLATION - Trawlers = 1 000 francs CFA per gross ton per year	US $ 2.11 per G.T.	LEGISLATION Foreign fishing in territorial waters reserved for local vessels or vessels from other countries or categories thereof on basis of reciprocity. (Ordinance No. 68-38, 1968 Art. 8) Foreign fishing in territorial waters reserved for foreign vessels holding Benin authorization. (Decree 76-92, 1976 Art 2)	LEGISLATION Local fishing vessel defined as fishing vessel at least half owned by Benin nationals or by nationals of another state with which reciprocal agreement concluded. Where vessel belongs to a company, head office must be in Benin, the Chairman of the Board, the General Manager and the majority of the members of the Board must be Benin nationals and at least 50 % of the share capital must be held by Benin nationals or nationals of another state with which reciprocal agreement concluded. Exemptions from these conditions may be accorded by decree in favour of neighbouring states not having any maritime frontier and public bodies, companies and nationals of such states. (Merchant Shipping Code, 1968 Art. 16)
	- Shrimp vessels = 3 500 francs CFA per gross ton per year (Ordinance No. 73-40, 1973 Art.2)	US $ 7.37		
	AGREEMENTS -By virtue of unwritten reciprocal arrangement Nigerian and Benin vessels operate in each other's zones. (ENTRY VERIFIED - OCTOBER 1985)			
BRAZIL	LEGISLATION Registration fee = US$ 500 + US$ 20 per net ton of the vessel (Fees payable in Brazilian currency)	US$ 500 US$ 20 per n.r.t.	LEGISLATION The conditions for the establishment of joint ventures are defined by SUDEPE in its informative bulletin No. 016 of 1976, p. 29-31.	LEGISLATION Local fishing vessel = fishing vessel owned by nationals or companies organized in Brazil. - Authorizations for chartering foreign fishing vessels may be

TABLE B

LICENCE FEES, BILATERAL AGREEMENT OR JOINT VENTURE REQUIREMENTS AND NATIONALITY CRITERIA

STATE	Licence fees, royalties and other payments		Requirements concerning bilateral framework agreements or joint venture participation	Nationality criteria for fishing vessels
	Local currency	US$ Equiv.		
BRAZIL (Cont'd)	Apparently Brazil no longer licences foreign fishing, except under joint venture. (Source NMFS-IFR-84/69)		Apparently Brazil no longer licences foreign fishing, except under joint venture (Source NMFS-IFR-84/69) AGREEMENTS *Framework agreements with Barbados (15 Feb. 1978) and with Trinidad and Tobago (8 May 1978) -the Brazilian partner must hold at least 60% of the capital and 51% of the voting shares. -the joint venture must have its head office in Brazil but may also be registered as carrying on business in Trinidad and Tobago. -Joint venture must not interfere with activities of small scale fishermen.	granted to local companies provided majority of share capital held by native born Brazilians (Decree No. 68.45, 1 71, Art.3) Note: New legislation under consideration
BULGARIA	NO INFORMATION			
BURMA	NO INFORMATION			

TABLE B

LICENCE FEES, BILATERAL AGREEMENT OR JOINT VENTURE REQUIREMENTS AND NATIONALITY CRITERIA

STATE	Licence fees, royalties and other payments: Local currency	US$ Equiv.	Requirements concerning bilateral framework agreements or joint venture participation	Nationality criteria for fishing vessels
CAMEROON	LEGISLATION Francs CFA -Trawling = 5 000 per G.T. -Shellfish = 10 000 per G.T. -Clupeidae = 2 500 per G.T. (Decree No. 75.528 of 16 July 1975 Art. 3) AGREEMENTS Agreement with Equatorial Guinea of 26 November 1981 (valid for 2 years renewable unless denounced) -Provides for reciprocal fishing rights. (ENTRY VERIFIED-SEPTEMBER 1984)	 US$10.5 per G.T. US$21 per G.T. US$ 5.2 per G.T.		LEGISLATION Local fishing vessel defined as fishing vessel at least half owned by Cameroon nationals or by nationals of another state with which reciprocal agreements concluded. Where vessels belong to a company, head office must be in Cameroon, the Chairman of the Board, the General Manager and the majority of the members of the Board must be Cameroon nationals and at least 50% of the share capital must be held by Cameroon nationals or nationals of another state with which reciprocal agreement concluded.
CANADA	LEGISLATION Access/Licence Fee: =$1.90 per GRT Amendment Fee: = $300 per amendment Daily Fishing Fee: -For squid fishery = 20 cents per G.R.T. per day on fishing ground; -For cod fishery = 32 cents per G.R.T. per day on fishing ground; -Other fisheries except Subarea 0 = 23 cents per GRT/day on ground	 US$1.38 US$219 US$0.15 US$0.23 US$0.17	Restrictive attitude toward joint ventures (Criteria for evaluation of fishing joint ventures, 9 Feb. 1977)	LEGISLATION Local fishing vessel - (a) fishing vessel registered or licenced in Canada or not required to be registered or licenced and not registered or licenced elsewhere; and (2) owned by Canadian citizens or persons resident and domiciled in Canada and having principal place of business in Canada. (Coastal Fisheries Protection Act S.2)

TABLE B

LICENCE FEES, BILATERAL AGREEMENT OR JOINT VENTURE REQUIREMENTS AND NATIONALITY CRITERIA

STATE	Licence fees, royalties and other payments: Local currency	Licence fees, royalties and other payments: US$ Equiv.	Requirements concerning bilateral framework agreements or joint venture participation	Nationality criteria for fishing vessels
CANADA (Cont'd)	Lump Sum Fishing Fee - Subarea 0 = $1 250 for non-EEC Member vessels Lump Sum Licence Fee = $5 000 for pelagic longliners (No Access Fee) (Fees for 1985) (ENTRY VERIFIED - DECEMBER 1985)	US$912 US$3 650		
CAPE VERDE	LEGISLATION New legislation under consideration AGREEMENTS *Agreement with Portugal 20 April 1980(valid for 3 years renewable unless denounced). -"Fishing conditions" to be agreed upon annually by representatives of both countries. *Agreement with Spain of 25 September 1981(valid for 3 years, renewable for 1-year unless denounced -Fees not specified in the Agreement. Spanish shipowners to enter into contracts with Capeverdean National Co. providing for the "economic conditions" of fishing operations. -Spain to set up of an ice plant in Cape Verde; to undertake 2 scientific research programmes into demersal and pelagic stocks and fishing		LEGISLATION Licences may be issued only where bilateral agreement in force between Cape Verde and the flag state. (Decree Law No. 126-77, 31 Dec. 1977, art.8).	

TABLE B

LICENCE FEES, BILATERAL AGREEMENT OR JOINT VENTURE REQUIREMENTS AND NATIONALITY CRITERIA

STATE	Licence fees, royalties and other payments: Local currency	Licence fees, royalties and other payments: US$ Equiv.	Requirements concerning bilateral framework agreements or joint venture participation	Nationality criteria for fishing vessels
CAPE VERDE (Cont'd)	methods; to supply 2 tuna boat skippers during 3 years for Capeverdean vessels; to fund a biologist to carry out tuna research ; to grant 5 annual scolarships. *Agreement with Senegal of 29 March 1985 with implementing annual protocol (valid for 2 years, renewable unless denounced) -Licences may be granted to Senegalese boats, on request made through the Senegalese Government. -No licence fees specified. (ENTRY VERIFIED - JULY 1985)			*Agreement with Senegal of 29 March 1985 with implementing annual protocol National vessels defined as vessels flying the flag of 1 of the countries which belongs at least 51% to national of Senegal or Cape Verde or to a company of which at least 51% of capital held by Senegalese or Cape Verdeans and having its head office in one of the two countries, a Board of Directors of which the Chairman and the majority of the members are nationals and a manager or director-general who is a national of Senegal or Cape Verde. Art. 4
CHILE	LEGISLATION Tuna fishing: Registration fee = US$ 800 + Licence fee = (valid 100 days) U.S.$60 per n.r.t. Decree No. 130 of 11 Feb.1959) (ENTRY VERIFIED - OCTOBER 1985)	US$ 800 + US$ 60 per nrt	LEGISLATION Foreigners may participate in offshore fishing operations in Chilean waters only through participation in Chilean incorporated joint venture company at least 51% Chilean owned. (Source NMFS-IFR-80/2)	LEGISLATION Chilean merchants shipping laws require 51% Chilean ownership for vessels granted Chilean registration (Source NMFS-IFR-80/2.)

TABLE B

LICENCE FEES, BILATERAL AGREEMENT OR JOINT VENTURE REQUIREMENTS AND NATIONALITY CRITERIA

STATE	Licence fees, royalties and other payments		Requirements concerning bilateral framework agreements or joint venture participation	Nationality criteria for fishing vessels
	Local currency	US$ Equiv.		
CHINA	NO INFORMATION			
COLOMBIA	LEGISLATION Licence fees - vessels over 25 G.T. working for Colombian companies (affiliated or chartered):			
	-Bottom trawling = 400 pesos per G.T.	US$29.40		
	-Tuna longlining, pole and line, purse seining, and mid-water trawling = 300 pesos per G.T.	US$ 2.20		
	-Lines and traps = 200 pesos per G.T.	US$ 1.47		
	- vessels under 25 G.T. pay registration fees calculated on same basis. (Industrial commercial fishing licence valid 1 year renewable. Commercial exploration fishing licence valid up to 6 months renewable).			

TABLE B

LICENCE FEES, BILATERAL AGREEMENT OR JOINT VENTURE REQUIREMENTS AND NATIONALITY CRITERIA

STATE	Licence fees, royalties and other payments		Requirements concerning bilateral framework agreements or joint venture participation	Nationality criteria for fishing vessels
	Local currency	US$ Equiv.		
COLOMBIA (Cont'd)	- Special permit for vessels not fishing for Colombian Companies - valid only for tuna & live bait 10 000 pesos per G.T. (valid 30 days - renewable once only).	US$73.5		
	(Vessels also required to hold Certificate of Registration = 50 000 pesos)	US$368		
	- Permit for scientific fishing - 4 000 pesos.	US$29		
	- over 25 G.T. scientific fishing permit at 100 pesos per G.T.	US$0.74		
	(Order No. 0052 of 19 December - 1978)			
COMORO ISLANDS	LEGISLATION Licence fee fixed by Minister for Fisheries, by decree and revised periodically. (Act No. 82-015 of 6 May 1982) (ENTRY VERIFIED - OCTOBER 1985)			LEGISLATION Local fishing vessel defined as one wholly owned by Comorian citizens or by state or company, society or association formed under Comorian law of which at least half of the shares are owned by Comorian citizens companies or the State (Act No. 82-015, Art. 1)
CONGO	LEGISLATION -		LEGISLATION Licences may be issued to foreign fishing vessels only	LEGISLATION Fishing vessel defined as fishing vessel at least half owned by

TABLE B

LICENCE FEES, BILATERAL AGREEMENT OR JOINT VENTURE REQUIREMENTS AND NATIONALITY CRITERIA

STATE	Licence fees, royalties and other payments: Local currency	US$ Equiv.	Requirements concerning bilateral framework agreements or joint venture participation	Nationality criteria for fishing vessels
CONGO (Cont'd)	AGREEMENTS *Agreement with Gabon of 9 November 1982 -Provides for reciprocal fishing rights. No fees specified.		where bilateral reciprocal agreement in force with flag state. (Ordinance No. 22-70 of 14 July 1970, Art. 4)	Congolese nationals or by nationals of another state with which agreements of reciprocity concluded. Where vessels belong to a company, head office must be in the Congo, the Chairman of the Board, the General Manager and the majority of the members of the Board must be Congolese nationals and at least 50% of the share capital must be held by Congolese nationals or nationals of another state with which reciprocal agreement concluded.
COSTA RICA	LEGISLATION Registration fee (valid 1 year) = 5 pesos per n.r.t. to be applied for in December (10 pesos per n.r.t. if applied for during year) Fishing permit -(valid for 60 days) -for vessels up to 400 n.r.t. = 30 pesos per n.r.t. (15 pesos for live bait fishery) -for vessels over 400 n.r.t. = 60 pesos per n.r.t. (30 pesos for live bait fishery) Note: Foreign vessels under 400 n.r.t. landing all or at least 100 tons of catch in local port within 60 days of validity of permit, validity of permit extended for 60 days free of charge (Law No. 6267, 1978, Art. 5)	 US$ 5 US$ 10 US$ 30 US$ 15 US$ 60 US$ 30		LEGISLATION Foreign vessels under contract to land specified quantity of catch to domestic companies treated as Costa Rican flag vessels for purposes of licencing. Foreign firms or companies means those in which Costa Ricans do not own more than 50% of the shares. (Law No. 6267, 1978 Art. 11)

TABLE B

LICENCE FEES, BILATERAL AGREEMENT OR JOINT VENTURE REQUIREMENTS AND NATIONALITY CRITERIA

STATE	Licence fees, royalties and other payments		Requirements concerning bilateral framework agreements or joint venture participation	Nationality criteria for fishing vessels
	Local currency	US$ Equiv.		
COSTA RICA (Cont'd)	AGREEMENTS *Agreement with Panama and USA, 14 March 1983valid until withdrawal TUNA FISHING -For 5 Contracting Parties = US$ 60 per nrt. -For additional Contracting Parties (coastal states) fees increased up to maximum of US$ 100 per nrt Note: Increases to be determined by Council set up under agreement - minimum increase of US$ 10 per nrt for each additional Contracting Party (coastal state) after 6th. Fees to be reduced on withdrawal by any Contracting Party (coastal state) as determined by Council down to minimum of US$ 60 per nrt. Fees to be paid in full before licence issued Licences valid until end year in which issued Proceeds of fees less up to 10% for administrative costs, to be distributed to Coastal States in proportion to amount of tuna taken in respective 200 mile areas Note: AGREEMENT NOT YET IN FORCE			

TABLE B

LICENCE FEES, BILATERAL AGREEMENT OR JOINT VENTURE REQUIREMENTS AND NATIONALITY CRITERIA

STATE	Licence fees, royalties and other payments		Requirements concerning bilateral framework agreements or joint venture participation	Nationality criteria for fishing vessels
	Local currency	US$ Equiv.		
CUBA	LEGISLATION No regulations currently in force, requests considered on case to case basis (Source: NMFS-IFR-81/69)		LEGISLATION In order to ensure optimum utilisation of fishing resources, under bilateral agreement, the Republic of Cuba shall give access to vessels of other States to the surplus of the TAC that will not be harvested by Cuban vessels, pursuant to relevant Cuban regulations (Decree-Law No.2, 1977 Art.4)	
CYPRUS	NO INFORMATION			
DENMARK	Licences issued by E.E.C. within the common fishing zone. No fees. See entry under European Community		Access to common fishing zone of E.E.C. governed by bilateral agreements with third countries on a reciprocal basis.	Local fishing vessel defined as fishing vessel owned by a national or a company in which 2/3 of the partners are Danish.
DJIBOUTI	LEGISLATION Fishing operations in territorial seas and EEZ must be authorized by Minster of Agriculture. Licence fees not specified. (Law no. 52/AN/78, 9 January 1979)			LEGISLATION
DOMINICA	Licences no longer issued to foreign vessels. New legislation under consideration			

TABLE B

LICENCE FEES, BILATERAL AGREEMENT OR JOINT VENTURE REQUIREMENTS AND NATIONALITY CRITERIA

STATE	Licence fees, royalties and other payments		Requirements concerning bilateral framework agreements or joint venture participation	Nationality criteria for fishing vessels
	Local currency	US$ Equiv.		
DOMINICAN REPUBLIC	LEGISLATION - Vessel licence = free - Fishermen's licence = C 25 per fisherman	US$ 25 per fisherman	LEGISLATION	LEGISLATION Local fishing vessel defined as fishing vessel owned by Dominican nationals or companies established under Dominican Law having at least 51% of capital owned by Dominican nationals. (Decree No.5914 of 1962)
ECUADOR	LEGISLATION Registration fee (valid one year) = U.S. $ 2 000 Permit fee (valid for 1 trip - up to 50 - 90 days depending on origin of vessel) = U.S. $ 160 per n r.t. (Fees expressed in U.S. dollars). Vessels over 600 nrt prohibited (Decree No. 477 of 8 August 1980) (ENTRY VERIFIED - OCTOBER 1985)	US$ 2 000 US$160 per nrt		
EGYPT	NO INFORMATION			
EL SALVADOR	LEGISLATION Permit and licence fees to be set by Law (Art 35) -Fishing for pelagic and migratory species subject to special regime:		LEGISLATION By way of exception and in order to fulfill development plans, Salvadorian enterprises holding high seas and	LEGISLATION Local fishing vessel defined as vessel owned by nationals, cooperative associations or companies with a majority holding by local citizens.

TABLE B

LICENCE FEES, BILATERAL AGREEMENT OR JOINT VENTURE REQUIREMENTS AND NATIONALITY CRITERIA

STATE	Licence fees, royalties and other payments		Requirements concerning bilateral framework agreements or joint venture participation	Nationality criteria for fishing vessels
	Local currency	US$ Equiv.		
EL SALVADOR (Cont'd)	Vessels required to hold, in addition to special fishing licence,- -General Permit (valid 1 year) 10 colones per n.r.t. (Art.77) -Special permit (valid 90 days) 75 colones per n.r.t.(Art.79) (General Law on Fisheries Activities, 1981)	 US$ 2.47 US$ 18.5	distant water fishing licences may be authorized to contract foreign fishing vessels as principal or auxiliary fleet units for a period up to 3 years. Authorization to be granted by Executive Order on payment of appropriate fees. (Art 40) All inshore (up to 12 mi.) fisheries and high seas (12 to 200 mi) demersal fisheries reserved for nationals, cooperatives and Salvadorean companies in which more than 50% of capital or shares owned by Salvadorean nationals. (Art. 25) -Foreign Governments not permitted to hold shares in enterprises dedicated to artisanal, inshore or high seas (dermersal) fisheries. (General Law on Fisheries Activities, 1981 Art. 28)	(General Law on Fisheries Activities, 1981, Art 26)

TABLE B

LICENCE FEES, BILATERAL AGREEMENT OR JOINT VENTURE REQUIREMENTS AND NATIONALITY CRITERIA

STATE	Licence fees, royalties and other payments		Requirements concerning bilateral framework agreements or joint venture participation	Nationality criteria for fishing vessels
	Local currency	US$ Equiv.		
EQUATORIAL GUINEA	LEGISLATION -		-	-
	AGREEMENTS *Agreement with Spain, 31 Oct. 1979. in force from 14 April 1982 Freezer Trawlers - Licence "A" (fishing allowed anywhere in zone) = 1 000 000 pesetas per vessel per year.	US$ 2 105		
	- Licence "B" (fishing only beyond 12 mi) 600 000 pesetas per vessel per year.	US$ 1 263	-	
	Fresh fish 200 000 pesetas per vessel per year	US$ 421		
	Tuna freezer vessels 50 000 pesetas per vessel per year.	US$ 105		
	-Spain to provide credit of up to US$ 10 000 000 for implementation of several fishing projects (cold storage, distribution network, etc)	US$ 10 000 000		
	*Agreement with Rep. of Cameroon signed 1980 valid for 2 years automatically renewed unless denounced Reciprocal fishing agreement no fee			
	*Agreement with Nigeria 27 Nov.1981 valid for 5 years, automatically renewed unless denounced.			*Agreement with Nigeria 27 Nov.1981 Nigerian vessel defined as one flying the Nigerian flag, whose crew are not

TABLE B

LICENCE FEES, BILATERAL AGREEMENT OR JOINT VENTURE REQUIREMENTS AND NATIONALITY CRITERIA

STATE	Licence fees, royalties and other payments		Requirements concerning bilateral framework agreements or joint venture participation	Nationality criteria for fishing vessels
	Local currency	US$ Equiv.		
EQUATORIAL GUINEA (Cont'd)	-50 tonnes of fish for each boat per year -20% of catch by purseiners per boat per year +licence fee of US$ 2 000 per boat per year *Agreement with EEC, 1983, valid thru' 1986 ECU 20 per ton of fish caught (ECU 40 000 paid in advance) + ECU 180 000 annually for development projects to be increased proportionately if tuna catches exceed 4 000 tons. Agreement provides for authorizations for 27 tuna freezer vessels Additional authorizations may be accorded on request of one party on terms to be agreed. (Text published in EC Official Journal No. L 237/13 of 26/8/1983) (ENTRY VERIFIED - AUGUST 1983)	 US$ 2 000 US$ 17.4 US$ 34 800 US$ 156 600		less than 50% Africans, and which belongs to a company at least 50% of the capital of which belongs to Nigerians. Art 11.
ETHIOPIA	LEGISLATION -			LEGISLATION Local vessels must be wholly owned by (a) Ethiopian subjects, or (b) Bodies corporate established under Ethiopian law and having principal place of

TABLE B

LICENCE FEES, BILATERAL AGREEMENT OR JOINT VENTURE REQUIREMENTS AND NATIONALITY CRITERIA

STATE	Licence fees, royalties and other payments		Requirements concerning bilateral framework agreements or joint venture participation	Nationality criteria for fishing vessels
	Local currency	US$ Equiv.		
ETHIOPIA (Cont'd)				business in Ethiopia, or (c) foreigners domiciled and having principal place of business in Ethiopia. (Maritime Code, Proclamation No. 164, 1960 Art. 4)
EUROPEAN COMMUNITY	Licences issued by E.E.C. within the common fishing zone. No fees.	-	Access to common fishing zone of E.E.C. governed by bilateral agreements with third countries on a reciprocal basis.	Nationality criteria set out in the national legislation of each member state of the EEC.
FIJI	LEGISLATION - F$ 50 plus 5% of the landed value of the catch. (Minister has power to exempt) (Marine Spaces (Foreign Fishing Vessels) Regulations 1979 Reg 10) Note: No vessels at present licens- under foreign fishing vessel licens ing provisions. Only vessels categorized as local licensed. (ENTRY VERIFIED - OCTOBER 1985)	US$ 43 + 5%		LEGISLATION Fiji fishing vessel means any fishing vessel which is registered in Fiji or the operations of which are based on a place in Fiji and which is wholly owned by, or is under exclusive charter to, a natural person who is a resident of, or a company incorporated in, Fiji. (Marine Spaces Act, 1977, S.2).
FINLAND	NO INFORMATION			

TABLE B

LICENCE FEES, BILATERAL AGREEMENT OR JOINT VENTURE REQUIREMENTS AND NATIONALITY CRITERIA

STATE	Licence fees, royalties and other payments		Requirements concerning bilateral framework agreements or joint venture participation	Nationality criteria for fishing vessels
	Local currency	US$ Equiv.		
FRANCE	Licences issued by E.E.C. within the common fishing zone. No fees. See entry under European Community		Access to common fishing zone of E.E.C. governed by bilateral agreements with third countries on a reciprocal basis.	LEGISLATION Local fishing vessel defined as vessel at least half owned by French nationals or wholly owned by companies whose head office is situated in the territory of France or in a convention state and meeting the following conditions: (a) for public companies, the Chairman of the Board, and the majority of the members of the Board, the Directors general and the auditors must be French; or (b) for partnerships, the managers and the majority of the members of the supervisory Board must be French; (c) for limited liability companies, collective name companies, limited partnerships and civil companies, the managers must be French and half the capital must be held by French nationals. French nationality may also be given to vessel on bareboat charter where French charterer assumes full control

TABLE B

LICENCE FEES, BILATERAL AGREEMENT OR JOINT VENTURE REQUIREMENTS AND NATIONALITY CRITERIA

STATE	Licence fees, royalties and other payments		Requirements concerning bilateral framework agreements or joint venture participation	Nationality criteria for fishing vessels
	Local currency	US$ Equiv.		
FRANCE (Cont'd)				and management etc. of vessel and flag state law allows relinquishing of its flag. (Act No. 67-5 of 3 January 1967 Art.3 as amended by Act No. 75/300 of 29 April 1978 Art. 1)
French Dependent Territ. - New Caledonia	LEGISLATION Licence issued by Governing Council Valid 1 year, or until quota filled The Governing Council may, in exchange for a fishing licence, require fees according to the size of the vessels, or to the actual authorized catches		LEGISLATION The Governing Council may, in exchange for a fishing licence, require general agreements in order to facilitate commercial exchanges or to supply the Territory with scientific and technical data. (Resolution No 163, 21 Feb. 1979, S. 8)	LEGISLATION See entry under FRANCE
French Dependent Territ.	AGREEMENTS *Agreement with Japan, 14 Aug. 1982 valid through August 1983			LEGISLATION See entry under FRANCE
	- 0.23 F/kg for New Caledonia	US$ 0.02		
	- 0.27 F/kg for Wallis and Futuna	US$ 0.03		
	- 0.36 F/kg for Indian Ocean Isl.	US$ 0.04		
	- 0.32 F/kg for French Polynesia	US$ 0.03		
	Alternative fee formulation (for a global quota 10 700 t.=F.2 865 000)	US$ 301 579		
	-1 276 000 F for New Caledonia (5 550 tons)	US$ 134 316		

TABLE B

LICENCE FEES, BILATERAL AGREEMENT OR JOINT VENTURE REQUIREMENTS AND NATIONALITY CRITERIA

STATE	Licence fees, royalties and other payments: Local currency	Licence fees, royalties and other payments: US$ Equiv.	Requirements concerning bilateral framework agreements or joint venture participation	Nationality criteria for fishing vessels
French Dependent Territ. (Cont'd)	- 364 500 F for Wallis and Futuna (1 350 tons)	US$ 38 368		
	-1 152 000 F for French Polynesia (3 600 tons)	US$ 121 263		
	- 72 000 F Indian Ocean Islands (200 tons)	US$ 7 579		
	*Agreement with Korea (Republic of) Nov. 1981, valid through 19 Jan.83. Lump sum payment of US$ 481 000 for 300 vessels (in French Polynesia and Wallis and Futuna) (ENTRY VERIFIED - OCTOBER 1982)	US$ 481 000		
GABON	LEGISLATION - Fishing for Ethmalosa or sardinella = 7 500 francs CFA per gross ton per year;	US$ 15 per G.R.T.	LEGISLATION Fishing by foreigners only within framework of joint ventures for industrial or artisanal fisheries, in accordance with conditions set down by regulations and subject to international agreements. (Law No 1/82 of 22 July 1982 Basic Law on Water and Forests, Art. 73)	LEGISLATION National fishing vessel defined as vessel at least half owned by Gabon nationals or by nationals under law recognized as equivalent by reciprocal agreements. Where vessels belong to a company, head office must be in Gabon, the Chairman of the Board, the General Manager and the majority of the members of the Board must be Gabon nationals and at least 50 % of the
	- Bottom trawling = 15 000 francs CFA per gross ton per year;	US$ 31.6 per G.R.T.		
	-Tuna fishing = 15 000 francs CFA per gross ton per year;	US$ 31.6 per G.R.T.		

TABLE B

LICENCE FEES, BILATERAL AGREEMENT OR JOINT VENTURE REQUIREMENTS AND NATIONALITY CRITERIA

STATE	Licence fees, royalties and other payments: Local currency	Licence fees, royalties and other payments: US$ Equiv.	Requirements concerning bilateral framework agreements or joint venture participation	Nationality criteria for fishing vessels
GABON (Cont'd)	- Fishing for crustacean = 30 000 francs CFA per gross ton per year; (Ordinance No. 24 75 of 10 April - 1975 Art. 2). AGREEMENTS *Agreement with Congo of 9 November 1982 Reciprocal fishing rights agreement *Agreement with Rep. of Korea, December 1984 350 ton trawler licensed to fish January to July 1985 against payment of US$8 500. (Source: FNI - April 1985) (ENTRY VERIFIED - OCTOBER 1985)	US$ 63 per G.R.T.		share capital must be held by Gabon nationals or nationals of another state with which reciprocal agreement. (Act No. 10-63 of 12 January 1963, Art. 9.
GAMBIA	LEGISLATION -Trawlers (other than shrimp) 400 hp or more = D.250 per GT p.a. less than 400hp = D.200 per GT p.a. -Lobster vessels= D.125 per GT p.a. -Factory vessels= D. 60 per GT p.a. -Tuna vessels = D.0.02 per Kg of (fees payable in advance) -Multipurpose vessels: 400 hp or more = D.250 per GT p.a.	 US$ 63 US$ 40 US$ 31 US$ 15 US$ 0.005 US$ 40 US$ 63		LEGISLATION Local fishing vessel defined as a vessel - (1) wholly owned by one or more persons who are citizens of the Gambia; or (2) wholly owned by companies established under the Gambian laws of which a) at least 51% of the shares are held by citizens;

TABLE B

LICENCE FEES, BILATERAL AGREEMENT OR JOINT VENTURE REQUIREMENTS AND NATIONALITY CRITERIA

STATE	Licence fees, royalties and other payments		Requirements concerning bilateral framework agreements or joint venture participation	Nationality criteria for fishing vessels
	Local currency	US$ Equiv.		
GAMBIA (Cont'd)	less than 400hp = D.200 per GT p.a. -Shrimp trawlers = D.100 per GT pa. -Seiners = D.100.50 per GT p.a. -Others = D.50 per GT p.a. (Fisheries (Amendment) Regulations 1982. AGREEMENTS *Agreement with Senegal of 22 October 1982(valid for 2 years, renewable on tacit understanding) -Reciprocal fishing rights agreement; fishing rights for industrial vessels to be determined annually by mixed commission. (ENTRY VERIFIED - SEPTEMBER 1984)	US$ 50 US$ 25 US$ 25 US$ 13		b) chairman and a majority of members of the Board are citizens. (Fisheries Act 1977 S.2)
GERMAN DEM. REP.	NO INFORMATION			
GERMAN FED. REP.	Licences issued by E.E.C. within the common fishing zone. No fees. See entry under European Community		Access to common fishing zone of E.E.C. governed by bilateral agreements with third countries on a reciprocal basis.	

TABLE B

LICENCE FEES, BILATERAL AGREEMENT OR JOINT VENTURE REQUIREMENTS AND NATIONALITY CRITERIA

STATE	Licence fees, royalties and other payments		Requirements concerning bilateral framework agreements or joint venture participation	Nationality criteria for fishing vessels
	Local currency	US$ Equiv.		
GHANA	LEGISLATION - Foreign fishing restricted to tuna fisheries. - Fees for tuna vessels: - where partly owned by nationals = C 50 per G.R.T. per annum; - where foreign or chartered = US$ 150 per G.R.T. per annum; or 10% of catch - foreign tuna vessels or carriers used for tuna transshipments = US$ 200 per call; - longliners which call at Ghana ports not more than twice a year = US$ 2 000 per call. (Fisheries Regulations 1979 2nd schedule)	US$ 0.94 US$ 150 US$ 200 US$ 2 000	Foreign tuna companies required to enter into 50/50 joint ventures with Ghanian companies on understanding that Ghanian partners will eventually assume full ownership. (Source: Marine Fisheries Review vol. 43 No. 8, August 1981 p. 29)	LEGISLATION Local fishing vessel defined as fishing vessel defined as fishing vessels wholly owned by nationals or by companies in which all shares are held by nationals. (Fisheries Decree 1979 S.3)
GREECE	Licences issued by E.E.C. within the common fishing zone. No fees See entry under European Community		Access to common fishing zone of EEC governed by bilateral agreements with third countries on a reciprocal basis.	

TABLE B

LICENCE FEES, BILATERAL AGREEMENT OR JOINT VENTURE REQUIREMENTS AND NATIONALITY CRITERIA

STATE	Licence fees, royalties and other payments: Local currency	US$ Equiv.	Requirements concerning bilateral framework agreements or joint venture participation	Nationality criteria for fishing vessels
GRENADA	LEGISLATION To be determined by regulations of the Minister. (Marine Boundaries Act, 1978) Note: New legislation under consideration (ENTRY VERIFIED - OCTOBER 1985)			LEGISLATION Local fishing vessel - (a) wholly owned by citizens or by a body corporate whose members or share-holders are all citizens of Grenada, or (b) certified in writing by the Minister as having such substantial economic connections with Grenada in relation to its ownership as to be deemed, for purposes of Act, a Grenadian vessel. (Marine Boundaries Act, 1978, S.2)
GUATEMALA	LEGISLATION A. Pacific Ocean 1.vessels over 91 n.r.t.= Q 500 per month; 2.vessels over 30 n.r.t.= Q 300 per month; 3.vessels over 12 n.r.t.= Q 150 per month; 4.vessels under 11.99 n.r.t.= per month Q 50	US$ 500 US$ 300 US$ 150 US$ 50	LEGISLATION Joint ventures with partici-pation by local citizens encouraged by preferential licence fee.	LEGISLATION Local fishing vessel defined as fishing vessel owned by Guatemalan companies with over 50% Guatemalan capital. (Decree No. 14-70 of 1961)

TABLE B

LICENCE FEES, BILATERAL AGREEMENT OR JOINT VENTURE REQUIREMENTS AND NATIONALITY CRITERIA

STATE	Licence fees, royalties and other payments: Local currency	US$ Equiv.	Requirements concerning bilateral framework agreements or joint venture participation	Nationality criteria for fishing vessels
GUATEMALA (Cont'd)	B. Atlantic Ocean			
	1. vessels over 91 n.r.t.= Q 250 per month;	US$ 250		
	2. vessels over 30 n.r.t.= Q 175 per month;	US$ 175		
	3. vessels over 12 n.r.t.= Q 75 per month;	US$ 75		
	4. vessels under 11.99.n.r.t.= per month Q 25	US$ 25		
	Regulations governing the granting of special marine fishing licences, 1979 Art. 46.			
GUINEA	LEGISLATION Fees for locally based foreign fishing vessels to be set by decree Fees for other foreign fishing vessels set in access agreement or failing which by decree. (Code de la Peche Maritime, 1985 Art. 20) -Foreign vessels operating to Guinean enterprise:-		LEGISLATION Access agreement required with flag state before foreign fishing vessel may be authorized to fish in waters under the jurisdiction of Guinea, with exception of locally based foreign fishing vessels. As exceptional and interim measure, Minister may authorize issue of licences without access agreement. (Code de la Peche Maritime, 1985, Art 10)	LEGISLATION Local vessel defined as one wholly owned by Guinean State, or at least 51% owned by Guinean citizens or by Guinean company of which at least 51% of capital belongs to Guinean citizens, with head office in Guinea, and with a Board of Directors or Supervisory Board of which Chairman and a majority of the members are Guinean citizens, and with a Guinean sole administrator, Manager or Managers. (Code de la Peche Maritime 1985 Art 7) Locally based foreign fishing vessel
	-Bond of US$2 000 per boat;	US$2 000		
	-Export tax of US$35 per tonne fish plus fishing fees of	US$35 /tonne		
	-For Trawlers = US$200 per GRT p.a.	US$ 200		
	-Shrimp boats = US$220 per GRT p.a.	US$ 220		

TABLE B

LICENCE FEES, BILATERAL AGREEMENT OR JOINT VENTURE REQUIREMENTS AND NATIONALITY CRITERIA

STATE	Licence fees, royalties and other payments: Local currency	US$ Equiv.	Requirements concerning bilateral framework agreements or joint venture participation	Nationality criteria for fishing vessels
GUINEA (Cont'd)	-Seiners = US$ 60 per GRT p.a.	US$ 60		defined as foreign fishing vessels based in Guinea and landing all their catch in Guinea or for Guinean based companies. (Code de la Peche Maritime, 1985, Art. 7)
	-Pole/Liners=US$3 000 per vessel/yr	US$3 000		
	-Tunaseiners=US$9 000 per vessel/yr	US$9 000		
	plus -Free delivery of 2 equipped boats ate least 9 metres long within 3 months of signing of agreement.			
	-Foreign vessels operating to foreign enterprise:-			
	-Bond of US$2 000 per boat;	US$2 000		
	-Export tax of US$40 per tonne fish	US$40 /tonne		
	plus fishing fees of			
	-For Trawlers = US$300 per GRT p.a.	US$300		
	-Shrimp boats = US$320 per GRT p.a.	US$320		
	-Seiners = US$100 per GRT p.a.	US$100		
	-Pole/Liners=US$5000 per vessel/yr.	US$5000		
	-Tunaseiners=US$15000 per vessel/yr	US$15000		
	(Ordinance No 039 PRG/85 -General Regulations, Annex II Fishing Fees for Industrial Fishing Vessels)			
	AGREEMENTS		AGREEMENTS	
	*Agreement with Nigeria, 28 August 1981(Valid for 5 years)		*Framework agreement with Ghana, 18 Aug. 1978 provides for joint Ghanean/Guinean fishing operations and formation of one joint venture.	
	-167 metric tons of fish per trawler p.a. and 28% of the catch per purse seiner p.a.			
	-Each fishing vessel to pay an annual tax of US$7,920.	US$7,920		

TABLE B

LICENCE FEES, BILATERAL AGREEMENT OR JOINT VENTURE REQUIREMENTS AND NATIONALITY CRITERIA

STATE	Licence fees, royalties and other payments		Requirements concerning bilateral framework agreements or joint venture participation	Nationality criteria for fishing vessels
	Local currency	US$ Equiv.		
GUINEA (Cont'd)	-For each fishing vessel deposit of a Guarantee Fee of US$20,000 to guarantee correct execution of commitments.	US$20,000		
	*Agreement with EEC of August 1982 valid from 1 January 1983 to 31 December 1985			
	Either 100ECU/GRT/year or delivery of part of the catch at Conakry (in any case delivery of a minimum of 200 tons per vessel per year) plus non reimbursable financial compensation of 2,100,000ECU and	US$ 87 US$1 827 000		
	and contribution of 200,000ECU to a Guinean fish research programme.	US$174 000		
	*Protocol of 28 October 1983(valid for one year)under the Agreement with USSR of 1981			
	-Licensing of up to 11 Soviet vessels in exchange for sale of 10,000 tons of fish to Guinea. Payment by Guinea of US$412 per ton of fish.			
	*Agreement with Spain of 30 April 1984 valid for 3 years			
	-Granting of renewable 3-month fishing licences for up to 47 vessels Payment in the form of supply of semi-industrial trawlers and seiners of an average length of 13mts			

TABLE B

LICENCE FEES, BILATERAL AGREEMENT OR JOINT VENTURE REQUIREMENTS AND NATIONALITY CRITERIA

STATE	Licence fees, royalties and other payments: Local currency	Licence fees, royalties and other payments: US$ Equiv.	Requirements concerning bilateral framework agreements or joint venture participation	Nationality criteria for fishing vessels
GUINEA (Cont'd)	according to conditions set out in an annex to the Agreement. *Arrangements concluded with 7 private companies for 1984 -Payment of a fee from US$200/GRT to US$220/GRT per year plus landing of 200tons of catch per vessel/year If vessels operate less than one year, landing of 25 tons of catch per month. (ENTRY VERIFIED- OCTOBER 1985)	US$200 US$220		
GUINEA BISSAU	LEGISLATION New legislation under consideration AGREEMENTS *Agreement with USSR of 11 April 1985 (valid for 10 years, renewable for 5-year periods unless denounced Protocol of December 1984(valid for one year) -Vessels allowed to operate on payment of 15% of the global production once processed and sold. *Agreement with Portugal 20 May1977 US$ 160 per GRT per year *Agreement with EEC 27 February1980 as amended on 15 March 1983 valid for three years	US$ 160	LEGISLATION Licence required even if under bilateral agreement Agreement with Portugal of 20 May 1977 -Joint Portuguese/Guinean fishing operations and creation of joint ventures are provided for on a general basis.	LEGISLATION -

TABLE B

LICENCE FEES, BILATERAL AGREEMENT OR JOINT VENTURE REQUIREMENTS AND NATIONALITY CRITERIA

STATE	Licence fees, royalties and other payments		Requirements concerning bilateral framework agreements or joint venture participation	Nationality criteria for fishing vessels
	Local currency	US$ Equiv.		
GUINEA BISSAU (Cont'd)	-Trawlers :120 or 100ECU/GRT/year	US$104/US$ 87		
	-Tuna Boats:20 ECU per ton of fish caught,plus financial compensation of 4,275,000 ECU (1,425,000/year)	US$17.4 US$3 719 250 US$1 239 750/p.a		
	-Contribution of 250,000 ECU to scientific research programme	US$217 500		
	-Grant of 10 scholarships for 3 yrs			
	Preferential access regime for Senegalese vessels under the Agreement of 22 December 1978			
	-Up to a global tonnage of 3,500GRT			
	-50,000CFA/GRT/year, plus	US$105		
	-landing of 15 tons of fish/vessel/year, plus			
	-sale of sole(at FOB prices in Dakar) to local industries according to size of vessels (up to 100 GRT - 3 tons/year; from 101 GRT to 160 GRT - 4 tons/year;			
	-Outside the global tonnage of 3,500 GRT			
	US$200/GRT/year plus landing of 10 tons of varied fish in Bissau	US$200		
	or US$250/GRT/year without landing of catch.	US$250		
	-Tuna vessels			

TABLE B

LICENCE FEES, BILATERAL AGREEMENT OR JOINT VENTURE REQUIREMENTS AND NATIONALITY CRITERIA

STATE	Licence fees, royalties and other payments		Requirements concerning bilateral framework agreements or joint venture participation	Nationality criteria for fishing vessels
	Local currency	US$ Equiv.		
GUINEA BISSAU (Cont'd)	25,000CFA/GRT/year	US$55		
	Vessels operating without agreement US$300/GRT/year	US$300		
	*Agreement with Spain, 15 Oct. 1985 valid 5 years. Licences to be issued to 10 Spanish vessels of up to 300 tons each. Licence fees to be paid by shipowners, level of fees unknown, plus scholarships for Guinean fisheries technicians, plus financing of purchase of oceanographic vessel by Guinea-Bissau (Source: Marchés Tropicaux 8/11/85) (ENTRY VERIFIED-NOVEMBER 1985)			
GUYANA	LEGISLATION Any fishing boat operating in fishing zone but not from base in Guyana = G$ 100 000	US$ 23 256	LEGISLATION The Minister may by order designate any country whose fishing boats may fish in Guyana waters. (Maritime Boundaries Act 1977, S.25)	LEGISLATION Local fishing boat defined as a fishing boat registered in Guyana. (Maritime Boundaries Act 1977 S.2)
	Any foreign owned fishing boat exceeding 100 ft operating from base in Guyana = G$ 50 000	US$ 11 628		
	Any foreign owned fishing boat less than 100 ft operating from base in Guyana = G$ 12 500	US$ 2 907		
	Authorization valid one year			

TABLE B

LICENCE FEES, BILATERAL AGREEMENT OR JOINT VENTURE REQUIREMENTS AND NATIONALITY CRITERIA

STATE	Licence fees, royalties and other payments		Requirements concerning bilateral framework agreements or joint venture participation	Nationality criteria for fishing vessels
	Local currency	US$ Equiv.		
GUYANA (Cont'd)	(Maritime Boundaries (Fishery Zone Fees) (Amendment) Regulations 1977 Schedule) AGREEMENTS *Agreement with USSR -Experimental fishing by 2 Soviet shrimp trawlers for 1 year. No fees All shrimp to be landed locally. By-catch transhipped to Soviet collector vessel. Costs of operation Soviet vessels to be met from proceeds of sale of shrimp in hard currency; any profits for Guyana. *Agreement with Cuba, 1978 (valid 1 year renewable. -12% of total shrimp catch for 4 to 30 shrimp trawlers, plus locally based foreign fishing fee & contribution in joint research projects. No exemption from taxes. *Agreement with German Dem Rep 1979 -Exploratory commercial fishing for 1 vessel, one fishing trip, no fees (ENTRY VERIFIED - OCTOBER 1985)		AGREEMENTS	

TABLE B

LICENCE FEES, BILATERAL AGREEMENT OR JOINT VENTURE REQUIREMENTS AND NATIONALITY CRITERIA

STATE	Licence fees, royalties and other payments: Local currency	Licence fees, royalties and other payments: US$ Equiv.	Requirements concerning bilateral framework agreements or joint venture participation	Nationality criteria for fishing vessels
HAITI	LEGISLATION Registration fee: 2 000 gourdes Licence fee: 1. base fee 2. multiplied by gross tonnage of vessel 3. multiplied by variable coefficient according to the type of fishing - -bottom fish = 1 -sardines = 1/2 -tuna = 1/3 -crustaceans = 2 (Decree of 27 October 1978 Art.17) (Note:Basic fee appears to be G.250 for industrial fishing (Art.10)	US$ 400 US$ 50	LEGISLATION Licences may be issued only where bilateral or multilateral agreements in force. (Declaration establishing a 200 mile EEZ of 6 April 1977	LEGISLATION Local fishing vessel defined as owned by nationals or companies incorporated under the Haitian laws and registered in Haiti, in which at least 51% of the share capital with voting rights is held by nationals. (Decree of 27 October 1978, Art. 64).
HONDURAS	LEGISLATION L. 0.20 per net ton (Decree No. 154 of 1959) State to issue legislation on licensing including fees and other forms of remuneration. (Law on Utilization of Marine Natural Resources 1980 Art. 4 (a)) Note: New legislation under consideration (ENTRY VERIFIED - OCTOBER 1985)	US$ 0.10	LEGISLATION Fishing in territorial sea restricted to Honduran residents or Honduran companies at least 51% owned by Honduran nationals and to vessels flying Honduran flag (Decree No. 154 of 1959)	LEGISLATION Local fishing boat defined as fishing vessel under Honduran flag owned by Honduran nationals or residents or by a company incorporated under local laws with at least 51% of capital owned by Honduran nationals. Master of the boat must be a native of Honduras. (Decree No. 154 of 1959)

TABLE B

LICENCE FEES, BILATERAL AGREEMENT OR JOINT VENTURE REQUIREMENTS AND NATIONALITY CRITERIA

STATE	Licence fees, royalties and other payments		Requirements concerning bilateral framework agreements or joint venture participation	Nationality criteria for fishing vessels
	Local currency	US$ Equiv.		
ICELAND			Licence may be issued only where bilateral agreement in force.	
INDIA	LEGISLATION -squid jigging = Rs 1 000 per tonne of fish allowed. -fishing by trawling = Rs 2 000 per tonne of fish allowed. -fishing by long-line and gill net =Rs 1 500 per tonne of fish allowed -fishing for tuna by long-lining/ purse seining/pole and line fishing =Rs 1 000 per tonne of fish allowed -transporting of fish = Rs 500 per tonne of fish carrying capacity of vessel for each voyage. -for any other purpose = Rs 200 per G.R.T. of craft for each voyage. In all cases, applications to be accompanied by a non-refundable fee of Rs 500. (Maritime Zones of India (Regulation of Fishing by Foreign Vessels) Rules, 1982 Schedule I.)	 US$ 82 US$ 164 US$ 124 US$ 82 US$ 41 US$ 16 US$ 41		LEGISLATION Indian vessel means: (I) a vessel owned by Government or by a corporation established by a Central Act or by a Provincial State Act, or (II) a vessel (i)which is owned wholly by persons to each of whom any of the following descriptions applies: - (1) a citizen of India; (2) a company in which not less than 60(sixty) per cent of the share capital is held by citizens of India; (3) a registered cooperative society every member whereof is a citizen of India or where any other co-operative society is a member thereof, every individual who is member of such other cooperative society is a citizen of India; and which is registered under the Merchant Shipping Act,

TABLE B

LICENCE FEES, BILATERAL AGREEMENT OR JOINT VENTURE REQUIREMENTS AND NATIONALITY CRITERIA

STATE	Licence fees, royalties and other payments		Requirements concerning bilateral framework agreements or joint venture participation	Nationality criteria for fishing vessels
	Local currency	US$ Equiv.		
INDIA (Cont'd)				1958, or under any other Central Act or any Provincial or State Act. (Maritime Zone of India (Regulation of Fishing by Foreign Vessels) Act, 1981)
INDONESIA	LEGISLATION 1. Registration(fishing permit)fee = US$ 3 per GRT + 2. Royalties on catches = For Longliners = US$69 per tonne Pole/line vessels = US$82 per tonne Purseseiners = US$85 per tonne Gillnetters = US$44 per tonne Fee for changes to permit = US$100 Fees for joint venture vessels range from US$500 to US$1000 per vessel, plus royalties on exported fish: Shrimp: = 2% of check price Tuna: = 1.5% of FOB price Skipjack= 1.5% of FOB price Pearl = 1.5% of FOB price Other species = 1% of FOB price (ENTRY VERIFIED - OCTOBER 1985)	US$500-US$1000	LEGISLATION Guidelines for joint ventures specified. -Undertakings not to compete with small-scale or traditional artisanal fisheries; -investor to be bona fide company; -investment to lead to foreign exchange earnings; -Share ratio for Indonesian partner to start at 20% rising to at least 40% in 5 years and 51% within 10 yrs	

TABLE B

LICENCE FEES, BILATERAL AGREEMENT OR JOINT VENTURE REQUIREMENTS AND NATIONALITY CRITERIA

STATE	Licence fees, royalties and other payments		Requirements concerning bilateral framework agreements or joint venture participation	Nationality criteria for fishing vessels
	Local currency	US$ Equiv.		
IRAN	LEGISLATION -			LEGISLATION local fishing vessel = owned by nationals or by an Iranian corporation in which at least 51% of the shares are held by nationals (Maritime Code 1964, Art. 1)
IRAQ	NO INFORMATION			
IRELAND	Licences issued by E.E.C. within the common fishing zone. No fees See entry under European Community		Access to common fishing zone of E.E.C. governed by bilateral agreements with third countries on a reciprocal basis.	Irish sea-fishing boat defined as: -a boat registered in the state under the local law; -a boat the owner or the managing owner of which resides or has his principal place of business in the state. (Fisheries Consolidation) Act, 1959 S.219.
ISRAEL	NO INFORMATION			
ITALY	Licences issued by E.E.C. within the common fishing zone. No fees See entry under European Community		Access to common fishing zone of EEC governed by bilateral agreements with third countries on a reciprocal basis.	

TABLE B

LICENCE FEES, BILATERAL AGREEMENT OR JOINT VENTURE REQUIREMENTS AND NATIONALITY CRITERIA

STATE	Licence fees, royalties and other payments		Requirements concerning bilateral framework agreements or joint venture participation	Nationality criteria for fishing vessels
	Local currency	US$ Equiv.		
IVORY COAST	LEGISLATION - AGREEMENTS *Agreement with Senegal, 11 June 1979 - both Governments grant reciprocal fishing rights for tuna in their EEZ's. AGREEMENTS *Liberia-Ivory Coast Cooperation Agreement -Reciprocal fishing rights for 3 bona fide Liberian and Ivory Coast fishing vessels (Shrimp trawlers, approx 70 ft350 H.P. with refrigeration capacity of 25 tons)-no fees-Other provisions on exchange information, joint studies.		LEGISLATION Licences may be issued to a foreign vessel for fishing in territorial waters only where reciprocal agreement in force. (Merchant Shipping Code, Law No. 61/349 of 9 November 1961, Art. 129)	LEGISLATION Ivory Coast fishing vessel = fishing vessel at least half owned by local nationals or by nationals under law recognized as equivalent by reciprocal agreements. Where vessel belongs to a company, head office must be in Ivory Coast, the Chairman of the Board, the General Manager and the majority of the members of the Board must be local nationals or nationals under law recognized as equivalent by reciprocal agreements and at least 50% of the share capital must be held by local nationals or nationals under law recognized as equivalent by reciprocal agreement. (Merchant Shipping Code, 1961 Art. 6)
JAMAICA	New legislation under consideration (ENTRY VERIFIED - OCTOBER 1985)			No distinction made in existing legislation between local and foreign fishing vessels (Fishing Industry Act, 1975) New legislation under consideration

TABLE B

LICENCE FEES, BILATERAL AGREEMENT OR JOINT VENTURE REQUIREMENTS AND NATIONALITY CRITERIA

STATE	Licence fees, royalties and other payments		Requirements concerning bilateral framework agreements or joint venture participation	Nationality criteria for fishing vessels
	Local currency	US$ Equiv.		
JAPAN	LEGISLATION Prescribed by the Cabinet. (Law on Provisional Measures relating to the Fishing Zone Law No. 31 of 2 May 1977, Art. 8).			
JORDAN	NO INFORMATION			
KAMPUCHEA	NO INFORMATION			
KENYA	LEGISLATION - Unspecified at the discretion of the Director of Fisheries; - Licences issued in respect of fishermen not vessels. (Fish Industry Act 1968 S.8) New legislation uncer consideration			LEGISLATION Local fishing vesel defined as fishing vessel owned by nationals or companies incorporated under the laws of Kenya and having principal place of business in Kenya. (Merchant Shipping Act CAP 389 S. 3)
KIRIBATI	LEGISLATION - Permits subject to payment of such fees and royalties as may be determined by the Chief Fisheries Officer with the approval of the Minister.			LEGISLATION "local fishing vessel" means any fishing vessel- (a) owned by one or more persons resident and domiciled in Kiribati; or

TABLE B

LICENCE FEES, BILATERAL AGREEMENT OR JOINT VENTURE REQUIREMENTS AND NATIONALITY CRITERIA

STATE	Licence fees, royalties and other payments: Local currency	US$ Equiv.	Requirements concerning bilateral framework agreements or joint venture participation	Nationality criteria for fishing vessels
KIRIBATI (Cont'd)	(Fisheries Ordinance 1977 S. 5 (4)) (Note: In practice fees set in access agreements) AGREEMENTS *Agreement with Japan, (Federation of Japan Tuna Fisheries Cooperative Associations), August 1984, valid 1 Sept 1984 thru 31 Aug 1985) (longline and pole and line)			(b) owned by any company or fisheries cooperative society registered or incorporated under the laws of Kiribati, and having its principal place of business in Kiribati; (Fisheries Ordinance 1977, S.2.)
	Goods and services =Yen 35 000 000+	US$ 140 000		
	Registration fee=Y. 30 000 per boat	US$ 120		
	+ Licence fee calculated as follows For longliners: -Vessels under 100 GRT:			
	Yen 29 382 per MT estimated fish catch per trip based on historical catch data (39 MT Sept/Oct 1984)	US$ 118		
	-Vessels over 100 GRT: Yen 29 302 per MT estimated fish catch per trip based on historical catch data (48 MT Sept/Oct 1984)	US$ 117		
	For Pole and Line Vessels: Yen 6 298 per MT estimated fish catch per trip based on historical catch data (51 MT Sept '84/Apr '85)	US$ 25		
	Note: Fee levels revised automatically to reflect changes in market prices at "basket" of markets according to			

TABLE B

LICENCE FEES, BILATERAL AGREEMENT OR JOINT VENTURE REQUIREMENTS AND NATIONALITY CRITERIA

STATE	Licence fees, royalties and other payments		Requirements concerning bilateral framework agreements or joint venture participation	Nationality criteria for fishing vessels
	Local currency	US$ Equiv.		
KIRIBATI (Cont'd)	formula = Initial licence fee per MT x Amount of catch per trip (MT) x (Monthly catch price : initial catch price			
	Initial prices are:			
	For longline fish = Yen 767 per kg	US$ 3		
	Pole and line fish = Yen 169 per kg	US$ 0.7		
	*Agreement with Rep. of Korea of 12 Nov 1984 valid thru' 11 Nov 1985			
	- Lump sum payment of US$ 200 000 for up to 60 boats.	US$ 200 000		
	For any additional vessels over 60 fee = US$ 5 000 per vessel	US$ 5 000		
	*Agreement with Sobryflot (USSR) August 1985 valid for 1 year			
	-Permits to be issued in respect of 5 large purse-seiners, 2 small purse-seiners, 3 small longliners and 1 processing/factory vessel with 6 catcher boats, for lump-sum payment of A$2 400 000 payable in 3 instalments	US$ 1 578 947		
	*Note:Agreement between Government Kiribati, Micronesia Maritime Authority, Palau Maritime Authority, and AMERICAN TUNABOAT ASSOCIATION, of 1 Jan 1983 valid thru' 31 Dec 1984 has now lapsed.			
	(ENTRY VERIFIED - OCTOBER 1985)			

TABLE B

LICENCE FEES, BILATERAL AGREEMENT OR JOINT VENTURE REQUIREMENTS AND NATIONALITY CRITERIA

STATE	Licence fees, royalties and other payments		Requirements concerning bilateral framework agreements or joint venture participation	Nationality criteria for fishing vessels
	Local currency	US$ Equiv.		
KOREA DEM. REP.	NO INFORMATION			
REP. OF KOREA	LEGISLATION UNSPECIFIED			LEGISLATION Local fishing vessel defined as fishing vessel owned by nationals or companies incorporated under the local laws. (Fisheries Code 1967)
KUWAIT	LEGISLATION Fees to be specified in access agreement. (Decree Promulgating Law No. 46 of 1980 on Conservation of Fisheries Resources Art. 2) (ENTRY VERIFIED - JULY 1985)		LEGISLATION Fishing only authorized under licence issued by Minister in accordance with an agreement specifying the conditions and fees to be paid. (Decree Promulgating Law No. 46 of 1980 on Conservation of Fisheries Resources A. 2)	LEGISLATION Local vessel defined as any fishing vessel owned by a resident of Kuwait, without prejudice to provision of Law on Marine Commerce. (Decree Promulgating Law No. 46 of 1980 on Conservation of Fisheries Resources Art. 3)
LEBANON	NO INFORMATION			

TABLE B

LICENCE FEES, BILATERAL AGREEMENT OR JOINT VENTURE REQUIREMENTS AND NATIONALITY CRITERIA

STATE	Licence fees, royalties and other payments: Local currency	Licence fees, royalties and other payments: US$ Equiv.	Requirements concerning bilateral framework agreements or joint venture participation	Nationality criteria for fishing vessels
LIBERIA	LEGISLATION Vessels over 50 feet = $ 225 up to 50 feet = $ 150 gill netters = $ 50 beach seiners = $ 40 sport fishing = $ 30 Kru fishermen = $ 15 (Revised fishing rules and regulations 1973) AGREEMENTS *Liberia-Ivory Coast Cooperation Agreement -Reciprocal fishing rights for 3 bona fide Liberian and Ivory Coast fishing vessels (Shrimp trawlers, approx 70 ft 350 H.P. with refrigeration capacity of 25 tons)-no fees- Other provisions on exchange information, joint studies. (ENTRY VERIFIED - OCTOBER 1983)	 US$ 225 US$ 150 US$ 50 US$ 40 US$ 30 US$ 15		LEGISLATION Local fishing vessel defined as fishing vessel owned by nationals or companies in which a controlling interest is held by nationals. (Revised fishing rules and regulations 1973)
LIBYA	LEGISLATION -		LEGISLATION Fishing by foreign vessels prohibited except under agreement or where of economic advantage to country. (Act No. 8 of 1962 Art. 6)	LEGISLATION -

TABLE B

LICENCE FEES, BILATERAL AGREEMENT OR JOINT VENTURE REQUIREMENTS AND NATIONALITY CRITERIA

STATE	Licence fees, royalties and other payments		Requirements concerning bilateral framework agreements or joint venture participation	Nationality criteria for fishing vessels
	Local currency	US$ Equiv.		
MADAGASCAR	LEGISLATION New legislation under consideration		LEGISLATION Access to fishing grounds within territorial waters only under bilateral agreements. (Code of Merchant Shipping, No. 66-007 of 1966, Art. 5.2.01)	LEGISLATION Local fishing vessel = owned by nationals (at least 50%) or owned by companies meeting following criteria: (a) registered in Madagascar; (b) Chairman of the Board and majority of Directors must be nationals; (c) at least 50% of the share capital must be held by nationals. (Code of Merchant Shipping, No. 66-007 of 1966, Art. 2.2.03)
	AGREEMENTS *Agreement with EEC 1985 valid 3yrs renewable automatically for periods 2 years unless notice denunciation Tuna-fishing: licences to be issued for 27 ocean-going freezer tuna boats (no more than 18 at one time) Financial Contribution for fisheries development projects: flat-rate fixed at minimum of 900 000 ECU for	US$ 783 000		
	duration of Protocol payable in 3 equal annual instalments. If catch exceeds 6 000 tonnes tuna per year contribution to be increased accordingly up to maximum of 3 000 000ECU	US$ 2 610 000		
	for duration protocol ie 1 000 000 ECU per year. +	US$ 870 000		
	Contribution of 350 000 ECU towards financing scientific programme +	US$ 304 500		
	Licence Fee of 20 ECU per tonne	US$ 17.4		
	of fish caught in fishing zone payable by shipowners; 15 000 ECU to be paid as non-reimburable advance	US$ 13 050		
	2 Malagasy seamen to be signed on permanently for tuna fleet, failing which payment flat-rate 50% wages to be used for training seamen			

TABLE B

LICENCE FEES, BILATERAL AGREEMENT OR JOINT VENTURE REQUIREMENTS AND NATIONALITY CRITERIA

STATE	Licence fees, royalties and other payments		Requirements concerning bilateral framework agreements or joint venture participation	Nationality criteria for fishing vessels
	Local currency	US$ Equiv.		
MADAGASCAR (Cont'd)	Other fishing: licences to be granted for up to annual average of 5 000 GRT per month for fishing for Nephrops, crab, deep-water shrimp, & other species Financial Contribution for fisheries development projects: flat-rate of 375 000 ECU per year for duration of reconnaissance campaigns, + Licence Fees: = 25 ECU per GRT p.a. At Government request fees may be replaced in part by landing of fish (ENTRY VERIFIED - OCTOBER 1985)	US$ 326 250 US$ 22		
MALAYSIA	LEGISLATION Permits subject to payment of such sum of maoney as the Director General may specify. Director-General may also require payment of sum of money by way of security for activities of vessel. (Fisheries Act 1984 S. 18) Licence fees for foreign owned fishing boats and fishing boats not wholly owned by Malaysians:- (Fees per gear per annum)		LEGISLATION International fishery agreement with flag state and fishing permit both required (Fisheries Act 1984 S. 15)	LEGISLATION Local fishing vessel defined as vessel not registered outside Malaysia, which is wholly owned by natural persons who are citizens of Malaysia; or by a statutory corporation established under the laws of Malaysia; or by the Government of Malaysia or a State of Malaysia; or by a body corporate or incorporate established in Malaysia and wholly owned by persons described above or by body corporate or incorp-

TABLE B

LICENCE FEES, BILATERAL AGREEMENT OR JOINT VENTURE REQUIREMENTS AND NATIONALITY CRITERIA

STATE	Licence fees, royalties and other payments: Local currency	US$ Equiv.	Requirements concerning bilateral framework agreements or joint venture participation	Nationality criteria for fishing vessels
MALAYSIA (Cont'd)	-Trawl nets used with engined boats			orate wholly owned by persons described above (Fisheries Act 1984 S. 2)
	250 GT and above = R. 6 000	US$ 2 459		
	150-250 GT = R. 3 000	US$ 1 223		
	100-150 GT = R. 2 250	US$ 922		
	70-100 GT = R. 1 500	US$ 615		
	Fish purse seine and Anchovy purse seine nets used with engined boats			
	250 GT and above = R. 9 000	US$ 3 689		
	150-250 GT = R. 6 000	US$ 2 459		
	100-150 GT = R. 4 500	US$ 1 844		
	70-100 GT = R. 3 000	US$ 1 223		
	(Fisheries (Maritime)(Amendment) Regulations 1982) (ENTRY VERIFIED - MARCH 1985)			
MALDIVES ISLANDS	AGREEMENTS			
MALTA	LEGISLATION -			LEGISLATION Foreign fishing boat defined as fishing vessel not registered in Malta. (Act. No. 12 of 1953 S.2)

TABLE B

LICENCE FEES, BILATERAL AGREEMENT OR JOINT VENTURE REQUIREMENTS AND NATIONALITY CRITERIA

STATE	Licence fees, royalties and other payments: Local currency	Licence fees, royalties and other payments: US$ Equiv.	Requirements concerning bilateral framework agreements or joint venture participation	Nationality criteria for fishing vessels
MAURITANIA	LEGISLATION Export Fishing Fee Product	Amount	LEGISLATION	LEGISLATION Local fishing vessel -
	1) Fresh or chilled fish	(% FOB value)		(1) owned by nationals (at least 51% or
	A) Demersal fish including cephalopoda :			(2) owned by companies
	a) high-value species: seabasses giltheads, common seabream, dentex, groupers and related, red mullets, halibuts, flat fishes, cephalopoda, etc.			(a) registered in Mauritania; (b) Chairman of the Board and majority of Directors must be nationals;
	1 - shore processing	8 %		(c) at least 51% of the share capital must be held by nationals, and (3) all members of crew and at least 75% of officers must be nationals (except special circumstances).
	2 - processing aboard	11 %		(Code of Merchant Shipping 1978, Art. 10)
	b) other species: grey mullets, "toyos", meagres, drums, hakes etc.			
	1 - shore processing	7 %		
	2 - processing on board	13 %		
	B) Pelagic fish			
	a) tunas and tunalike species			
	1 - shore processing	7 %		
	2 - processing aboard	17,5 %		
	b) other species:mackerels,horse mackerels, sardinellas			
	1 - shore processing	6.5 %		

TABLE B

LICENCE FEES, BILATERAL AGREEMENT OR JOINT VENTURE REQUIREMENTS AND NATIONALITY CRITERIA

STATE	Licence fees, royalties and other payments		Requirements concerning bilateral framework agreements or joint venture participation	Nationality criteria for fishing vessels
	Local currency	US$ Equiv.		
MAURITANIA (Cont'd)	2 - processing aboard	11 %		
	2) Frozen fish			
	A) Processing aboard			
	a) Demersal, including cephalopoda :			
	1 - caught by Mauritanian vessels	10 %		
	2 - caught by chartered foreign vessels	16,5 %		
	b) Pelagic fish	11,5 %		
	B) Shore processing			
	a) Demersal, including cephalopoda	6 %		
	b) Pelagic			
	1 - tunas and tunalike fish	7 %		
	2 - other	3 %		
	3) Salted, dried and smoked fish	5 %		
	4) Spiny lobsters	20 %		
	5) "Poutargue"	20 %		
	6) Fish meal	7 %		
	7) Fish oil	15 %		
	9) Canned preserves	10 %		
	11) Other fishery products	8 %		
	(Art. 11 of Ordonnance No. 80-011 of 28 February 1980 as amended by Ordinances No. 80-326 of 27 December 1980 and No. 83-132 of 22 February 1983).			

TABLE B

LICENCE FEES, BILATERAL AGREEMENT OR JOINT VENTURE REQUIREMENTS AND NATIONALITY CRITERIA

STATE	Licence fees, royalties and other payments		Requirements concerning bilateral framework agreements or joint venture participation	Nationality criteria for fishing vessels
	Local currency	US$ Equiv.		
MAURITANIA (Cont'd)	AGREEMENTS			
	*Agreement with Republic of Korea of May 1981 (valid for 5 years renewable for 2-year periods unless denounced) with implementing procès verbal of May 1983 as subsequently amended			
	-Trawlers fee = US$450 per GRT/year all catch to be landed Nouadhibou;	US$ 450		
	plus US$ 120 tax per ton of fish caught and exported. Total tonnage authorized = 4 500 GRT.	US$ 120		
	-Financial grant of 1 Million US $ per year for 3 years.	US$ 1 000 000		
	*Agreement with Senegal of 11 August of 1983(valid for two years, renewable unless denounced) with Protocol (valid for one year, renewable unless denounced)			
	-Pelagic trawlers 200 US$ GRT/year			
	-Sardine vessels 200 US GRT/year			
	-Tuna vessels 200 US$ GRT/campaign			
	Contracts with French interests for 1985			
	-US$ 110/GRT/year for pole and line	US$ 110		

TABLE B

LICENCE FEES, BILATERAL AGREEMENT OR JOINT VENTURE REQUIREMENTS AND NATIONALITY CRITERIA

STATE	Licence fees, royalties and other payments		Requirements concerning bilateral framework agreements or joint venture participation	Nationality criteria for fishing vessels
	Local currency	US$ Equiv.		
MAURITANIA (Cont'd)	tuna boats -US$3 500/GRT/year for lobster vessels	US$3 500		
	-US$ 200/GRT/year for shrimp vessels	US$ 200		
	*Contracts with Spanish interests for 1985 -US$ 200/GRT/year for shrimp boats	US$ 200		
	*Most foreign vessels are under time-charter to Mauritanian based companies. Under normal contracts about 31% of the demersal catch and between 27% and 31% of the pelagic catch supplied to the Mauritanian companies. (ENTRY VERIFIED - JULY 1985)			
MAURITIUS	LEGISLATION 100 Rupees base fee plus 200 rupees per G.R.T. per annum (Government Notice No. 23 of 1978 as amended by G.N. No. 344 of 1981) Note: New legislation under consideration (ENTRY VERIFIED - OCTOBER 1985)	US$7-US$13	LEGISLATION Licence required, even if under bilateral agreement. Licence issued under the authority of Prime Minister. (Maritime Zones (Fishing licences) Regs. 1978, Reg. 3)	LEGISLATION Local fishing vessel - owned by citizens or by approved companies substantially owned and controlled by citizens. Licence application form to reveal shareholding. (Maritime Zones (Fishing Licences)

TABLE B

LICENCE FEES, BILATERAL AGREEMENT OR JOINT VENTURE REQUIREMENTS AND NATIONALITY CRITERIA

STATE	Licence fees, royalties and other payments: Local currency	US$ Equiv.	Requirements concerning bilateral framework agreements or joint venture participation	Nationality criteria for fishing vessels
MEXICO	LEGISLATION Tuna: Permit fee = 2 500 pesos per vessel per trip (up to 60 days) + Exploitation fee = 1 380 pesos per n.r.t. per trip (up to 60 days) Other species: 2 000 Pesos per n.r.t. up to 1 year (Federal Law on Fees 1982) (ENTRY VERIFIED - FEBRUARY 1983)	 US$ 10 US$ 5.7 per n.r.t. US$ 8.26	LEGISLATION Fisheries Department give preference to foreign vessels from countries granting equal conditions of reciprocity to Mexican vessels. (Decree amending Art. 37 of the Federal Law on Fisheries Development 1976)	LEGISLATION Local fishing vessel defined as vessel owned by nationals or cooperatives or statutory corporations or commercial companies constituted and registered under the local laws in which at least 51% of the share capital with voting rights is held by nationals, or Mexican companies whose constitions exclude foreigners, and whose consitutions establish that the majority of the administrators are to be designated by Mexican shareholders and that Mexican persons must be designated (Federal Law on Fisheries Development 1972 Art. 27)
MONACO	NO INFORMATION			
MOROCCO	LEGISLATION Fees determined by gross tonnage of vessel: Fees payable range from 100 dirhams for vessels up to 15 G.T. up to 10 000 dirhams (for vessels over 1 000 G.T.) vessels under 2 G.T. exempted. (Decree No. 2.37.167 of 24 November 1973 as amended by Decree No. 279.339 of 29 June 1979, Art. 2)	 US$ 9.6 US$ 960	LEGISLATION Fishing reserved for vessels under Moroccan flag or operated by nationals or Moroccan companies. (Act No. 1-73-211 of 1973 Art. 5).	LEGISLATION Local fishing vessel=fishing vessel owned by Moroccan nationals or Moroccan company having its head office in Morocco, and with at least half its capital held by Moroccan nationals and of which a majority of members of the Board of Directors and the chairman of the Board are nationals, or partnerships where all partners are

TABLE B

LICENCE FEES, BILATERAL AGREEMENT OR JOINT VENTURE REQUIREMENTS AND NATIONALITY CRITERIA

STATE	Licence fees, royalties and other payments		Requirements concerning bilateral framework agreements or joint venture participation	Nationality criteria for fishing vessels
	Local currency	US$ Equiv.		
MOROCCO (Cont'd)	AGREEMENTS *Agreement with Spain of 1 August 1983 valid through 31 July 1987 Licences granted for a degressive global tonnage of vessels - 138,602 GRT by 1 August 1983 and 81,961GRT after 1 August 1986. All vessels to pay a progressive annual fee defined in Special Drawing Rights (SDR) per Gross Registered Ton by type of vessel and payable in convertible currency.			nationals. (Act No. 1-73-210 of 1973, Art. 2) Art. 2).
	-North of Cape Noun For vessels of less than 100GRT-87,14SDR from 1 July 1984;96,48SDR from 1 January 1985; 105,82SDR from 1 January 1986.	US$87,US$96 US$105		
	For vessels of more than 100GRT-149,14SDR from 1 July 1984; 166,12 SDR from 1 January 1985; 181,10SDR from 1 January 1986.	US$149,US$166 US$181		
	-South of Cape Noun Sardine vessels-99,22SDR from 1 July 1984; 109,85SDR from 1 January 1985; 120,48SDR from 1 January 1986	US$99 US$109 US$120		
	Artisanal vessels-62,17SDR from 1 July 1984; 68,83SDR from 1 January	US$62 US$68		

TABLE B

LICENCE FEES, BILATERAL AGREEMENT OR JOINT VENTURE REQUIREMENTS AND NATIONALITY CRITERIA

STATE	Licence fees, royalties and other payments		Requirements concerning bilateral framework agreements or joint venture participation	Nationality criteria for fishing vessels
	Local currency	US$ Equiv.		
MOROCCO (Cont'd)	1985; 75,49SDR from 1 January 1986.	US$75		
	Cephalopoda freezer vessels-186,23 SDR from 1 July 1984; 206,18SDR from 1 January 1985; 226,13SDR from 1 January 1986.	US$186 US$206 US$226		
	Other cephalopoda vessels-136,33 SDR from 1 July 1984; 150,93SDR from 1 January 1985; 165,53SDR from 1 January 1986.	US$136 US$150 US$165		
	Merluza vessels- 70,53SDR from 1 July 1984; 78,09SDR 1 January 1985; 85,65SDR from 1 January 1986.	US$70 US$78 US$85		
	PLUS Spain to supply for the period of the agreement two credits of US$400Million and US$150Milliom respectively on conditions defined in the Agreement. (ENTRY VERIFIED - OCTOBER 1985)	US$400M and US$150M		
MOZAMBIQUE	LEGISLATION Conditions of authorization for foreign fishing vessels to be set by Minister of Industry and Energy. (Decree No. 32/76 of 19 August 1976 Art. 3.) Fees set annually. Level of fees depends on whether fishing commercial or experimental.			

TABLE B

LICENCE FEES, BILATERAL AGREEMENT OR JOINT VENTURE REQUIREMENTS AND NATIONALITY CRITERIA

STATE	Licence fees, royalties and other payments		Requirements concerning bilateral framework agreements or joint venture participation	Nationality criteria for fishing vessels
	Local currency	US$ Equiv.		
	Commercial licences issued annually experimental licences issued for between 3 months and 1 year Fees payable in kind (catch) or freely convertible currency AGREEMENTS *Agreement with Portugal, 1982 valid thru' end 1983 Licences issued to Portuguese vessels to fish in Mozambique EEZ No licence fees mentioned Qota of 700 tons of shrimp fixed for 1983 for Portuguese market 4 study places allocated to Mozambique nationals at Portuguese institutions 1 specially equipped Portuguese vessel to carry out scientific and technical survey and train Mozambique nationals (ENTRY VERIFIED - MAY 1983)			
NAMIBIA	----			

TABLE B

LICENCE FEES, BILATERAL AGREEMENT OR JOINT VENTURE REQUIREMENTS AND NATIONALITY CRITERIA

STATE	Licence fees, royalties and other payments: Local currency	US$ Equiv.	Requirements concerning bilateral framework agreements or joint venture participation	Nationality criteria for fishing vessels
NAURU	LEGISLATION Fees to be prescribed by Minister (Marine Resources Act 1978 S. 20) Note: No access agreements (ENTRY VERIFIED - OCTOBER 1985)			
NETHER-LANDS	Licences issued by E.E.C. within the common fishing zone. No fees. See entry under European Community	--	Access to common fishing zone of E.E.C. governed by bilateral agreements with third countries on a reciprocal basis.	
NEW ZEALAND	LEGISLATION -squid by jigging =$25 350 per year + $169 per tonne of fish taken under the licence over 150 tonnes; -squid by trawling = $114 per tonne of fish permitted; -trawling (Management Area E)= $40 per tonne of fish permitted; -trawling (other than Area E)= $59 per tonne of fish permitted; + $11 per tonne of orange roughy (Hoplostethus atlanticus) caught) bottom-lining = $84 per tonne of fish permitted; -longlining - albacore and yellow fin tuna = $7 500 per year	US$ 11 471 US$ 76 US$ 52 US$ 18 US$ 27 US$ 5 US$ 38 US$ 3 394	LEGISLATION Allowable catch for foreign fishing craft to be apportioned among foreign countries by the Minister. (In practice bilateral access agreements required). Individual foreign fishing craft must be licensed. (Territorial Sea and Exclusive Economic Zone Act 1977 S. 13).	LEGISLATION New Zealand Fishing craft means a fishing craft (a)That is a New Zealand ship within the meaning of Section 2(1) of the Shipping and Seamen Act, 1952; or b) That is an aircraft registered in New Zealand under the Civil Aviation Act 1964; or c) in which no person who is not a New Zealand citizen has any legal or equitable interest (except by way of security only for any advance made by him to the owner.) (Territorial Sea and Exclusive Economic Zone Act 1977 S.2)

TABLE B

LICENCE FEES, BILATERAL AGREEMENT OR JOINT VENTURE REQUIREMENTS AND NATIONALITY CRITERIA

STATE	Licence fees, royalties and other payments		Requirements concerning bilateral framework agreements or joint venture participation	Nationality criteria for fishing vessels
	Local currency	US$ Equiv.		
NEW ZEALAND (Cont'd)	-Longlining - southern blue fin tuna = $74 000 per year -fish carriers = $5 per tonne of fish carrying capacity per voyage; -support craft =$2.50 per G.R.T. per voyage (The Exclusive Economic Zone (Licence Fees for Foreign Fishing Craft) Regs. 1978 as amended) AGREEMENTS *Agreements in force with Republic of Korea, USSR, and Japan, but fees set in Regulations cited above (ENTRY VERIFIED - FEBRUARY 1985)	US$ 33 484 US$ 2 US$ 1		
NEW ZEALAND DEPENDENT TERRITORIES				
- Tokelau	LEGISLATION Fees to be prescribed by regulation (Tokelau (Territorial Sea and Exclusive Economic Zone) Act 1977 S. 8) (Note: In practice fees set in access agreements)	-	LEGISLATION Governor General may make regulations providing for apportionment of surplus of total allowable catch. (Tokelau (Territorial Sea and Exclusive Economic Zone) Act 1977, S. 11)	LEGISLATION Tokelauan fishing craft means a fishing craft in which no person who is not a Tokelauan has any legal or equitable interest (except by way of security only for any advance made by him to the owner. (Tokelau (Territorial Sea and Exclusive Economic Zone) Act 1977 S. 2)

TABLE B

LICENCE FEES, BILATERAL AGREEMENT OR JOINT VENTURE REQUIREMENTS AND NATIONALITY CRITERIA

STATE	Licence fees, royalties and other payments		Requirements concerning bilateral framework agreements or joint venture participation	Nationality criteria for fishing vessels
	Local currency	US$ Equiv.		
NEW ZEALAND DEPENDENT TERRITORIES (Cont'd)	AGREEMENTS *Note:Agreement between Government Kiribati, Micronesia Maritime Authority, Palau Maritime Authority, and AMERICAN TUNABOAT ASSOCIATION, of 1 Jan 1983 valid thru' 31 Dec 1984 has now lapsed. (ENTRY VERIFIED - OCTOBER 1985)			
NEW ZEALAND ASSOCIATED STATES -Cook Islands	LEGISLATION Such fees as may from time to time be prescribed. (Territorial Sea and Exclusive Economic Zone Act, 1977 S. 16) (Note: In practice fees set in access agreements)		LEGISLATION Allowable catch to be apportioned by the Minister among foreign countries. Criteria for apportionment specified. Individual foreign fishing	LEGISLATION Cook Islands fishing craft means any fishing vessel based in and operating from the Cook Islands. (Territorial Sea and Exclusive Economic Zone Act 1977 S.2)

TABLE B

LICENCE FEES, BILATERAL AGREEMENT OR JOINT VENTURE REQUIREMENTS AND NATIONALITY CRITERIA

STATE	Licence fees, royalties and other payments		Requirements concerning bilateral framework agreements or joint venture participation	Nationality criteria for fishing vessels
	Local currency	US$ Equiv.		
NEW ZEALAND ASSOCIATED STATES -Cook Islands (Cont'd)	AGREEMENTS Notes: No access agreements in force Agreement with Rep. of Korea (Nov.1982-valid thru' Nov. 1983) (now lapsed) (Agreement with Taiwanese Fishermens' Association 7 Oct. 1981 valid thru' 6 October 1982)(now lapsed) Agreement between Government Kiribati, Micronesia Maritime Authority, Palau Maritime Authority, and AMERICAN TUNABOAT ASSOCIATION, of 1 Jan 1983 valid thru' 31 Dec 1984 has now lapsed. (ENTRY VERIFIED - OCTOBER 1985)		craft must be licensed. (Territorial Sea and Exclusive Economic Zone Act 1977, S. 11)	
- Niue	LEGISLATION Such fee as may from time to time be prescribed. (Territorial Sea and Exclusive Economic Zone Act, 1978, S. 16) In practice fees set in agreements	-	LEGISLATION Licences required for all vessels (Territorial Sea and Exclusive Economic Act 1978 S. 12)	LEGISLATION Foreign fishing vessels defined as fishing vessel which is owned or controlled by a person or persons not ordinary resident in Niue. (Territorial Sea and Exclusive Economic Zone Act 1978, S. 2)

TABLE B

LICENCE FEES, BILATERAL AGREEMENT OR JOINT VENTURE REQUIREMENTS AND NATIONALITY CRITERIA

STATE	Licence fees, royalties and other payments		Requirements concerning bilateral framework agreements or joint venture participation	Nationality criteria for fishing vessels
	Local currency	US$ Equiv.		
- Niue (Cont'd)	AGREEMENTS *Note: Agreement between Government Kiribati, Micronesia Maritime Authority, Palau Maritime Authority, and AMERICAN TUNABOAT ASSOCIATION, of 1 Jan 1983 valid thru' 31 Dec 1984 has now lapsed. (ENTRY VERIFIED - OCTOBER 1985)			
NICARAGUA	LEGISLATION - Licence fee (annual) Vessels up to 16 feet long and 4 feet wide = US$ 10 Vessels over these dimension pay additional US$ 1 per foot - Plus percentage of profits ("utilidad") from fishing operations as follows: - profits up to 15% of gross revenue = 3% of profits; - profits from 15% to 30% = 3% plus 0.2% per each 1% over 15% - profits over 30% = 3% plus 0.2% for each 1% over 15% up to 30% plus 0.4% for each 1% over 30% (Ley Especial Sobre Explotación de la Pesca, 1961) Art. 26-28)	US$ 10 US$ 1 per ft.		LEGISLATION Local fishing vessel = - Vessels of Nicaraguan registry or vessels operating under the authority of a Nicaraguan licence. (Ley Especial Sobre Explotación de la Pesca, Act 1)

TABLE B

LICENCE FEES, BILATERAL AGREEMENT OR JOINT VENTURE REQUIREMENTS AND NATIONALITY CRITERIA

<table>
<tr><th rowspan="2">STATE</th><th colspan="2">Licence fees, royalties and other payments</th><th rowspan="2">Requirements concerning bilateral framework agreements or joint venture participation</th><th rowspan="2">Nationality criteria for fishing vessels</th></tr>
<tr><th>Local currency</th><th>US$ Equiv.</th></tr>
<tr><td>NIGERIA</td><td>LEGISLATION
Fishing in territorial waters reserved for Nigerian flag vessels (Conditions under which a vessel may be granted permission to fish in Nigerian Territorial Waters)
Fishing in exclusive economic zone (i.e. 30-200 miles) also apparently reserved for Nigerian flag vessels

Foreign flag vessels may be licensed only to fish outside Nigerian EEZ though may land fish in Nigeria
Licence fees are:
G.R.T. / Annual / Quarterly
Under 20 / N. 40 / N. 12
20 - 199 / N.100 / N. 30
200- 999 / N.200 / N. 60
1000 and up / N.400 / N.120
(Conditions for the licensing of distant water motor fishing boats)

(ENTRY VERIFIED - DECEMBER 1983)</td><td>

US$ 45-US$ 14
US$114-US$ 34
US$227-US$ 68
US$455-US$136</td><td>LEGISLATION
Fishing reserved for Nigerian flag vessels.
Foreign Fishing allowed only under joint venture with Nigerian national interests

All joint ventures must have at least 51% of the capital provided by Nigerial nationals.</td><td>LEGISLATION
Vessel must be owned by Nigerian national or Nigerian Corporate body registered according to the prevailing rules and regulations.
(Conditions under which a vessel may be granted permission to fish in Nigerian Territorial Waters)
To qualify for registration of vessels under Nigerian flag, joint venture companies should theoretically have at least 51% Nigerian shareholding, though recent practice indicates more flexible requirements, so long as substantial Nigerian interest in the company.
AGREEMENTS
Agreement with Equatorial Guinea, 27 Nov. 1981
A Nigerian vessel is a vessel owned by the Nigerian Government or a Nigerian Company flying the Nigerian flag; whose crew is made up of not less than 50% African nationals and
-belonging to a company whose capital is owned for no less than 50% by Nigerians (art. 11).</td></tr>
</table>

TABLE B

LICENCE FEES, BILATERAL AGREEMENT OR JOINT VENTURE REQUIREMENTS AND NATIONALITY CRITERIA

STATE	Licence fees, royalties and other payments		Requirements concerning bilateral framework agreements or joint venture participation	Nationality criteria for fishing vessels
	Local currency	US$ Equiv.		
NORWAY	LEGISLATION Licence issued by Director of Fisheries Licence fees not specified in the basic legislation or regulations (Regulations relating to foreign fishing in the EEZ of Norway 1977, S. 5)			LEGISLATION Norwegian citizens = 1. Persons resident in Norway, 2. Joint stock companies or other limited liability companies provided the head office and the Board of Directors of such company are located in Norway and the Directors are shareholders, resident in Norway and Norwegian citizens and at least six-tenths of the share capital is owned by Norwegian citizens 3. The State. establishments and funds directed by the State and Norwegian municipalities. In special cases the King may permit a joint stock company or other limited liability company which does not satisfy the conditions in poitn 2 above, and which engages in the processing of fish products pursuant to concession granted under the Act of 14 December 1917 concerning the acquisition of waterfalls, mines and other real property, to engage in business which according to this Act is reserved for the persons and companies mentioned in the preceding

TABLE B

LICENCE FEES, BILATERAL AGREEMENT OR JOINT VENTURE REQUIREMENTS AND NATIONALITY CRITERIA

STATE	Licence fees, royalties and other payments: Local currency	Licence fees, royalties and other payments: US$ Equiv.	Requirements concerning bilateral framework agreements or joint venture participation	Nationality criteria for fishing vessels
NORWAY (Cont'd)				paragraph. The permission can only be granted for such business as is naturally related to the company's processing plant in Norway. Whenever the public interest so requires, the permit may be made subject to certain requirements. -Norwegian vessel is for the purposes of this Act deemed to include vessels owned by persons resident in Norway provided the vessel is not of such size as to be subject to compulsory registration under the Ship Registration Act of 4 May 1901 (Maritime Act of 20 July 1983, S.5).
OMAN	LEGISLATION Minister to issue regulations prescribing fees for fishing licences (Sultanic Decree No 53/81 promulgating the Law on Marine Fisheries and Conservation of Living Aquatic Resources, Art. 4) -Fishing Boat Licence = 1 Rial for up to 50 hp. + 100 pisas per additional hp. up to max. of 200 Rials	US $ 3 US $ 580		

TABLE B

LICENCE FEES, BILATERAL AGREEMENT OR JOINT VENTURE REQUIREMENTS AND NATIONALITY CRITERIA

STATE	Licence fees, royalties and other payments		Requirements concerning bilateral framework agreements or joint venture participation	Nationality criteria for fishing vessels
	Local currency	US$ Equiv.		
OMAN (Cont'd)	(licence valid 1 year) + -Fisherman's Licence (including master and crew) = 3 Rials (licence valid 3 years) (Art. 11) Omani fishery companies and institutions operating in Omani fishing zones not to use foreign owned boats unless permitted by competent authority which has power to levy appropriate tolls on use (Art. 24) (Ministerial Decree No. 3/82 on the Executive Regulations for the Marine Fisheries and Protection of Living Resources Law) AGREEMENTS 30% of catch (in kind or equivalence) (Agreement with Korean Company)	US $ 9		
PAKISTAN	LEGISLATION -registration fee = fishing craft RS 50 fishing gear RS 10 to 50 -licence fees = RS 100 per year per vessel	 US$ 3 US$ 0.6 to 3 US$ 6	Joint venture guidelines: -Bank guarantee of Rs200 000 -Vessel GRT 300-500 only; -Area of operation beyond 35 miles from coast only;	LEGISLATION Local fishing vessel Owned by nationals or companies incorporated under the local law.

TABLE B

LICENCE FEES, BILATERAL AGREEMENT OR JOINT VENTURE REQUIREMENTS AND NATIONALITY CRITERIA

STATE	Licence fees, royalties and other payments		Requirements concerning bilateral framework agreements or joint venture participation	Nationality criteria for fishing vessels
	Local currency	US$ Equiv.		
PAKISTAN (Cont'd)	-permit fee = RS 50 per vessel -identity card = RS 5 per card (Exclusive Fishery Zone (Regulation of Fishing) Rules 1976 Schedule) Government Royalty = 10% of value of catch in foreign exchange. Local party to receive 27%.	US$ 6 US$ 0.3	-Catch to be exported in frozen form through Pak. port; -Tax holidays; -Provisions specfied regarding respnsibilties of local and foreign party.	
PANAMA	LEGISLATION Licence fee for tuna fishing B 30 per n.r.t. per 6 months (Decree No. 8 of 1976) Navigation permit = B 600 AGREEMENTS *Agreement with Costa Rica and USA 14 March 1983 valid until withdrawal TUNA FISHING -For 5 Contracting Parties = US$ 60 per nrt. -For additional Contracting Parties (coastal states) fees increased up to maximum of US$ 100 per nrt	 US$ 30 US$ 600		LEGISLATION Local fishing vessel Owned by nationals, locally registered companies, or foreigners domiciled in the country. (Decree Law No. 17 of 1959 Art. 5)

TABLE B

LICENCE FEES, BILATERAL AGREEMENT OR JOINT VENTURE REQUIREMENTS AND NATIONALITY CRITERIA

STATE	Licence fees, royalties and other payments		Requirements concerning bilateral framework agreements or joint venture participation	Nationality criteria for fishing vessels
	Local currency	US$ Equiv.		
PANAMA (Cont'd)	Note: Increases to be determined by Council set up under agreement - minimum increase of US$ 10 per nrt for each additional Contracting Party (coastal state) after 6th. Fees to be reduced on withdrawal by any Contracting Party (coastal state) as determined by Council down to minimum of US$ 60 per nrt. Fees to be paid in full before licence issued Licences valid until end year in which issued Proceeds of fees less up to 10% for administrative costs, to be distributed to Coastal States in proportion to amount of tuna taken in respective 200 mile areas Note: AGREEMENT NOT YET IN FORCE (ENTRY VERIFIED - OCTOBER 1984)			
PAPUA NEW GUINEA	LEGISLATION Licence fees made up of 3 different components 1.Boat Licensing Fee = K. 30 per metre length per year, or K. 7.50 per metre length for quarterly licences +	US$ 29 US$ 7.3		Papua New Guinea boat means a boat the operations of which are based on a place in PNG and that is wholly owned by a natural person who is a resident of, or a company incorporated, PNG, being a boat that- (a)was built in PNG; or

TABLE B

LICENCE FEES, BILATERAL AGREEMENT OR JOINT VENTURE REQUIREMENTS AND NATIONALITY CRITERIA

STATE	Licence fees, royalties and other payments		Requirements concerning bilateral framework agreements or joint venture participation	Nationality criteria for fishing vessels
	Local currency	US$ Equiv.		
PAPUA NEW GUINEA (Cont'd)	2. Operational fee of 5% of value of fish caught under licence 3. Fisherman Licensing fee = 1 kina per fisherman employed on board vessel per year (Fisheries Regulations 1975) (For domestically based fisheries duty of 5% F.O.B. value of unprocessed tuna exported + 2.5% of F.O.B.value for bait fees) AGREEMENTS *Japanese/Papua New Guinea Fishing Arrangement (valid 7 August 1981 until 3 months after either party gives notice of termination) Fees as above. Operation fee determined by formula (Estimated catch per trip in tonnes) x (F.O.B. Price in Kina per tonne) x (Unit Rate in percentage) x (Operation Ratio) x (Duration Ratio for Longliners and group purse-seiners or number of trips per year for single purse-seiners - nothing for pole and liners) x (Factor - for single purse-seiners only)	US$ 1.32		(b) has been lawfully imported into PNG, otherwise than for a limited period; or (c) has been sold or otherwise disposed of in PNG after having been forfeited or distrained under an Act or an Act of Australia. (Fisheries Act 1974 S. 2)

TABLE B

LICENCE FEES, BILATERAL AGREEMENT OR JOINT VENTURE REQUIREMENTS AND NATIONALITY CRITERIA

STATE	Licence fees, royalties and other payments		Requirements concerning bilateral framework agreements or joint venture participation	Nationality criteria for fishing vessels
	Local currency	US$ Equiv.		
PAPUA NEW GUINEA (Cont'd)	F.O.B. Price calculated in accordance with agreed formula from average of Yaizu market prices over previous 3 months. Note: Agreement with American Tuna Boat Association, 1982, valid thru' 31 December 1982) now lapsed (ENTRY VERIFIED - OCTOBER 1985)			
PERU	LEGISLATION FOR TRAWLERS:		LEGISLATION	
	Registration fee = US$ 2 000 (valid 1 year) +	US$ 2 000 +	Joint ventures allowed where foreign capital not more than 49% depending on the size of the enterprise, the amount of foreign capital invested, the technology and the kind of fishery. (Decree Law No. 18810 Art 57)	
	Navigation Permit Fee=US$20 per GRT (valid 1 year) +	US$20 per GRT		
	Fishing Permit fee = US$250 per NRT (valid 1 year) (Supreme Decree 012-84-PE of 1984)	US$250 per NRT		
	FOR TUNA FREEZER VESSELS:			
	Registration fee = US$ 2 000 (valid 180 days) +	US$ 2 000		
	Navigation Permit Fee=US$20 per NRT (valid 180 days) +	US$20 per GRT		
	Fishing Permit fee = US$250 per NRT	US$250 per NRT		
	Permit fee - up to: (valid 180 days) (Supreme Decree 008-84-PE of 1984) (ENTRY VERIFIED - JANUARY 1985)			

TABLE B

LICENCE FEES, BILATERAL AGREEMENT OR JOINT VENTURE REQUIREMENTS AND NATIONALITY CRITERIA

<table>
<tr><th rowspan="2">STATE</th><th colspan="2">Licence fees, royalties and other payments</th><th rowspan="2">Requirements concerning bilateral framework agreements or joint venture participation</th><th rowspan="2">Nationality criteria for fishing vessels</th></tr>
<tr><th>Local currency</th><th>US$ Equiv.</th></tr>
<tr><td>PHILIP-
PINES</td><td>LEGISLATION
Fees and other charges for foreign fishing boats operating under charter, lease or lease-purchase agreement with Philippine national or company are :
Application fee = P.100 US$
Fisherman's licence (annual)= P. 20 US$
Boat licence (annual)
-below 100 G.T. = P. 1 000 US$
-100 - 250 G.T. = P. 3 000 US$
-over 250 G.T. = P. 5 000 US$
Foreign Fisherman's licence = P 20 US$
(Fisheries Administrative Order No. 121, 1976 Sects. 10 & 11)</td><td>

6
1

57
170
283

1</td><td>LEGISLATION
Exploration and exploitation of natural resources restricted to citizens or corporations or associations with at least 60% of capital owned by citizens. National Assembly may allow citizens to enter into service contracts for financial, technical, management or other forms of assistance with foreign person or entity. (Constitution, SEC. 9)
Foreign fishing must be under charter, lease or or lease-purchase agreement with Philippine national or company (at least 70% Philippine owned)(Fisheries Administrative Order No. 121,1976</td><td>LEGISLATION
See entry in previous column</td></tr>
<tr><td>POLAND</td><td>LEGISLATION
Determined by the Minister of Marine
(Sea Fishing Act, 21 May, 1963 S.7)</td><td></td><td>LEGISLATION
Foreign fishing vessels shall not fish in Polish territorial waters unless otherwise stipulated in any</td><td>LEGISLATION
1. A Polish vessel is a vessel which is owned by:
1) a body corporate having its seat in Poland;</td></tr>
</table>

TABLE B

LICENCE FEES, BILATERAL AGREEMENT OR JOINT VENTURE REQUIREMENTS AND NATIONALITY CRITERIA

STATE	Licence fees, royalties and other payments		Requirements concerning bilateral framework agreements or joint venture participation	Nationality criteria for fishing vessels
	Local currency	US$ Equiv.		
POLAND (Cont'd)			international agreement antered into by the Polish state (Sea Fishing Act, 1963 S. 5)	2) the State Treasury; 3) a Polish citizen resident in Poland. 2. A Polish vessel is also a vessel which is owned at least as to 50 per cent by bodies or persons mentioned in S. 1 provided that her operator is resident, or has the seat of his head office or a branch office, in Poland. (Maritime Code Act, 1961 Art. 14)
PORTUGAL	LEGISLATION Fees to be established by decree Product of fees from licences to go by priority to fisheries sector in the subareas where fishing allowed (Decree-Law No 52/85 1985 Art. 8)		LEGISLATION Framework agreements required, and individual licences (Decree-Law No 52/85 of 1 March 1985 Art. 8)	
QATAR	LEGISLATION Minister to issue regulations prescribing fees for fishing licences (Law No. 4 of 1983 on Exploitation and Conservation of Living Aquatic Resources in Qatar, Art. 5) -Fishing Boat Licence = 100 Rials	US $28		

TABLE B

LICENCE FEES, BILATERAL AGREEMENT OR JOINT VENTURE REQUIREMENTS AND NATIONALITY CRITERIA

STATE	Licence fees, royalties and other payments		Requirements concerning bilateral framework agreements or joint venture participation	Nationality criteria for fishing vessels
	Local currency	US$ Equiv.		
QATAR (Cont'd)	for initial licence and 10 Rials for its renewal (licence valid 1 year) +	US $ 2.8		
	-Fisherman's Licence (including master and crew) = 10 Rials (licence valid 3 years) (Art. 13)	US $ 2.8		
	Qatar fishery companies and institutions operating in Qatar fishing zones not to use foreign owned boats unless permitted by competent authority which has power to levy appropriate tolls on use (Art. 40) (Executive Regulations of Law No. 4 on the Exploitation and Conservation of Living Aquatic Resources in the State of Qatar) (ENTRY VERIFIED - OCTOBER 1985)			
ROMANIA	NO INFORMATION			
ST. LUCIA	LEGISLATION Such fees as may be prescribed plus such royalties or other charges as the Minister may determine. (S. 14) (The Fisheries Act No 10 of 1984) Fisheries Regulations not yet promulgated.		LEGISLATION No foreign fishing vessel licence to be issued unless there is in force an access agreement with the flag state or association representing the owners. Flag state includes regional	LEGISLATION Local fishing vessel defined as any fishing vessel (a) wholly owned by the Govt. of St. Lucia or any public corporation established by or under any law; or (b) wholly owned by one or more persons who are citizens of St. Lucia;

TABLE B

LICENCE FEES, BILATERAL AGREEMENT OR JOINT VENTURE REQUIREMENTS AND NATIONALITY CRITERIA

STATE	Licence fees, royalties and other payments		Requirements concerning bilateral framework agreements or joint venture participation	Nationality criteria for fishing vessels
	Local currency	US$ Equiv.		
ST. LUCIA (Cont'd)	(ENTRY VERIFIED - OCTOBER 1985)		organization with delegated power to make agreements. Requirement does not apply to licences issued for test fishing operations or locally based fishing operations. (The Fisheries Act No 10 of 1984 S. 8)	or (c) wholly owned by any company, society or other association of persons incorporated or established in St. Lucia of which at least 51% of the voting shares are held by citizens locally based foreign fishing vessel defined as one based in Antigua & Barbuda which lands all its catch there (The Fisheries Act No 10 of 1984 S. 2)
ST.VINCENT	New legislation under consideration			
SAO TOME AND PRINCIPE	LEGISLATION Tax = DB 3 800 per G.T. per year plus royalty = up to 20% of international value of catch, both payable in convertible currency. Royalty payable at end of 3 month periods in respect of preceding periods. (Decree-Law No. 63/81, 1981 Art 22) AGREEMENTS *Agreement with Portugal of Oct. 1979 -Portuguese vessels allowed to	US$ 85 + 20%	LEGISLATION Access to the fishing zone only under bilateral agreements, with other States or private institutions. Agreements must include one or more of following conditions: a) Technical training of Tomean citizens; b) financing for development of S.Tomean fishing industry c) payment of fees;	

TABLE B

LICENCE FEES, BILATERAL AGREEMENT OR JOINT VENTURE REQUIREMENTS AND NATIONALITY CRITERIA

STATE	Licence fees, royalties and other payments: Local currency	US$ Equiv.	Requirements concerning bilateral framework agreements or joint venture participation	Nationality criteria for fishing vessels
SAO TOME AND PRINCIPE (Cont'd)	operate in Sao Tomean waters: -fees to be established according to S.T. laws and regulations. -Parties shall seek to establish fishing joint ventures. *Agreement with the EEC, 1983, valid thru' 1986 -ECU 20 per ton of fish caught (ECU 40 000 paid in advance) + ECU 180 000 annually for development projects to be increased proportionately if tuna catches exceed 4 000 tons. Agreement provides for authorizations for 27 tuna freezer vessels Additional authorizations may be accorded on request of one party on terms to be agreed. (Text published in EC Official Journal No. L 282/567, 14/10/1983) (ENTRY VERIFIED - OCTOBER 1983)	 US$ 17.4 US$ 34 800 US$ 156 600	d) delivery to S. Tome of a percentage of the catch; e) carrying of S. Tomean inspectors on board foreign vessels; f) inclusion of S. Tomean citizens in crews. (Decree-Law No. 63/81, 1981 Art 4)	
SAUDI ARABIA	LEGISLATION Fishing by foreign vessels only allowed under permit from Minister of Agriculture and Water. Level of fees not specified.			

TABLE B

LICENCE FEES, BILATERAL AGREEMENT OR JOINT VENTURE REQUIREMENTS AND NATIONALITY CRITERIA

STATE	Licence fees, royalties and other payments		Requirements concerning bilateral framework agreements or joint venture participation	Nationality criteria for fishing vessels
	Local currency	US$ Equiv.		
SAUDI ARABIA (Cont'd)	(Fishing Regulation, Exploitation and Conservation of Living Aquatic Resources Scheme Art. 9) Note: New legislation under consideration (ENTRY VERIFIED - OCTOBER 1985)			
SENEGAL	LEGISLATION - Sardine freezer boats CFA 1 500 000 per vessel - Trawlers - if land all catch in Senegal = CFA 7 500 per G.T. - if not required to land all catch CFA 15 000 per G.T. - if from states not having concluded a fishing agreement with Senegal CFA 25 000 per G.T. - Tuna vessels - royalty payment per kilo of fish landed fixed annually by regulation - vessels participating in Senegalese fishing operations = 1x basic rate - vessels not participating in Senegalese fishing operations = 2x basic rate	 US$ 3 158 US$ 16 US$ 32 US$ 53	LEGISLATION Bonds must be posted to guarantee performance of obligations where no bilateral agreement in force. (Act No. 76-86 of 2 July 1976 as amended by Act No. 79-23 of 24 January 1979 Art. 24)	LEGISLATION Local fishing vessels = 1) owned by nationals (at least 51%) or owned by companies meeting following criteria: a) has head office in Senegal; b) Chairman of the Board and majority of Directors must be nationals; c) at least 50% of the share capital must be held by nationals. d) director general or manager must be national; 2) Crew and officers must be all nationals except where special provisional exemption granted by the maritime authority where it is imposible to recruit the necessary technicians locally.

TABLE B

LICENCE FEES, BILATERAL AGREEMENT OR JOINT VENTURE REQUIREMENTS AND NATIONALITY CRITERIA

STATE	Licence fees, royalties and other payments		Requirements concerning bilateral framework agreements or joint venture participation	Nationality criteria for fishing vessels
	Local currency	US$ Equiv.		
SENEGAL (Cont'd)	- vessels from states not having concluded a fishing agreement with Senegal = 3x basic rate (Decree No. 76-836 of 24 July 1976 Art. 2-4)			(Act No. 62-32 of 22 March 1962, (Merchant Shipping Code) as amended by Act No. 73-53 of 4 December 1973 Art. 15)
	AGREEMENTS *Agreement with EEC, 15 June 1979 as amended Jan. 1982 and Jan. 1984 (Valid until denounced) Fees set on following scale: (a) trawlers landing their entire catch (licences to be issued for up to 2 500 GRT):			
	= CFA 8 500 per G.R.T. per year for shrimp boats;	US$ 18		
	= CFA 7 500 per G.R.T. per year for fish boats;	US$ 16		
	(b) trawlers not landing their entire catch and fishing throughout the year (up to 5 000 GRT for year)			
	= CFA 17 000 per G.R.T. per year for shrimp boats,	US$ 46		
	= CFA 15 000 per G.R.T. per year for fish boats;	US$ 41		
	(c) freezer trawlers not landing their entire catch and fishing for			

TABLE B

LICENCE FEES, BILATERAL AGREEMENT OR JOINT VENTURE REQUIREMENTS AND NATIONALITY CRITERIA

STATE	Licence fees, royalties and other payments		Requirements concerning bilateral framework agreements or joint venture participation	Nationality criteria for fishing vessels
	Local currency	US$ Equiv.		
SENEGAL (Cont'd)	a specific four-month period for each vessel (up to 9 000 GRT additional to the 5 000 GRT referred to under (a) = CFA 10 500 per G.R.T.;	US$ 28		
	(d) tuna boats landing their entire catch (up to 3 000 GRT): = CFA 2 per kg of fish caught	US$ 0.005		
	(e) tuna boats not landing their entire catch (up to 23 300 GRT): = CFA 6 per kg of fish caught	US$ 0.016		
	PLUS financial compensation for the period 16 Jan. 1984 to 15 Jan. 1986 of CFA 3 000 000 000 plus	US$ 6 757 000		
	CFA 100 000 000 contribution towards the financing of a Senegalese scientific programme.	US$ 270 000		
	*Agreement with Gambia of 22 October 1982 (valid for two years, renewable on tacit understanding) -Reciprocal fishing rights agrement; fishing rights for industrial vessels to be determined yearly.			
	*Agreement with Ivory Coast 11 June 1979 - Ivory Coast vessels allowed to fish upon payment of fees laid down by national legislation - Ivory Coast to allow duty-free imports of fishing products from Senegal up to 13 000 tons per year.			

TABLE B

LICENCE FEES, BILATERAL AGREEMENT OR JOINT VENTURE REQUIREMENTS AND NATIONALITY CRITERIA

STATE	Licence fees, royalties and other payments		Requirements concerning bilateral framework agreements or joint venture participation	Nationality criteria for fishing vessels
	Local currency	US$ Equiv.		
SENEGAL (Cont'd)	*Agreement with Nigeria of 8 November 1982 (valid for 2 years, renewable on tacit understanding) -Fees and other payments to be agreed upon subsequently through implementing protocols. (ENTRY VERIFIED - AUGUST 1985)			
SEYCHELLES	LEGISLATION The fees for licences shall be the subject of negotiation between the Government and the owner of the foreign fishing vessel. (Foreign Fishing Vessels (Amendment) Regulations, 1983 Reg. 2) Note: Fee schedules originally set out in Schedule 2 of the Foreign Fishing Vessels Regulations, 1979 now repealed. AGREEMENTS *Agreement with EEC (Valid from 11.1.1984 to 10.1.1987) - 27 tuna vessels of which only 18 may fish at any one time. 1 000 GRT of other fishing vessels			LEGISLATION local fishing vessel= - wholly owned by citizens or by a statutory corporation established under the laws of Seychelles; - wholly owned by any company of which at least 51% of the shares are held by citizens of Seychelles. (Control of Foreign Fishing Vessels Decree, 1979, S.2)

TABLE B

LICENCE FEES, BILATERAL AGREEMENT OR JOINT VENTURE REQUIREMENTS AND NATIONALITY CRITERIA

STATE	Licence fees, royalties and other payments: Local currency	Licence fees, royalties and other payments: US$ Equiv.	Requirements concerning bilateral framework agreements or joint venture participation	Nationality criteria for fishing vessels
SEYCHELLES (Cont'd)	- Fees of 20 ECU per ton of catch payable by vessel operators	US$ 17.4		
	(ECU 120 000 paid in advance)	US$ 104 400		
	-Financial compensation =300 000ECU	US$ 261 000		
	+ 50 ECU per ton if catch exceeds 6 000 tons per year up to a ceiling	US$ 43		
	of 1 000 000 ECU per year. +	US$ 870 000		
	250 000 ECU over 3 years to finance scientific programmes.	US$ 217 500		
	*Agreement with 2 private fishing companies, March 1984 valid 5 years automatically renewed for further periods of 1 year unless denounced. Fishing permits to be given to 2 tuna purse-seiners. Fees set at 10% of 50% of total catches in the Western Indian Ocean FOB Victoria. Payments to be made six-monthly Vessels to be based preferentially in Victoria and at least 80% of transshipments and revictualling to be carried out in Victoria.			
	*Agreement with Spain, I June 1984 valid for 5 years, renewed automatically for periods of 1 year unless denounced 6/3 months before expiry) For up to 15 tuna purse-seiners: Fees fixed at 10% of landed value of 50% of catch FOB Victoria. Payment to be made every six months.			
	*Agreement with French, Ivorian & Mauritian Companies indefinite duration - Annual fees per vessel not published			
	(ENTRY VERIFIED - OCTOBER 1985)			

TABLE B

LICENCE FEES, BILATERAL AGREEMENT OR JOINT VENTURE REQUIREMENTS AND NATIONALITY CRITERIA

STATE	Licence fees, royalties and other payments		Requirements concerning bilateral framework agreements or joint venture participation	Nationality criteria for fishing vessels
	Local currency	US$ Equiv.		
SIERRA LEONE	LEGISLATION Licence fee = according to the length of vessels: Le 30 p.a. for vessels up to 20 ft. to Le. 450 for vessels over 20 ft. plus royalty fee = -for fish = Le. 45 per G.R.T. -for shell fish = Le. 75 per G.R.T. (Fisheries (Royalty fees) Regulations as amended) AGREEMENTS *Agreement with USSR of 14 May 1976 (valid for 5 years, renewable for 3-year periods on tacit understanding) -Fishing conditions laid down by implementing protocols. Under implementing protocol now in force, 12% of catch supplied to Sierra Leone. Remaining 88% retained by USSR but the Sierra Leone Fishing Company may buy up to 38% of this amount at a preferential pre-agreed price. (Source: West Africa, May/June, 1984, p. 1129) Agreement renewed 30 October 1985 (Source Marchés tropicaux 15/11/85)	US$ 15 US$ 99 US$ 8 US$ 13		
SINGAPORE	-			

TABLE B

LICENCE FEES, BILATERAL AGREEMENT OR JOINT VENTURE REQUIREMENTS AND NATIONALITY CRITERIA

STATE	Licence fees, royalties and other payments: Local currency	Licence fees, royalties and other payments: US$ Equiv.	Requirements concerning bilateral framework agreements or joint venture participation	Nationality criteria for fishing vessels
SOLOMON ISLANDS	LEGISLATION -Foreign fishing permits subject to payment of such fees and royalties as may be determined by the Principal Licensing Officer with the approval of the Minister. (Fisheries Act 1972 S. 7 (3) (b)) In practice fees set in agreements -Export duty on frozen tuna fish payable at following rates: 1st 10 000 tonnes = 10% 10 000 - 15 000 tonnes = 8% 15 000 - 20 000 tonnes = 7% 20 000 - 25 000 tonnes = 6% over 25 000 tonnes = 5% (applicable to local joint venture operation only) (Customs and Excise (Duties) Amendment (No 4) Order 1981 S.2 (10.1) AGREEMENTS * Agreement with Japanese Tuna Fisheries Co-operative Associations under Japanese Head Agreement of 1978 (Jan. 1984 valid thru' Dec. 1984 - extended thereafter until 6 months after notice given of intent to terminate) Tuna longlining and pole and line fishing operations:	 10% 8% 7% 6% 5%		LEGISLATION Local fishing vessel means any fishing vessel: (a) owned by one or more persons domiciled and resident in the Solomon Islands; (b) owned by any company or fishermen's cooperative society incorporated under the laws of the Solomon Islands, and having its principal place of business in the Solomon Islands, and does not include any vessel registered in any country outside the Solomon Islands. (Fisheries Act 1972, S. 2)

TABLE B

LICENCE FEES, BILATERAL AGREEMENT OR JOINT VENTURE REQUIREMENTS AND NATIONALITY CRITERIA

STATE	Licence fees, royalties and other payments		Requirements concerning bilateral framework agreements or joint venture participation	Nationality criteria for fishing vessels
	Local currency	US$ Equiv.		
SOLOMON ISLANDS (Cont'd)	a) Permit fee of = Y 27 000 per vessel (valid 1 year) +	US$108		
	b) Permit Activation Fee (Valid for one trip) Permit activation fee calculated on basis of value of fish to be caught during permit activation period, according to formula: Initial Price per metric ton x Catch per trip x monthly "all tuna" or "skipjack" price divided by initial all tuna or skipjack price.			
	Longline Vessels:			
	Initial price - Jan. 1984 = Y21 500	US$ 86		
	Initial "all tuna" price = Y590 /kg	US$ 2.4		
	Pole and line vessels:			
	Initial price - Jan. 1984 = Y 6 500	US$ 26		
	Initial "skipjack" price = Y209 /kg	US$ 0.8		
	Note: Price calculated on approximate bas is of 5% of market value of catch Maximum allowable catch for Japanese fishing vessels set at 6 000 tonnes for pole and line vessels and 6 500 tonnes for longline vessels per year.			
	Note: Agreement with Deep-Sea Fisheries Association of Rep. of Korea 1980 (valid from 12 Jan 1982 thru' 11			

TABLE B

LICENCE FEES, BILATERAL AGREEMENT OR JOINT VENTURE REQUIREMENTS AND NATIONALITY CRITERIA

STATE	Licence fees, royalties and other payments		Requirements concerning bilateral framework agreements or joint venture participation	Nationality criteria for fishing vessels
	Local currency	US$ Equiv.		
SOLOMON ISLANDS (Cont'd)	Jan. 1983 - for longliners) and Agreement with SPFC - Vanuatu (valid thru' Jan 1981 - longliners) AGREEMENTS NO LONGER IN FORCE (ENTRY VERIFIED - OCTOBER 1985)			
SOMALIA	AGREEMENTS 20% of value of catch = US$ 4000 per ton for lobster = US$ 1000 per ton for fish (Agreements in force 1980) *Somalia/Rep. of Korea Agreement on Fisheries, valid 1 March thru' 31 May 1985. Total of 20 boats to be licensed at fee of US$4 000 per boat, targetting primarily on tuna. (Source: INFOFISH Trade News Feb. 1985)	 US$ 4000 US$ 1000 US$4 000		LEGISLATION Any vessel whether built or owned locally or abroad, may be registered as a Somali vessel provided it complies with the necessary standards (Maritime Code, 1959 Art. 41)
SOUTH AFRICA	LEGISLATION From Rands 2 to 20 Rds 60 for each vessel equipped with trawl nets Rds 150 for whalers factory ships From Rds 100 to 300 (Sea Fisheries Act Regs. 1973 Schedule M.)	 US$1 to US$ 10 US$ 30 US$ 75 US$ 50 to US$ 150	LEGISLATION The State President may enter into an agreement with any foreign state providing for any vessel registered in such state to be used as a fishing boat within the fishing zone. (Sea Fisheries Act 1973)	

TABLE B

LICENCE FEES, BILATERAL AGREEMENT OR JOINT VENTURE REQUIREMENTS AND NATIONALITY CRITERIA

STATE	Licence fees, royalties and other payments: Local currency	Licence fees, royalties and other payments: US$ Equiv.	Requirements concerning bilateral framework agreements or joint venture participation	Nationality criteria for fishing vessels
SOUTH AFRICA (Cont'd)	*Agreement with Japan of 6 Dec.1977 - South Africa to collect reasonable fees from Japanese vessels. *Agreement with Spain of 14 August 1979 - Spanish vessels to pay such fees as the Govt. of South Africa may impose. (Art. 4)			
SPAIN	LEGISLATION AGREEMENTS *Agreement with EEC April 1980 valid 5 years and further periods of 5 years each unless renounced. Reciprocal fishing arrangements - No fees. Note: On 1 January 1986 Spain and Portu- will become members of the EEC. As from that date fishing in Spanish waters will be governed by	-	Access to the EEZ only under bilateral agreements with flag state to which quota assigned. Licence also required. Order No. 6640 of 2 Mar 1982 Establishment abroad (with Spanish participation) of joint ventures encouraged (at least 40% of the share capital must be owned by Spanish citizens or companies. (Crown Decree No. 2517 of 8 October 1976 Art. 4)	LEGISLATION Law allows the use of the Spanish flag for foreign fishing vessels (under conditions) on a provisional basis. (Crown Decree No. 2517 of 8 October 1976 Art. 2)

TABLE B

LICENCE FEES, BILATERAL AGREEMENT OR JOINT VENTURE REQUIREMENTS AND NATIONALITY CRITERIA

STATE	Licence fees, royalties and other payments		Requirements concerning bilateral framework agreements or joint venture participation	Nationality criteria for fishing vessels
	Local currency	US$ Equiv.		
SPAIN (Cont'd)	agreements made by the EEC Licences will be issued by E.E.C. within the common fishing zone. No fees. See entry under European Community	-	After 1 January 1986, access to the common fishing zone of EEC will be governed by bilateral agreements with third countries on a reciprocal basis.	
SRI LANKA	LEGISLATION 0 and less than 100 GRT: = US$5 per GRT per month 100 and less than 500 GRT: = US$4 per GRT per month 500 and over : = US$4 per GRT per month (Foreign Fishing Boat Regulations 1981 - Second Schedule.) (ENTRY VERIFIED - NOVEMBER 1984)	- US$5 GRT/month US$4 GRT/month US$3 GRT/month	LEGISLATION Establishment of joint ventures is encouraged for certain fisheries and fishing areas.	LEGISLATION Local fishing vessel = wholly owned by - citizens of Sri Lanka; or - Government or any public corporation established by or under law of Sri Lanka; or - any company, society or other association of persons incorporated or established under local law in which a majority of voting shares held by citizens and registered under Merchant Shipping Act. (Fisheries (Regulation of Foreign Fishing Boats) Act, 1979, as amended 1982.S. 28)
SUDAN	LEGISLATION Vessel licence: = £ 10 per vessel per annum	US$ 4		

TABLE B

LICENCE FEES, BILATERAL AGREEMENT OR JOINT VENTURE REQUIREMENTS AND NATIONALITY CRITERIA

STATE	Licence fees, royalties and other payments		Requirements concerning bilateral framework agreements or joint venture participation	Nationality criteria for fishing vessels
	Local currency	US$ Equiv.		
SUDAN (Cont'd)	-Vessel may be required to make payment in form of share of catch. Each case considered separately (Marine Fisheries Ordinance Sched. 2, 1960 and country reply)			
SURINAME	LEGISLATION Fees to be determined by the Minister after consultation with the Council. (Decree of 31/12/ 1980 regulating the field of Sea Fishery, Art.19) S. Fls. 10 000 per vessel per annum AGREEMENTS *Reciprocal fishing agreement with Guyana, April 1979. (ENTRY VERIFIED - OCTOBER 1985)	US$ 5 650	LEGISLATION Licence may only be issued to owner or operator of an alien fishing vessel if international agreement governing fishing in the zone is in force with the country of registration of the vessel. (Decree of 31 December 1980 regulating the field of Sea Fishery Art. 2 (1))	LEGISLATION Suriname fishing vessel means a fishing vessel which (a) belongs for at least 50% to Suriname nationals, or for at least 25% to Surinamese nationals and at least 50% to residents of Suriname;and (b) regularly moors or will moor in Suriname; and (c) the owner is established in Suriname and is registered as such in the Register of the Chamber of Commerce and Factories. Suriname national includes besides individuals: 1. partnerships, limited or other, established in Suriname, of which all severally liable partners are Suriname nationals living in Suriname; 2. companies with limited liability, founded according to the law of Suriname and established in Suriname,

TABLE B

LICENCE FEES, BILATERAL AGREEMENT OR JOINT VENTURE REQUIREMENTS AND NATIONALITY CRITERIA

STATE	Licence fees, royalties and other payments		Requirements concerning bilateral framework agreements or joint venture participation	Nationality criteria for fishing vessels
	Local currency	US$ Equiv.		
SURINAME (Cont'd)				of which at least 50% of the invested capital stock belongs to Surinamese nationals living in Suriname; 3. incorporated associations or foundations, founded according to the law of Suriname and established in Suriname, of which the majority of the directors consists of Surinamese nationals living in Suriname. "Residents of Suriname" includes besides individuals: 1. partnerships, limited or other, established in Suriname, of which all severally liable partners are Surinamese nationals living in Suriname, or residents of Suriname; 2. companies with limited liability, founded according to the law of Suriname and established in Suriname, of which at least fifty percent of the invested capital stock belongs to Surinamese nationals living in Suriname, or to residents of Suriname; 3. incorporated associations or foundations, founded according to the

TABLE B

LICENCE FEES, BILATERAL AGREEMENT OR JOINT VENTURE REQUIREMENTS AND NATIONALITY CRITERIA

STATE	Licence fees, royalties and other payments: Local currency	Licence fees, royalties and other payments: US$ Equiv.	Requirements concerning bilateral framework agreements or joint venture participation	Nationality criteria for fishing vessels
SURINAME (Cont'd)				law of Suriname and established in Suriname, of which the majority of the directors consists of Surinamese nationals living in Suriname, or of residents of Suriname.
SWEDEN	LEGISLATION unspecified	-	LEGISLATION Access to the fishing zones of Sweden only under bilateral agreements.	LEGISLATION Local fishing vessel = owned to the extent of two-thirds by Swedish subjects or by a joint stock company, the Board of Directors of which has its registered office in Sweden and the share-helders of which are Swedish subjects. A managing part-owner must always be a Swedish subject residing in Sweden. (Maritime Law, 1981 as amended Art.1)
SYRIAN ARAB REPUBLIC	-		Special consideration for vessels from Arab countries subject to reciprocity.	-

TABLE B

LICENCE FEES, BILATERAL AGREEMENT OR JOINT VENTURE REQUIREMENTS AND NATIONALITY CRITERIA

STATE	Licence fees, royalties and other payments		Requirements concerning bilateral framework agreements or joint venture participation	Nationality criteria for fishing vessels
	Local currency	US$ Equiv.		
TANZANIA	LEGISLATION - According to the length of the boat = 200 shillings (non powered) sh. 1 000 up to 10 000 (powered) - fees according to the species - fees according to the species sh. 200 up to sh. 2 000 (if the species is specified in the licence); sh. 200 up to sh. 600 for other species - fee for export = licence = from sh 600 to sh 2 000 + tax = per kilo or per fish or ad valorem (Fisheries (General) (Amendment) Regs. 1978 Third Schedule)	 US$ 11 US$ 57 to US$ 568 US$ 11 to US$ 114 US$ 11 to 34 US$ 34 to 114		LEGISLATION Local fishing vessel defined as fishing vessel owned by local national or company registered in Tanzania.
THAILAND	NO FOREIGN FISHING AT PRESENT		LEGISLATION No licence may be issued to foreign vessels except under an agreement with the flag state.	LEGISLATION local fishing vessel = vessel owned by a Thai national, or partnership with all partners Thai, and at least 70% capital owned by Thais; or limited

TABLE B

LICENCE FEES, BILATERAL AGREEMENT OR JOINT VENTURE REQUIREMENTS AND NATIONALITY CRITERIA

STATE	Licence fees, royalties and other payments: Local currency	US$ Equiv.	Requirements concerning bilateral framework agreements or joint venture participation	Nationality criteria for fishing vessels
THAILAND (Cont'd)			(Act governing the Right to fish in Thai fishery waters, 1939 S. 7).	company with majority of investors Thai and at least 70% of capital owned by Thais. (Act governing the Right to fish in Thai waters, 1939 S. 5)
TOGO	LEGISLATION Licence (valid 6 months) to import fish: Fees set at following rates according to tonnage of vessel: - 0 - 50 n.r.t.= 120 000 francs CFA -50 -100 n.r.t.= 150 000 francs CFA (Order No 4/MDR/MFE of 26 March 1979)	 US $ 324 US $ 450	LEGISLATION In a spirit of interafrican solidarity, Togo undertakes to allow the hinterland countries to participate in the exploitation of the biological resource through bilateral or regional agreements. (Ordinance No. 24 of 16 August 1977, Art. 4)	LEGISLATION National fishing vessel defined as fishing vessel at least half owned by Togo nationals or by nationals of another state with which agreements of reciprocity concluded. Crew and officers must be nationals except where exemption granted by Minister. Where vessels belong to a company, head office must be in Togo, the Chairman of the Board, the General Manager and the majority of the members of the Board must be Togo nationals and at least 50% of the share capital must be held by Togo nationals or national of another state with which reciprocal agreement concluded. (Merchant Shipping Code, Ordinance 29 of 12 August 1971, Art. 7-8).

TABLE B

LICENCE FEES, BILATERAL AGREEMENT OR JOINT VENTURE REQUIREMENTS AND NATIONALITY CRITERIA

STATE	Licence fees, royalties and other payments: Local currency	Licence fees, royalties and other payments: US$ Equiv.	Requirements concerning bilateral framework agreements or joint venture participation	Nationality criteria for fishing vessels
TONGA	LEGISLATION -By arrangement between the Government of Tonga and the Government of the flag state or the owners of the vessels. (Fisheries Protection Act 1973 S. 3 AGREEMENTS - No licensed foreign fishing at present (ENTRY VERIFIED - OCTOBER 1985)		LEGISLATION Special provision may be made for fishing by foreign fishing vessels by arrangement between Government of Tonga of flag state or vessel owners. (Fisheries Protection Act, 1973 S. 3).	LEGISLATION Foreign fishing vessel means any vessel used commercially for fishing or for the processing or storage of fish which is either not registered in Tonga or is owned or controlled by a person or persons not ordinarily resident in Tonga, but does not include any canoe or any vessel used for the transport of fish or fish products as part of its general cargo. (Fisheries Protection Act, 1973 s.2)
TRINIDAD AND TOBAGO	LEGISLATION No licensing requirements under current fisheries legislation New legislation under consideration AGREEMENTS Fishing by nationals of Venezuela under conditions of reciprocity. No fees. (Agreement with Venezuela 1978) (ENTRY VERIFIED - OCTOBER 1985)		LEGISLATION - AGREEMENTS Agreements with Venezuela and Brazil provide for establishment of joint venture companies.	
TUNISIA	LEGISLATION Fees for fishing permits fixed by Joint Order of Director of Finances and Director of Public Works			

TABLE B

LICENCE FEES, BILATERAL AGREEMENT OR JOINT VENTURE REQUIREMENTS AND NATIONALITY CRITERIA

STATE	Licence fees, royalties and other payments		Requirements concerning bilateral framework agreements or joint venture participation	Nationality criteria for fishing vessels
	Local currency	US$ Equiv.		
TUNISIA (Cont'd)	(Decree of 26 July 1951 revising the legislation on the policing of marine fisheries, Art. 3)			
TURKEY	LEGISLATION Foreigners or companies whose share holders are foreigners are not allowed to fish in Turkish waters. (Fisheries Law, N° 1380)			LEGISLATION -
TUVALU	LEGISLATION -Foreign fishing permits subject to payment of such fees and royalties as may be determined by the Fisheries Officer with the approval of the Minister. (Fisheries Ordinance S. 5 (4) (b)) In practice fees set in agreements AGREEMENTS *Agreement with Deep-Sea Fisheries Association of Republic of Korea under Head Agreement with Government of Rep of Korea dated 1980 (Dec 1982 - valid thru' Dec 1983) Lump sum payment of US$ 70 000 for up to 60 vessels (Longlining only)	US$ 70 000		LEGISLATION "Local fishing vessel means any fishing vessel- (a) owned by one or more persons resident and domiciled in Tuvalu; or (b) owned by a company or fisheries cooperative society registered or incorporated under the laws of Tuvalu and having its principal place of business in Tuvalu. (Fisheries Ordinance 1978, S. 2.)

TABLE B

LICENCE FEES, BILATERAL AGREEMENT OR JOINT VENTURE REQUIREMENTS AND NATIONALITY CRITERIA

STATE	Licence fees, royalties and other payments		Requirements concerning bilateral framework agreements or joint venture participation	Nationality criteria for fishing vessels
	Local currency	US$ Equiv.		
TUVALU (Cont'd)	Note: Agreement renewed 31 Jan 1984 valid thru' 31 Jan. 1986. Changes to terms unknown. Note: Agreement between Governments of Niue, New Zealand (for Tokelau) Tuvalu and Western Samoa and AMERICAN TUNABOAT ASSOCIATION, Sept. 1983, valid thru' end 1984. AGREEMENT NO LONGER IN FORCE (ENTRY VERIFIED - OCTOBER 1985)			
USSR	LEGISLATION Unspecified	-	LEGISLATION Access to the fishing zone only under bilateral agreements (Decree of Presidium 10/12 1976 s.3)	LEGISLATION -
	AGREEMENTS *Agreement with Japan concerning Salmon quotas in North-West Pacific 1983. -Yen 4 250 000 for 42 500 tons of salmon	US$ 17 000		
	*Agreement with Japan, May 1983 375 Japanese vessels (45 more than 1982) to exploit seaweeds (LAMINARIA) around Kaigara Isle in the Shikotan Islands.			

TABLE B

LICENCE FEES, BILATERAL AGREEMENT OR JOINT VENTURE REQUIREMENTS AND NATIONALITY CRITERIA

STATE	Licence fees, royalties and other payments		Requirements concerning bilateral framework agreements or joint venture participation	Nationality criteria for fishing vessels
	Local currency	US$ Equiv.		
USSR (Cont'd)	-Yen 200 000 per boat Total fee of Yen 750 000 000 (Yen 9 000 000 up on 1982) is paid for 1983 (ENTRY VERIFIED - MAY 1983)	US$ 800 US$3 000 000 US$ 36 000		
UNITED KINGDOM	Licences issued by E.E.C. within the common fishing zone. No fees. See entry under European Community	-	Access to the common fishing zone of EEC governed by bilateral agreements with third countries on a reciprocal basis.	Local fishing vessel = 1) registered in the UK or exempted from registration under the Merchant Shipping Act of 1894 S. 373; or 2) owned wholly by person entitled to own British ship under the Merchant shipping Act. (Fishery Limits Act 1976 s. 8) At least 75% of crew of a British fishing boat must nationals of a member country of the European Community. (British Fishing Boats Order 1983)

TABLE B

LICENCE FEES, BILATERAL AGREEMENT OR JOINT VENTURE REQUIREMENTS AND NATIONALITY CRITERIA

STATE	Licence fees, royalties and other payments		Requirements concerning bilateral framework agreements or joint venture participation	Nationality criteria for fishing vessels
	Local currency	US$ Equiv.		
UNITED KINGDOM DEPENDENT TERRITOR.				
Bermuda	LEGISLATION B$ 1 000 per vessel per annum + B$ 1 per GRT per annum (Government Fees Regulations 1978)	US$ 1 000 + US$ 1 per GRT	-	LEGISLATION Foreign fishing boat defined as one not bona fide owned by person possessing Bermudian status under Immigration and Protection Act 1956. (Fisheries Act 1972, s.7)
British Virgin Is.	LEGISLATION Foreign fishing prohibited except for scientific research			LEGISLATION Foreign fishing boat defined as fishing boat owned and operated by a person not deemed to be "a belonger" or owned and operated by a person not resident in the territory. (Fisheries Ordinance, 1979 s.2)
Cayman Is.	-	-	-	-
Montserrat	LEGISLATION Fees and royalties to be determined by the Governor in Council (Fisheries Ordinance 1982 S. 6)			LEGISLATION "Local fishing vessel" defined as: (a) owned by one or more persons resident and domiciled in Montserrat; (b) owned by a company or co-operative society registered or incorporated under the laws of Montserrat and

TABLE B

LICENCE FEES, BILATERAL AGREEMENT OR JOINT VENTURE REQUIREMENTS AND NATIONALITY CRITERIA

STATE	Licence fees, royalties and other payments: Local currency	Licence fees, royalties and other payments: US$ Equiv.	Requirements concerning bilateral framework agreements or joint venture participation	Nationality criteria for fishing vessels
UNITED KINGDOM DEPENDENT TERRITOR. Montserrat (Cont'd)				having its principal place of business in Montserrat; (Fisheries Ordinance 1982 S. 2)
Pitcairn Islands	LEGISLATION Fees to be prescribed by Governor (Fisheries Zone Ordinance 1980 S.11)	-	-	-
Turks and Caicos	LEGISLATION Up to 20 ft ($ 10); 20-30 ft $50 over 30 ft. $100 (Fisheries Protection Regulations 1976 Schedule)	US$ 2 US$ 9 US$ 18	-	-
UNITED STATES OF AMERICA	LEGISLATION 1) Permit Application Fee = US$ 101 per vessel Note: 20% surcharge for Fishing Vessel and Gear Damage Compensation Fund waived for 1985 as Fund already sufficiently capitalized. 2) Plus poundage fee expressed in	US$ 101	LEGISLATION Access to the fishery zone of the United States only under bilateral agreements.	LEGISLATION Local fishing vessel Vessel must be documented as US flag vessel, which requires that: (a) vessel must be owned by nationals or companies incorporated under the local law; (b) where vessel owned by company,

TABLE B

LICENCE FEES, BILATERAL AGREEMENT OR JOINT VENTURE REQUIREMENTS AND NATIONALITY CRITERIA

STATE	Licence fees, royalties and other payments		Requirements concerning bilateral framework agreements or joint venture participation	Nationality criteria for fishing vessels
	Local currency	US$ Equiv.		
UNITED STATES OF AMERICA (Cont'd)	dollars per metric ton for each listed species: e.g. 1. Butterfish = $160 2. Hake, red = $ 96 3. Hake, silver = $102 4. Herring, river = $ 46 5. Mackerel, Atlantic = $ 49 6. Other finfish, Atlantic= $ 69 7. Squid, Illex = $ 57 8. Squid, Loligo = $114 9. Atlantic shark = $110 10.Shrimp, royal red Reserved 11.Pollock, Alaska = $ 32 12.Cod, Pacific = $ 73 13.Pacific ocean perch = $100 14.Other rockfish (Alaska)= $ 94 15.Mackerel, Atka = $ 52 16.Squid, Pacific = $ 59 17.Flatfish, Gulf Alaska, Bering Sea Aleutian Isles = $ 34 18.Sablefish, Gulf Alaska = $159 Bering Sea Aleutian Isles = $ 64 19.Other species = $ 39 20.Snails = $ 66 21.Whiting, Pacific = $ 32 22.Sablefish = $143 23.Pacific ocean perch = $124 24.Other rockfish = $119 25.Flounders = $155			management must be controlled by nationals, (i.e. majority of board of directors must be US nationals) (no restrictions on ownership of shares by non-nationals as such); (c) vessel must be built in US; and (d) vessel must be under the sea-going command of US nationals.

TABLE B

LICENCE FEES, BILATERAL AGREEMENT OR JOINT VENTURE REQUIREMENTS AND NATIONALITY CRITERIA

STATE	Licence fees, royalties and other payments: Local currency	Licence fees, royalties and other payments: US$ Equiv.	Requirements concerning bilateral framework agreements or joint venture participation	Nationality criteria for fishing vessels
UNITED STATES OF AMERICA (Cont'd)	26.Mackerel, jack 27.Other species 28.Coral (per kilogram) 29.Wahoo 30.Dolphin fish 31.Wahoo 32.Sharks, Pacific 33.Striped marlin 34.Pacific billfish 35.Pacific swordfish (Note: 1985 poundage fees calculated on basis of 24.2 % of the adopted value (ex-vessel value) of each species.) (Foreign Fishing; Poundage Fee Schedule, 1985 50 CFR 460, Jan 4, 1985 and 50 CFR 611, 1 March 1985) 3.Plus entire cost of US observers on board vessel, including shore-side support. (ENTRY VERIFIED - OCTOBER 1985)	= $ 55 = $154 = $ 53 = $103 = $1 428 = $571 = $286 = $428 = $514 = $514		
U.S. TRUST TERRIT. Federated States of Micronesia	LEGISLATION Fees and other forms of compensation for right to exploit living resources within extended fishery		LEGISLATION Foreign fishing permits will only be issued in accordance with an approved foreign	LEGISLATION "Foreign fishing" means fishing by vessels: (a) not registered in Micronesia; or

TABLE B

LICENCE FEES, BILATERAL AGREEMENT OR JOINT VENTURE REQUIREMENTS AND NATIONALITY CRITERIA

STATE	Licence fees, royalties and other payments		Requirements concerning bilateral framework agreements or joint venture participation	Nationality criteria for fishing vessels
	Local currency	US$ Equiv.		
U.S. TRUST TERRIT. Federated States of Micronesia (Cont'd)	limits of Micronesia shall be established in the [approved foreign fishing] agreement. Fishery Zones Jurisdiction of FSM (Trust Territory Code Title 52 S. 154 (7))		fishing agreement. (Not applicable for research, survey, recreational or non-commercial fishing) (Fishery Zones Jurisdiction of FSM Trust Territory Code Title 52 S. 154 (2))	(b) not wholly owned by citizens of Micronesia; or (c) not wholly controlled by citizens of Micronesia. (Fishery Zones Jurisdiction of FSM Trust Territory Code Title 52 S. 2.)
	AGREEMENTS			
	*Agreement with Japanese Fishing Associations of 25 Jan. 1984 (valid from 10 Feb thru' 9 Aug. 1984) (Longline, pole and line and purse seine - up to 650 vessels)			
	Lump sum payment of Yen 285 000 000 for six month period of validity	US$ 1 140 000		
	New agreement signed 26 July 1984 effective from 10 August 1984 and continuing in force thereafter until expiry of 120 days from notice of intent to terminate-Fees unknown			
	*Agreement with Kaohsiung Fishery Association of 16 July 1982, valid thru' 15 July 1983 extended to 15 July 1984)			
	2 Seiner groups (1 group = 1 purse-seiner + 2 carriers) = Lump sum of US$ 26 000 for 2 groups	US$ 26 000		

TABLE B

LICENCE FEES, BILATERAL AGREEMENT OR JOINT VENTURE REQUIREMENTS AND NATIONALITY CRITERIA

STATE	Licence fees, royalties and other payments		Requirements concerning bilateral framework agreements or joint venture participation	Nationality criteria for fishing vessels
	Local currency	US$ Equiv.		
U.S. TRUST TERRIT. Federated States of Micronesia (Cont'd)	Note: lump sum based on 5% of estimated value of landed catch NOTE: AGREEMENT APPARENTLY NO LONGER IN FORCE Note: Agreement with Republic of Korea 14 November 1980 - valid thru' 13 November 1981); Agreement between Government of Kiribati, Micronesia Maritime Authority, Palau Maritime Authority, and AMERICAN TUNABOAT ASSOCIATION, valid 1 Jan 1983 thru' 31 Dec 1984; Agreement with Samyong Enterprise Co. Ltd. 19 Oct 1982 valid thru' 31 Dec 1983; Agreement with Mar Fishing Co. Inc (Philippines), 29 Dec 1982 valid 1 Jan 1983 thru' 31 Dec 1983 AGREEMENTS NO LONGER IN FORCE (ENTRY VERIFIED - OCTOBER 1985)			

TABLE B

LICENCE FEES, BILATERAL AGREEMENT OR JOINT VENTURE REQUIREMENTS AND NATIONALITY CRITERIA

STATE	Licence fees, royalties and other payments		Requirements concerning bilateral framework agreements or joint venture participation	Nationality criteria for fishing vessels
	Local currency	US$ Equiv.		
- Marshall Islands	LEGISLATION - Marshall Islands Maritime Authority may make regulations fixing terms of licensing including payment of fees and other forms of remuneration and compensation in the field of financing, equipment and technology relating to the fishing industry.(S. 8.409) - Marshall Islands Maritime Authority delegated authority to negotiate foreign fishing agreements and issue permits thereunder.(S. 8.408) (Marshall Islands Marine Resources Jurisdiction Act of 1978) - Fee of US$ 450 per vessel/month payable for locally based foreign fishing vessels fishing in EEZ (Cabinet Directive November 1985) AGREEMENTS *Agreement with Japanese Fisheries Associations, May 1985 (valid thru' April 1986 and thereafter until 6 months after notice of termination by either party-Longline/pole line) Registration Fee (all vessels): = Yen 36 000 +	 US$ 150	LEGISLATION Foreign fishing permits will only be issued in accordance with the regulations promulgated [under the Act] and applicable [foreign fishing] agreements. (Marshall Islands Marine Resources Jursdiction Act of 1978 S. 8.413.)	LEGISLATION "Foreign fishing" means fishing by a person or vessel other than a person or vessel of the Republic of Marshall Islands. (Marshall Islands Marine Resources Jursdiction Act of 1978 S. 8.402 as amended by Secretarial Order 3039)
	Variable Per Vessel Per trip fee: Fees for May 1985 =			
	Longliners = Yen 801 680	US$ 3 340		
	Pole and liners = Yen 544 320	US$ 2 268		
	Fees subject to monthly variation thereafter to reflect market fluctuations. (See entry under Solomon Islands for price formula) (ENTRY VERIFIED - DECEMBER 1985)			

TABLE B

LICENCE FEES, BILATERAL AGREEMENT OR JOINT VENTURE REQUIREMENTS AND NATIONALITY CRITERIA

STATE	Licence fees, royalties and other payments		Requirements concerning bilateral framework agreements or joint venture participation	Nationality criteria for fishing vessels
	Local currency	US$ Equiv.		
-Palau	LEGISLATION -Fees and other forms of compensation for the right to exploit living resources within the territorial sea or fishery zones of Palau District shall be established in the [foreign fishing] agreement. Public Law No. 6-7-14 S. 14		Foreign fishing permits will only be issued in accordance with an approved foreign fishing agreement. (Not applicable for research, recreational or other non-commercial fishing) Public Law No. 6-7-14 S. 14	"Foreign fishing" means fishing by vessels not wholly owned or chartered by citizens of Palau Public Law No. 6-7-14 S. 2
	AGREEMENTS *Agreement with Japan, Nov. 1983 (valid Jan 1 thru. 31 Dec. 1984) Lump sum payment of equipment/aid to value of Y 65 000 000 for up to 290 vessels (longline/pole and line/purseseine) Parties to explore alternative fee systems for next agreement based on pre-determined fee levels for individual vessels.	US$ 260 000		
	Agreement renewed thru' Dec. 1985 by exchange of letters. Lump sum payment apparently = US$263 000 (Source FFA)	US$263 000		
	*Agreement with Sino-Palau Fishing Co. Ltd. signed 27 July 1982, valid for 1 year, automatically renewed for further periods of 1 year unless			

TABLE B

LICENCE FEES, BILATERAL AGREEMENT OR JOINT VENTURE REQUIREMENTS AND NATIONALITY CRITERIA

STATE	Licence fees, royalties and other payments		Requirements concerning bilateral framework agreements or joint venture participation	Nationality criteria for fishing vessels
	Local currency	US$ Equiv.		
U.S. TRUST TERRIT. - Palau (Cont'd)	notice given of intent to terminate Lump sum of US$ 14 800 for 1 long-line vessel under 200 GRT + 2 long-line vessels under 100 GRT + 8 small seine fishing vessels under 50 GRT. Note: Agreement between Government of Kiribati, Micronesia Maritime Authority, Palau Maritime Authority, and AMERICAN TUNABOAT ASSOCIATION, valid 1 Jan 1983 thru' 31 Dec 1984. AGREEMENT NO LONGER IN FORCE (ENTRY VERIFIED - OCTOBER 1985)	US$ 14 800		
URUGUAY	LEGISLATION Licence fees fixed every year. Double for: - refrigerator vessels. - factory ships; plus unspecified royalties (Act No. 13833 of 1969) Exemption from payment of licence fees for foreign vessels fishing with national firms. (Decree No. 711/971 of 1971)			LEGISLATION Local fishing vessel = As specified in Laws No. 10945 of 10 October 1974 and No. 12091 of 5 January 1954.

TABLE B

LICENCE FEES, BILATERAL AGREEMENT OR JOINT VENTURE REQUIREMENTS AND NATIONALITY CRITERIA

STATE	Licence fees, royalties and other payments: Local currency	US$ Equiv.	Requirements concerning bilateral framework agreements or joint venture participation	Nationality criteria for fishing vessels
URUGUAY (Cont'd)	Registration (valid 1 year) Registration fee = US$ 500; Permit (valid 120 days) permit fee = US$ 10 per n.r.t. double for freezer and factory ship (Decree No. 544 of 26 August 1971) All foreign fishing licences in 200 mile zone suspended 1974.	 US$ 500 US$ 10 per nrt		
VANUATU	LEGISLATION Such fees as may be prescribed plus such royalties or other charges as the Minister, after consulting the Minister responsible for Finance may determine. (S. 14) (The Fisheries Act No 37 of 1982) Fees Less than 100 tons = 10 000 Vatu 100 to 1 000 tons = 10 000 Vatu + 50 Vatu per ton in excess 1 000 tons or more = 55 000 Vatu (The Fisheries Regulations 1983) (ENTRY VERIFIED - OCTOBER 1985)	 US$ 92 US$ 97 and US$ 0.45 US$ 505	LEGISLATION Licences to be issued to foreign vessels only where access agreement in force with the flag state or vessel owners' association, or where vessel is locally based. (S. 4) Foreign investments in fisheries subject to approval. (The Fisheries Act No 37 of 1982) S. 8)	Local fishing vessel defined as any fishing vessel (a) wholly owned by the Govt. of Vanuatu or any public corporation established by or under any law of Vanuatu; or(b) wholly owned by one or more persons who are citizens of Vanuatu: or (c) wholly owned by any company, society or other association of persons incorporated or established in Vanuatu. locally based foreign fishing vessel defined as one based in Vanuatu and landing all its catch there. (The Fisheries Act No 37 of 1982) S. 1

TABLE B

LICENCE FEES, BILATERAL AGREEMENT OR JOINT VENTURE REQUIREMENTS AND NATIONALITY CRITERIA

STATE	Licence fees, royalties and other payments		Requirements concerning bilateral framework agreements or joint venture participation	Nationality criteria for fishing vessels
	Local currency	US$ Equiv.		
VENEZUELA	Monthly fee of at least US$ 467 based on vessel size. (Source: Milan A. Kravanja, Fishing Fees in Foreign Countries, National Marine Fisheries Service, prepared for the Workshop on Foreign Fees Washington D.C. June 1978)	US$ 467	Access to the EEZ under bilateral agreements.	-
VIETNAM	LEGISLATION Fees to be determined by interminis terial regulations of Ministries of Marine Products and Finance (Art 5) (Enactment No. 31 of 29 Jan. 1980) AGREEMENTS Agreement with USSR, Oct. 1982 USSR to give 25% of catch as licence fee. In 1982 1 800 tons of catch were turned over to Vietnam by the USSR		LEGISLATION Foreign fishing only allowed on the basis of agreements or understandings between Vietnam and concerned parties (Enactment No. 31 of 29 Jan. 1980 Art. 7)	
WESTERN SAMOA	LEGISLATION -Such fee as may from time to time be prescribed. (Exclusive Economic Zone Act 1977 S.8) In practice fees set in agreements	-	LEGISLATION No foreign fishing allowed except as expressly provided in an agreement or convention to which W. Samoa is a party. Minister may grant exemptions for fishery research or where otherwise	LEGISLATION Foreign fishing craft means any fishing craft that is not a Western Samoan fishing craft Western Samoan fishing craft means a fishing craft - (a) that is registered in Western Samoa under the Shipping Act 1972; or

TABLE B

LICENCE FEES, BILATERAL AGREEMENT OR JOINT VENTURE REQUIREMENTS AND NATIONALITY CRITERIA

STATE	Licence fees, royalties and other payments		Requirements concerning bilateral framework agreements or joint venture participation	Nationality criteria for fishing vessels
	Local currency	US$ Equiv.		
WESTERN SAMOA (Cont'd)	AGREEMENTS Note: Agreement between Governments of Niue, New Zealand (for Tokelau), Tuvalu and Western Samoa and AMERICAN TUNABOAT ASSOCIATION, Sept. 1983, valid thru' end 1984. AGREEMENT NO LONGER IN FORCE (ENTRY VERIFIED - OCTOBER 1985)		in the national interest. (Fisheries Protection Act 1972, S. 4)	(b) that is an aircraft registered in Western Samoa under the Civil Aviation Act 1963; or (c) in which no person who is not a Western Samoan citizen has any legal or equitable interest (except by way of security only for any advance made by him to the owner). (Exclusive Economic Zone Act 1977 S.2)
YEMEN ARAB REPUBLIC			LEGISLATION Foreign fishing may be authorized under permit or treaty. (Command Council Decree Law of 1976 S. 2)	
YEMEN DEMOCRATIC REPUBLIC	LEGISLATION No fees specified AGREEMENTS Pro-rata royalty fees based on species, sizes and grades. Payments to be made either in kind as percentage of catch, in cash or in delivery of catch at below market prices.		LEGISLATION Foreign fishing may be authorized by a special agreement with the Republic or permit from the competent authorities. (Act No. 45 of 1977 Art. 20) Yemeni share in any joint venture must be at least 51%	

TABLE B

LICENCE FEES, BILATERAL AGREEMENT OR JOINT VENTURE REQUIREMENTS AND NATIONALITY CRITERIA

STATE	Licence fees, royalties and other payments		Requirements concerning bilateral framework agreements or joint venture participation	Nationality criteria for fishing vessels
	Local currency	US$ Equiv.		
YEMEN DEMOCRATIC REPUBLIC (Cont'd)	AGREEMENTS *Agreement with USSR, 1969 renewed annually Licences granted to USSR trawlers and research vessels. Joint expedition in fishing for supply of fish for domestic consumption in the PDRY. Fisheries development projects provided by USSR on soft loans. *Agreement with LIBYA A joint company apparently establis hed in 1982. 60% shares held by Yemen. The Company charters fishing vessels from Yemen and catches are aimed at domestic markets of the two countries as well as for export			
YUGOSLAVIA			LEGISLATION Foreign citizens not permanently resident in Yugoslavia may be authorized to fish under conditions and in the manner specified by	

TABLE B

LICENCE FEES, BILATERAL AGREEMENT OR JOINT VENTURE REQUIREMENTS AND NATIONALITY CRITERIA

STATE	Licence fees, royalties and other payments		Requirements concerning bilateral framework agreements or joint venture participation	Nationality criteria for fishing vessels
	Local currency	US$ Equiv.		
YUGOSLAVIA (Cont'd)			an international agreement to which Yugoslavia is a party. (Basic Act on Marine Fisheries 27 February 1965, Art. 23)	
ZAIRE	Z. 4 000 Per vessel per year (Order No. 0001/CCE/ADRE/83) Ordonnance No. 79-224, 16 Oct 1979)	US$ 82		

TABLE C
COASTAL STATE REQUIREMENTS FOR FOREIGN FISHING

STATE	Foreign fishing vessel licence conditions (other than reporting requirements) [including observers, bonds, etc.]	Logbook and reporting requirements for foreign fishing
ALBANIA	NO INFORMATION	NO INFORMATION
ALGERIA	LEGISLATION Commercial fishing by foreign vessels forbidden in territorial waters. (Ordinance No. 76-84, 1976, art. 6)	
ANGOLA	LEGISLATION Conservation measures may be imposed as conditions of licence. Licence to be carried on board vessel. National flag to be flown and registration number to be displayed. (Decree on the Protection of Marine Resources No. 12-A/80 Arts. 5 & 6) AGREEMENTS *Agreement with Spain, 21 June 1980, valid for three years renewable upon tacit agreement. - Licences granted to catch up to 3 000 tons of prawn and 15 000 tons of shrimp; to 12 tuna purse seiners; to fish for the Spanish quota of ICSEAF for 1980 - Applications for licences to specify: name and official number of the vessel, total length and maximum gauge depth; gross and net tonnages, type of processing and freezing equipment, zones where they intend to operate, quantity of catch expected; other relevant data which may be requested by the Ministry of Fisheries. - Spain to conduct theoretical-practical course on fish population dynamics in Angola, to evaluate crustacean, and cephalopod fisheries and to assess the possibility of mussel and oyster farming, Angolan nationals to be taken on board research vessel.	AGREEMENTS *Agreement with Spain, 21 June 1980 - Before entry into Angolan waters Spanish tuna vessels must inform Angolan authorities of quantities of tunnidae and other species in their hold, fished in waters of other countries (Annex II - 3). - Advance notice to be given of transshipments so that Angolan authorities may supervise them. - Monthly report of catches to be made, to be submitted to Angolan authorities at least once every three months.

TABLE C
COASTAL STATE REQUIREMENTS FOR FOREIGN FISHING

STATE	Foreign fishing vessel licence conditions (other than reporting requirements) [including observers, bonds, etc.]	Logbook and reporting requirements for foreign fishing
ANGOLA (cont'd)	- Fishing zones for shrimp - north of 12° parallel beyond 12 nautical miles; tuna fishing outside 9 nautical miles. - Each Spanish fishing vessel to board two Angolan citizens. - Observers to be taken on board. *New Agreement with Spain signed end 1984 for crustaceans See entry in Table A for financial details. No further details on other terms and conditions. *Agreement on Experimental Fishing with Nigeria, 23 Feb.82 - Experimental fishing by vessels from Nigeria for an initial period of 90 days in specified areas of Angolan Fishing Zone. - 4 Angolans to be employed as crew.	
ANTIGUA AND BARBUDA	LEGISLATION Access agreements to include provision establishing responsibility of foreign country or association to take necessary measures to ensure compliance by its vessels with agreement and fishing laws. (S. 7(3)) -Fishing gear to be stowed except where authorized to fish -licences subject to general conditions to be prescribed, or specified by notice published in the Gazette and to special conditions specified by the Minister. (The Fisheries Act, No. 14 of 1983 S. 9 & 13) Note: New regulations specifying general conditions including reporting now under consideration	
ARGENTINA	LEGISLATION Foreign fishing within the territorial sea is prohibited, except for privately owned foreign companies from a group of predetermined countries (after an experimental period) which are authorized to fish up to an annual quota of	-

TABLE C
COASTAL STATE REQUIREMENTS FOR FOREIGN FISHING

STATE	Foreign fishing vessel licence conditions (other than reporting requirements) [including observers, bonds, etc.]	Logbook and reporting requirements for foreign fishing
ARGENTINA (Cont'd)	200 000 tons under joint venture with Argentinian companies. (Act No. 21.514, 1977 and Decree No. 190, 1977)	
AUSTRALIA	LEGISLATION - The conditions that may be specified in a licence include conditions relating to: - the class or classes of fish (taken, processed or carried); - the quantity of fish to be taken; - the rate at which fish may be taken; - the methods or equipment used to take, process or carry fish; - The Minister or the Secretary may, at any time, endorse a licence so as to extend it to authorize the boat to be brought into a specified port and the landing at that port of fish carried on board. - Observers may be designated by the Minister or the Secretary (Fisheries Act 1952-81) -Licensed vessel to display international call sign in prescribed manner so as to be visible from aircraft and surface vessels. (R. 12 D) -Name of vessel to be displayed on both sides of bow and on stern in contrasting colours. (R. 12 E) -Officer may inspect licensed foreign fishing boat, gear and catch. (R. 12 F) -Master not to obstruct inspecting officers and to produce registration papers, licences, records relating to fishing in Australian fishing zone together with written translation into English if required. (R. 12 F & J)	LEGISLATION The Governor General may make regulations, - providing for the reporting of the positions of foreign boats licensed within the fishing zone; - providing for the furnishing of information relationg to the use in the fishing zone of foreign boats. (Fisheries Act 1952-81, S. 17) -Master of licensed foreign fishing boat shall report position within 12 hours of each of the times specified in the licence by radio to the Australian Coastal Surveillance Centre through an Australian coast radio station operated by the Overseas Telecommunications Commission (R. 12C) -Master of licensed foreign fishing boat to maintain logbook in published form on daily basis (information to be recorded by end of following day. -Completed folios of logbook to be furnished as soon as practicable to officer or the Department in accordance with requirements set out in logbook. (R. 18) Fisheries Regulations. FOR TRANSIT BY UNLICENSED FISHING VESSELS -Nets must be stowed and secured; -transit through waters must be by shortest practicable route; -where vessel transitting to or from Australian port or authorized fishing area or between areas, approval

TABLE C

COASTAL STATE REQUIREMENTS FOR FOREIGN FISHING

STATE	Foreign fishing vessel licence conditions (other than reporting requirements) [including observers, bonds, etc.]	Logbook and reporting requirements for foreign fishing
AUSTRALIA (Cont'd)	-Master to embark and land observers at times and places specified and provide access to all parts of boat required and provide information reasonably requested. Observers to be provided with food and accomodation appropriate for junior officer and to be permitted to use facilities or operate equipment as required.(R. 12K) -master to transmit radio messages required by observer and deliver radio messages sent to observer promptly(R 12) (Fisheries Regulations) Foreign vessels operating under licence under the Torres Strait Fisheries Act in areas of Australian jurisdiction to bear distinguishing number assigned to it, consisting of boats international call-sign followed by the letter T (Torres Strait Fisheries Regulations 1985 Reg 7) AGREEMENTS *Australia/Japan Agreement on Tuna Longlining - Oct. 1983 valid through end Oct. 1984- - Fishing plan to be submitted for each vessel on licence application. *New Agreement with Japan signed 30 Oct 84 valid thru' end Oct. 1985 -agreement applies only to waters of AFZ north of 34° S. and waters south of that latitude adjacent to Lord Howe Island and thus excludes Japanese vessels from areas where significant fishing for bluefin tuna in the past. -Seasonal closures between Smokey Cape and Sidney and all other restrictions remain in force. (Source: AFZ Bulletin No.28 Oct 84) *Australia/Rep. of Korea-Agreement on Squid Fishing - renewed 16 Oct. 1984 valid thru' 15 Oct 1985 -Up to 12 Korean vessels permitted to fish for squid in designated area off Tasmania, Victoria & South Australia.	of authorities to be sought. Fisheries Act, S. 13AB (3) -Approval to be sought from Senior Co-ordinator, Australian Coastal Surveillance Centre (ACSC); -Approval to be sought by radio message or telx/telegram with pescribed code letters and specifying international radio call-sign, point and time of entry or other details of voyage Fisheries Regulations, R. 12B Foreign vessels operating under licence under the Torres Strait Fisheries Act may be required to maintain fishing log-books in prescribed form during prescribed periods. Where so required details of fishing etc. to be entered before end of day following that of operations. (Torres Strait Fisheries Regulations 1985 Reg 7) AGREEMENTS *Australia/Japan Agreement on Tuna Longlining - Oct. 1983 valid through end Oct. 1984- -Vessels licensed to fish in seasonally closed area off New South Wales to notify ACSC 12 hours in advance intention to enter and location and ETA, and provide catch and effort reports every 6 days and position reports daily; 12 hours notice for exit from area. -Licensed vessels required to: -notify ACSC 36 hours in advance intention to enter AFZ -report position at hour/on days specified in licence -notify 24 hours in advance sailing plan for travel in AFZ outside authorized fishing area. -notify 24 hours in advance intention to depart AFZ -report 36 hours in advance intention to enter Aus. port -report 24 hours in advance intention to depart Aus port -report within 12 hours time starts and stops fishing in authorized fishing area

TABLE C
COASTAL STATE REQUIREMENTS FOR FOREIGN FISHING

STATE	Foreign fishing vessel licence conditions (other than reporting requirements) [including observers, bonds, etc.]	Logbook and reporting requirements for foreign fishing
AUSTRALIA (Cont'd)	-Proportion of catch may be landed in Australia if required to provide source of raw material for local processing industry. -Vessels will be subject to strict inspection and reporting requirements and will be exclused from areas where interference with Australian fishermen could occur, partcularly rock lobster fishering areas adjacent South Australia and Vicotria. (Source: AFZ Bulletin No.27 May 84) *Australia/KKFC Pty Ltd. Agreement-Aug.1984 valid thru' end July 1985. -Each vessel to call in Darwin or Broome port for pre-fishing inspection by Australian authorities and for issue of logbooks, licences, briefing of master/radio operator. -After initial inspection, may be required to report to port for subequent pre-fishing inspections -KKFC to provide at own expense on request aircraft or vessel to carry out inspections of licensed vessels -Each vessel to call in Darwin or Broome port for post-fishing inspection by Australian authorities and for delivery of log-book. -KKFC may offer up to 15% of catch for sale to local processors, unless arrangements made for landing of higher proportion of catch, which will be permitted only if not detrimental to Australian fishing industry. -Master of vessel to comply with requirements under relevant laws relating to carriage of observers, and provision of samples for scientific purposes -KKFC also to provide available economic and marketing information in specified form. -Guild to ensure that if fishing vessel used in contravention of laws, that vessel shall not be further used for fishing in AFZ nor persons responsible for contravention.	*Australia/KKFC Pty Ltd. Agreement-Aug.1984 valid thru' end July 1985. -KKFC to provide on 15th day of each month lists of vessels proposing to enter Aus. port or AFZ next month -Reporting and log-book requirements as in publication "Notes for Guidance of Masters and Radio Operators on Licensed Foreign Fishing Vessels" See entry under Japan Agreement above for synopsis of requirements. -Position reports required every 2nd day; catch and effort reports every 6th days -Master of each vessel to keep daily record of particulars required in fishing log-book.

TABLE C
COASTAL STATE REQUIREMENTS FOR FOREIGN FISHING

STATE	Foreign fishing vessel licence conditions (other than reporting requirements) [including observers, bonds, etc.]	Logbook and reporting requirements for foreign fishing
AUSTRALIA (Cont'd)	-KKFC to remit promptly all fines imposed in respect of contraventions by its vessels, and facilitate claiming of all forfeitures ordered by Australian courts, meet costs and expenses of Government for court proceedings, and all hospital and medical care. -KKFC to ensure that no unlicensed fishing operations take place and to bear full responsibility for unlicensed operations to remit promptly all fines imposed in respect of unlicensed fishing operations and facilitate claiming of all forfeitures ordered by Australian courts meet costs and expenses of Government for court proceedings, and all hospital and medical care. -KKFC to take necessary measures to facilitate prompt and adequate settlement of claims for loss or damage for which licensed vessels are responsible. Note: -In accordance with the decision of the South Pacific Forum in August 1982 and as from 1 September 1983, no member of the Forum Fisheries Agency will licence a foreign vessel to fish for tuna in their fishing zone unless it is listed in good standing on the regional register maintained by the Forum Fisheries Agency. (Source: AFZ Information Bulletin Canberra May-July 1983)	
BAHAMAS	LEGISLATION - Such conditions and restrictions as appear to Minister to be necessary or expedient for regulating conservation and management of fisheries resources; - Licence shall contain conditions and restrictions: - as to requirements of any applicable management plan and regulations made to implement it;	

TABLE C
COASTAL STATE REQUIREMENTS FOR FOREIGN FISHING

STATE	Foreign fishing vessel licence conditions (other than reporting requirements) [including observers, bonds, etc.]	Logbook and reporting requirements for foreign fishing
BAHAMAS (Cont'd)	- as to requirement licence not to be used by another vessel; - as to requirements provided for in relevant fishery treaty; - as to requirements that vessel shall fish only in the area of the exclusive fishery zone for which the licence has been granted, and during seasons and periods indicated and that the vessel shall not engage in the cutting up, canning and packaging of any fishery resource except in said area (S.9) CONTROLS OVER TRANSIT BY UNLICENSED FISHING VESSELS - Fishery resources found on board any unlicensed fishing vessel within the exclusive fishing zone shall be deemed, unless the contrary be proved, to have been taken within the zone by person on board that fishing vessel (S.19-2) The Fisheries Resources (Jurisdiction and Conservation) Act, 1977. Note: New regulations now under preparation No licensed foreign fishing at present	
BAHREIN	LEGISLATION -Proprietor of vessel or person responsible for use not to cause damage to fish barriers of fishing gear and to furnish Fisheries Resources Department with information on vessel. (Art. 13) -Minister empowered to make regulations enforcing fishing vessels to display identification numbers (Art. 15) (Decree Promulgating Law No 5 of 1981 on Fishing Regulation)	LEGISLATION -Minister empowered to make regulations regarding statistics and data concerning fisheries resources (Decree Promulgating Law No 5 of 1981 on Fishing Regulation)

TABLE C

COASTAL STATE REQUIREMENTS FOR FOREIGN FISHING

STATE	Foreign fishing vessel licence conditions (other than reporting requirements) [including observers, bonds, etc.]	Logbook and reporting requirements for foreign fishing
BANGLADESH	LEGISLATION -Certain areas within the economic zone reserved for Bangladesh fishermen. (S. 6) -licence issued only by competent authority, subject to such conditions, limitations and restrictions as licensing authority may specify. (S. 5) (Territorial waters and Maritime Zones Rules, 1977) -Licences not transferrable -Licences valid only for species, fishing gear, method and location specified in licence -Fishing vessels not to interfere with navigation aids, shipping etc. in shipping lanes; -Licences subject to conditions prescribed by rules or endorsed on licence by Director; (Marine Fisheries Ordinance, 1983 SS. 11, 13, 15 & 16) -Information to be given on licence application specified -Licences valid only for activities, period, area, conditions, species, quantities, methods and gear as specified -Relevant laws and rules on fish conservation and management to be complied with; -By-catch not to exceed specified percentage; -Vessel to display assigned identification mark to be clearly visible from air and sea; -Owner to appoint and maintain local representative resident in Bangladesh, authorized to accept legal and financial responsibility on behalf owner in respect of fishing operations and accept service of notice, summons or other document in legal proceedings related to those operations -Owner to execute bond to guarantee performance of licence obligations if required by Director; -Compulsory inspection in Chittagong or Khulna on entry and in place specified by Director before departure zone; -Transhipments of fish only in Chittagong or Khulna under control of authorized officer unless otherwise authorized	-Licence holder to keep detailed information on catches and sales in prescribed form and submit copy to Director (Marine Fisheries Ordinance, 1983 S. 14 -Written records to be maintained on daily basis of fishing effort and catch in form specified by Director; -Records to be transmitted to Director monthly or at request of Director or authorized officer; -Master or local representative to notify estimated time and location of entry into Bangladesh waters at least 24 hrs. in adance giving fishing plan and arrival date in Chittagong or Khulna for initial inspection; -Master, if required by licence, to make radio reports weekly to Director giving name and licence number, position, quantity of fish of each species caught in Bangladesh waters, caught since last report and transferred, to other vessels since last report or inspection; -Master or local representative to notify estimated time and location of departure from Bangladesh waters at least 48 hours in advance giving expected date of arrival in Chittagong or Khulna for final inpsection, and species, quantity, condition of fish on board; -Vessel to maintain records and make reports in English -Vessel to use IMO International Code of Signals. (Marine Fisheries Rules, 1983)

TABLE C
COASTAL STATE REQUIREMENTS FOR FOREIGN FISHING

STATE	Foreign fishing vessel licence conditions (other than reporting requirements) [including observers, bonds, etc.]	Logbook and reporting requirements for foreign fishing
BANGLADESH (cont'd)	-Master to bring vessel to port for inspection if required -Vessel to fly national flag and Bangladesh courtesy flag while in Bangladesh waters; -Master to accept observers designated by Director and provide food and accomodation equivalent to officer, cooperate in performance duties, and allow access to radiotelephone facilities; -Master to comply with directions of authorized officers, stop vessel on request and allow boarding and inspection; -Vessel to carry communications and position fixing equipment as specified; -Vessel not authorized to fish to stow gear in prescribed manner; -Licensed vessels to emply at least 3 Bangladesh crew trained in Marine Fisheries Training Academy, Chittagong; -Minimum mesh sizes, permitted fishing areas for specified methods of fishing, prohibited fishing methods specified. (Marine Fisheries Rules, 1983)	
BARBADOS	LEGISLATION Foreign fishing vessel permits may contain -details of owner and vessel; -fishing area designated; -periods allowed for fishing and number of voyages authorized; -descriptions and quantities of fish permitted to be taken -method of fishing; -conditions respecting landing of fish and designated ports;	

TABLE C
COASTAL STATE REQUIREMENTS FOR FOREIGN FISHING

STATE	Foreign fishing vessel licence conditions (other than reporting requirements) [including observers, bonds, etc.]	Logbook and reporting requirements for foreign fishing
BARBADOS (Cont'd)	-permitted use of catch; -other terms and conditions; (Marine Boundaries and Jurisdiction Act 1978 S. 12). Note: New legislation being prepared	
BELGIUM	Specified in measures for foreign fishing adopted by the EEC. 12-mile coastal zone reserved in principle for local fishermen. Limited fishing by Netherlands and France in specified areas within the 6-12 mile coastal zone. (Council Regulation (EEC) No 170/83 of 25 January 1983)	Specified in measures for foreign fishing boats adopted by EEC.
BELIZE	LEGISLATION Minister may make regulations prescribing conditions of issue of licences to fish No distinction made between local and foreign fishing boats in present law (Fisheries Ordinance, CAP 174 S.13) Note: No licensed foreign fishing at present.	
BENIN	LEGISLATION -Trawling prohibited within 3 miles of coast. (Order No. 100 of 31 July 1968, Art. 1) -All foreign fishing vessels must hold valid licence from Benin authorities. -Vessels licenced for industrial fishing must be owned by Company having its head office in Benin and hold its accounts there, or by physical person residing in Benin or represented there and holding his accounts there.	

TABLE C
COASTAL STATE REQUIREMENTS FOR FOREIGN FISHING

STATE	Foreign fishing vessel licence conditions (other than reporting requirements) [including observers, bonds, etc.]	Logbook and reporting requirements for foreign fishing
BENIN (Cont'd)	- Vessels operating in industrial fisheries out of the port of Cotonu must be less than 7 years old. (Ordinance No. 73-40, 5 May 1973 Arts. 4 and 5). - Applications for licences for industrial fishing operations out of the port of Cotonu to be passed on by a special Commission. - Limits fixed on the number of trawlers operating out of Cotonu. -Freezer trawlers not permitted to land fish anywhere in country except within limits of quotas established by the authorities. -Licence holder to pay deposit of from 200 000 (US$ 667) to 400 000 CFA (US$ 1333) per boat depending on tonnage class. (Decree No. 290 of 16 July 1966) AGREEMENTS -Bilateral agreements have included provisions regarding training on board of foreign vessels and welfare protection (e.g. Agreement with France in 1975).	
BRAZIL	LEGISLATION -Foreign fishing only in the zone comprised between 100 to 200 miles off the coast (unless special authorization). -Certain fisheries reserved for national fishermen (lobster, shrimp). (Decree 68.459 of 1 April 1971). Licences valid maximum one year and renewable. Licences to specify methods of fishing and gear to be used. Vessels must be entered in General Fishing Register once licence granted. Captains of vessels to be familiar with and comply with Brazilian laws and regulations. Fishery inspectors to be allowed on licensed vessels. Transhipment of catch between vessels in territorial	LEGISLATION Captains of foreign vessels to inform Navy, Coast Patrol, Naval Police and Search and Rescue Service of day and hour of entry and exit of vessel into and from Brazilian territorial sea. Captains to give daily radio reports on position in territorial sea. Above reports to be submitted through SUDEPE radio telephone station or nearest coastguard station to Naval District Command. Captains to maintain official SUDEPE log books giving details of position, effort, catch and other relevant data, to be sent in to SUDEPE as required. (Decree Law No. 221 of 28 February 1967) (Note: New legislation under consideration).

TABLE C

COASTAL STATE REQUIREMENTS FOR FOREIGN FISHING

STATE	Foreign fishing vessel licence conditions (other than reporting requirements) [including observers, bonds, etc.]	Logbook and reporting requirements for foreign fishing
BRAZIL (Cont'd)	seas subject to prior authorization by SUDEPE. Local landings by foreign vessels are prohibited unless specifically authorized. Legal agents or representatives of the owner to be maintained during the period of the fishing operations in Brazil. Employment of nationals must meet standards set out in Brazilian Labour Laws. (Decree Law No. 221 of 28 February 1976) (Note: New legislation under consideration).	
BULGARIA	NO INFORMATION	
BURMA	LEGISLATION Licenses to be issued only with prior express permission of the Council of Ministers. (Territorial Sea and Maritime Zones Law, 1977, s. 20)	
CAMEROON	AGREEMENTS *Agreement with Equatorial Guinea of 26 November 1981 (valid for two years renewable on tacit agreement) - Guinean vessels to hold a permit from state of origin. - Operations forbidden in estuaries and within 2-mile zone reserved for artisanal fishing. - Each vessel must be less than 500 GRT. Catch may be landed only in ports of flag state.	

TABLE C

COASTAL STATE REQUIREMENTS FOR FOREIGN FISHING

STATE	Foreign fishing vessel licence conditions (other than reporting requirements) [including observers, bonds, etc.]	Logbook and reporting requirements for foreign fishing
CANADA	LEGISLATION Legal agents or representatives of the owner to be maintained in the State during the period of the fishing operations. Master to respect licence conditions concerning permitted quotas, minimum sizes, discards, etc. Fishing gear to be stowed while the vessel is within an area where not authorized to fish. Vessel to have required equipment, including communications equipment. Must allow observers on board and provide necessary facilities. Must display required identification markings. Must carry out agreed research and sampling programmes. (Coastal Fisheries Protection Regulations) Licences carry conditions relating inter alia to following Designation of Regional Director-General; Authorized Activities; Directed Fisheries; Explanatory Notes; Authorized Fishing Gear and Equipment; Prohibited Catches; Weekly Reporting Requirements. (Guidelines for Foreign Fishing Vessels Fishing National Allocations 1983)	LEGISLATION Master or agent to notify Regional Director General of estimated time of entry into Canadian fishery waters 24 hours in advance, together with location of entry and approximate schedule of activities and estimated time of departure not less than 72 hours in advance. Written records to be maintained on daily basis of fish caught, effort, transhipments/fish transported, fish processed.(Fishing log-books) Records to be transmitted by master: (a) during term of licence on request to protection officer or Reg. Director General; (b) not later than 60 days after expiry licence. Master or agent to notify Regional Director General of estimated time of entry of vessel into Canadian port at least 24 hours in advance.
	AGREEMENTS * Agreements concluded in the late 70's with foreign distant fishing nations - main features - Access to surplus after determination of TAC and Canadian harvesting capacity - Fishing operations to be conducted pursuant to Canadian laws and regulations. - Foreign State acknowledges that states in whose rivers anadromous stocks originate have the primary interest in and responsability for such stocks. Latest agreements require recognition by contracting	Master to report position, activities, catch statistics transhipments, etc., as required in licence. (Coastal Fisheries Protection Regulations) Original of assigned log-books shall be submitted to the Region responsible for issuing licence within 30 days of end of each calendar month during which vessel operating in Canadian zone. Radio reports to be made weekly covering period Monday A.M. through Sunday P.M. not later than Monday 23.59 GMT

TABLE C
COASTAL STATE REQUIREMENTS FOR FOREIGN FISHING

STATE	Foreign fishing vessel licence conditions (other than reporting requirements) [including observers, bonds, etc.]	Logbook and reporting requirements for foreign fishing
CANADA (Cont'd)	parties of special interest of Canada in conservation of certain stocks occurring both within and beyond the limits of the Canadian fishery zone, as recognized in the practice of the International Commission for the North West Atlantic Fisheries. * Exchange of letters with EEC of 30 December 1980 relating to the Agreement concluded with EEC on the same day (valid through 31 December 1987) - The maintenance of fish allocations to vessels flying the flag of EEC countries shall be contingent upon the fulfilment by the Community of its obligations with regard to commerical cooperation. - (Fishing quotas for EEC vessels in Canadian fishery zone linked to tariff quotas for import of Canadian fish products into EEC market) (Annexes I and II)	
CAPE VERDE ISLANDS	LEGISLATION Fishing in archipelagic waters and territorial sea and fishing for crustaceans in exclusive economic zones reserved to nationals. (Decree-Law No. 126-77 of 31 December 1977 Art. 8) AGREEMENTS *Agreement with Senegal of 29 March 1985 with implementing -Tuna boats allowed and "cordiers" allowed to operate in allareas under the jurisdiction of Cape Verde; sardine boats may operate only three miles from the baselines.	AGREEMENTS *Agreement with Senegal of 29 March 1985 with implementing protocol - Monthly returns of catch to be provided

TABLE C
COASTAL STATE REQUIREMENTS FOR FOREIGN FISHING

STATE	Foreign fishing vessel licence conditions (other than reporting requirements) [including observers, bonds, etc.]	Logbook and reporting requirements for foreign fishing
CHILE	LEGISLATION Permits issued for tuna and live bait fishing only. Other fishing operations subject to special authorization. - Registration valid for one year. - Permits valid for 100 days and renewable. - Permits may only be issued to freezer ships when acting as mother ships to licensed vessels. - All operations subject to control by local fisheries authorities, who will indicate restrictions, closed seasons and other technical conditions applicable. - Licensed vessels must not purchase fish from other fishermen in Chilean waters. - Licensed vessels must accept on board such observers as may be designated by local fisheries authorities and provide accomodation and food and must also receive on board any persons designated to carry out technical or statistical checks when operating in Chilean waters. - Fishing for albacore, anchoveta and sardine for fishmeal prohibited. - Transshipments at sea or in port prohibited except for exports, in which case transshipment to be carried out in port under supervision of authorities. - Licensed operators to respect conservation measures. - No fish to be sold on local market for local consumption unless authorized. (Decree No. 130 of 11 February 1959) No licenses have been issued in practice to foreign flag vessels since 1977 except for tuna fishing operations. (Source NMFS-IFR/80/2)	LEGISLATION Foreign vessels must provide Fisheries authorities with all the data and information they require pertaining to their fishing operations. Vessels must notify dates of entry into and departure from Chilean waters. (Decree No. 130 of 11 February 1959).
CHINA	NO INFORMATION	

TABLE C
COASTAL STATE REQUIREMENTS FOR FOREIGN FISHING

STATE	Foreign fishing vessel licence conditions (other than reporting requirements) [including observers, bonds, etc.]	Logbook and reporting requirements for foreign fishing
COLOMBIA	LEGISLATION Permit for industrial commercial fisheries: (foreign vessels apparently must be affiliated or under charter to local industries-Order No 0052 of 19/12 1978) -only valid for zones indicated and for operations on one coastline; -vessels 25 GT or over require fishing licence and under 25 GT require registration; -catch to be landed in Colombian ports; -specified proportion of catch to be destined for local market. -Permit qpplications to include information on applicant, location and shareholding of company applicants and plan of operations. Special commercial permit: -valid only for tuna live bait fishery; -permit holders do not need to be linked with local firm; -conditions to include fishing areas authorized target species, quotas, permitted fishing methods, expiry date and percentage or quota of catch to be destined for national market. Permit applications to include plans of operations	
	Commercial exploratory fisheries: -Conditions to include area of exploration; maximum catch limits; permitted fishing methods; requirements concerning final reports; performance bonds. Inderena to establish percentage of catch to be sold on local market -permit applications to include plans of operations (Decree No. 1681 of 1978, Title 11, Chapter 1) Shrimp fishing temporarily banned and lobster fishing regulated. Foreign nationals not legally domiciled in Colombia may fish only for tuna, live bait and cetaceans (Source NMFS/IFR/81/69)	Commercial exploratory fisheries: Permit holder to submit detailed final report on results obtained. (Decree No. 1681 of 1978, Art 36)

TABLE C

COASTAL STATE REQUIREMENTS FOR FOREIGN FISHING

STATE	Foreign fishing vessel licence conditions (other than reporting requirements) [including observers, bonds, etc.]	Logbook and reporting requirements for foreign fishing
COMORO ISLANDS	LEGISLATION Fishing by foreign vessels prohibited in territorial sea. Fishing in EEZ requires licence. Licence conditions may include area, seasons, species, quotas, fishing methods and gear, requirements concerning the processing, transport, transshipping and landing of catch, port inspection, requirements concerning statistical and vessel position reports, research and training programmes, obligation to carry licence on board, vessel identification marks, compliance with instructions, observers, transponders and other required equipment, etc. (Act No. 82-015 of 11 May 1982 Art. 5)	LEGISLATION Licence conditions may include requirement to report statistical information to competent authorities, including in particular, information on catch and effort and position of vessel. (Act No. 82-015 of 11 May 1982 Art. 5)
CONGO	LEGISLATION Fishing in territorial sea reserved to Congolese vessels. Vessels to bear clear identification marks and carry documents attesting nationality and marks. (Ordinance 22-70 of 14 July 1970, Art. 4 & 16)	
COSTA RICA	LEGISLATION Foreign fishing for export (fresh fish) market subject to following conditions: a) Motherships must keep in bays in sight of shore; b) fish not landed to local plants considered exported and subject to customs duties and other charges; c) motherships and other ships to pay transshipment fee on all fish transshipped to other ships. (Law on Fisheries and Marine Hunting, 1948 Art 16.)	Vessels encountered in jurisdictional waters and overflown by Costa Rican aircraft must put radio on frequency 8A to receive instructions. If no contact and aircraft overflies 3 time, vessel to go immediately to nearest port. CONTROLS OVER TRANSIT BY UNLICENSED FISHING VESSELS -fishing boats without fishing permits that need to cross Costa Rican waters must communicate entry and

TABLE C
COASTAL STATE REQUIREMENTS FOR FOREIGN FISHING

STATE	Foreign fishing vessel licence conditions (other than reporting requirements) [including observers, bonds, etc.]	Logbook and reporting requirements for foreign fishing
COSTA RICA (Cont'd)	-Foreign vessels fishing in 200 mile zone must register with Costarican authorities through consulates in San Diego, Panama or other authorized locations and must hold a fishing permit valid for one trip (up to max of 60 days) -Foreign vessels under contract to domestic companies to land specified quantity of catch enjoy same privileges as national vessels, but must board at least 75% Costa Rican crew. (Law No. 6267, 1978) Deposit required of 10% of amount of permit fee (Decree No. 8081-A, 1978 Art. 15) Commercial fishing by means of long lines prohibited within 100 miles of coast.(Decree No. 11580-A 9 June 1980) -Vessels over 400 NRT required to put down deposit in US$ of $60 per NRT ($30 per NRT for vessels under 400 NRT) (Decree No. 9822-A of 10 March 1979) Commercial long line fishing prohibited within 100 miles from coast. (Decree No. 11580-A, 9 June 1980) Commercial foreign fishing prohibited within 12-mile territorial sea. Licences for foreign commercial fishing operations in 12-200 mile zone valid for 1 sea only (Pacific or Caribbean) (Decree No. 12737-A, 23 June 1981) (ENTRY VERIFIED - JANUARY 1983)	departure to Costa Rican authorities. Vessels have 48 hours to effect transit or reach national port. (Law No. 6267, 1978, Art. 7) Requests for permit of passage to be made to Harbour Master at Puntarenas (Pacific) or Puerto de Limon. Information required on application for passage permit includes proposed course, place of entry and exit, time required for passage (up to 48 hours) characteristics of vessel, agreement to keep radio on on frequency 8A. (Decree No. 9996-S of 16 April 1979)
CUBA	NO INFORMATION	
CYPRUS	NO INFORMATION	

TABLE C
COASTAL STATE REQUIREMENTS FOR FOREIGN FISHING

STATE	Foreign fishing vessel licence conditions (other than reporting requirements) [including observers, bonds, etc.]	Logbook and reporting requirements for foreign fishing
DENMARK	Specified in interim measures for foreign fishing adopted by EEC. 12-mile coastal zone reserved in principle for local fishermen. Limited fishing by Netherlands, Germany and Belgium in specified areas within the 3-12 mile coastal zone. (Council Regulation (EEC) No 170/83 of 25 January 1983) AGREEMENTS *Agreement with EEC and Norway on the Regulation of Fisheries in the Skagerrak and the Kattegat in 1983 Valid from 1 Jan. to 31 Dec. 1983. Total cataches for Cod, Haddock, Whiting, Plaice and Kattegat specified and allocated. Directed fishing for Herring permitted only for human consumption. The period of fishing, size of vessels, use of trawls, purse seines and pair trawls specified. (Council Regulation (EEC) No. 621/83)	Specified in measures for foreign fishing adopted by EEC.
DJIBOUTI	LEGISLATION Fishing operations in territorial seas and EEZ must be authorized by Minster of Agriculture. Licence conditions not specified. (Law no. 52/AN/78, 9 January 1979)	
DOMINICA	Note: New legislation under consideration. No fishing licences issued for foreign fishing at present	

TABLE C
COASTAL STATE REQUIREMENTS FOR FOREIGN FISHING

STATE	Foreign fishing vessel licence conditions (other than reporting requirements) [including observers, bonds, etc.]	Logbook and reporting requirements for foreign fishing
DOMINICAN REPUBLIC	LEGISLATION Conditions may include - duration of fishing operations; time by which fishing to start; - type of fish to be caught; - type of equipment to be used; nature of operations. (Law No. 5914 of 1962)	
ECUADOR	LEGISLATION Fishing permits may be issued only to foreign flag vessels of 60 n.r.t. or less. Issue of permits to be suspended when volume of catch threatens local operations or reaches annual maximum catch 60-mile coastal zone reserved for local fishing except for vesels operating under charter or joint venture with locally established industries. (Decree No. 477 of 8 August 1980) Registration valid until 31 December each year. Permits valid for one voyage (transhipments deemed to terminate voyage). Controls over transhipments and fishing areas. Permits obtained from Directorate General of Fisheries or through Consulates abroad. Permits may also be obtained by radio message to accredited agent or representative in Ecuador at least 12 hours before entry into Ecuador waters Agent to pay fees and exhibit documents required. Notice of obtention of permit to be given to Maritime Authority through Naval Radio Station. -Observers to be permitted on board and given necessary information. Transhipments only in designated ports in accordance with specified conditions. (Regulations under the Act on Fisheries and Fisheries Development, Decree No. 759 of 1974 as amended by Decree No 1312 of 12 November 1982) Foreign fishermen required to appoint local agent (Source - NMFS/IFR/81/69)	LEGISLATION Detailed report of catch to be made, in which quantities, species and locations shall be specified. CONTROLS OVER TRANSIT BY UNLICENSED FISHING VESSELS -Vessels wishing to undertake innocent passage through Ecuadorian 200 mile sovereign waters must notify General Directorate of Merchant Marine through the Naval Radio Station of the following information: -Notice of wish to undertake innocent passage at least 12 hours in advance; -Position of vessel before entering Ecuadorian waters; -Date, hour and position of entry; -Route to be followed, speed of passage and estimated day, time of exit from Ecuadorian waters; -Whether or not fish is being carried, and if so weight and species of fish in holds; -Vessel cannot be authorised to carry out any other activity; -Vessel must report at least 24 hours before departure from Ecuadorian waters and may be inspected at any time while in Ecuadorian waters. (Regulations under the Act on Fisheries and Fisheries Development, Decree No. 759 of 1974 as amended by Decree No 1312 of 12 November 1982)

TABLE C
COASTAL STATE REQUIREMENTS FOR FOREIGN FISHING

STATE	Foreign fishing vessel licence conditions (other than reporting requirements) [including observers, bonds, etc.]	Logbook and reporting requirements for foreign fishing
EGYPT	NO INFORMATION	
EL SALVADOR	LEGISLATION Fishing in 12-mile coastal zone (Pesca de bajura) reserved for national and Central-American fishermen and local companies (at least 50 per cent local ownership - proof of ownership structure may be required). (Arts. 25 & 26) By way of exception and in order to fulfill development plans, Salvadorian enterprises holding high seas and distant water fishing licences may be authorized to contract foreign fishing vessels as principal or auxiliary fleet units for a period up to 3 years. Authorization to be granted by Executive Order on payment of appropriate fees. (Art. 40) - Foreign flag vessels in respect of which authorization granted under article 40 must carry on board documents required by competent maritime authorities, licence, permit, certificate of health and other required documents, and: - a) the Executive Order granting the authorization; b) international health certificate; c) international inspection certificate; (Art. 41) - Vessels must not tranship catch except in authorized ports, with the exception of auxiliary vessels which may receive transshipments provided supervised by the authorities. (Art. 42) - Authorized fishermen must: - a) catch only authorized species;	LEGISLATION - Authorized fishermen must: - -furnish information required in carrying out of their duties; -use forms prepared by Directorate-General to provide complete reports of each fishing trip; (General Law on Fisheries Activities, Decree No. 799 of 14 September 1981, Art. 50) CONTROLS OVER TRANSIT BY UNLICENSED FISHING VESSELS Foreign fishing vessels that need to transit jurisdictional waters must request permission by radio from the appropriate Harbour Master and have 48 hours to effect innocent passage or reach their port of destination. (General Law on Fisheries Activities, Decree No. 799 of 14 September 1981)

TABLE C
COASTAL STATE REQUIREMENTS FOR FOREIGN FISHING

STATE	Foreign fishing vessel licence conditions (other than reporting requirements) [including observers, bonds, etc.]	Logbook and reporting requirements for foreign fishing
EL SALVADOR (Cont'd)	b) comply with conservation measures; c) give free access to installations and boats to officers and employees of Directorate-General and furnish information required in carrying out of their duties; d) use gear and systems indicated by technology to avoid environmental contamination; e) land catch only at authorized landing places; f) use forms prepared by Directorate-General to provide complete reports of each fishing trip; g) make fixed fishing gear; h) do other things as required by law, regulation or orders of the competent authorities. (Art. 50) -Fishing for pelagic and migratory species subject to special regime applicable to the 12-200 mile area: -Nationals or foreigners wishing to fish must apply to Directorate General for Special Fishing licence (valid 1 year); (Art.76) -Vessels of authorized enterprises must be inscribed on register to be drawn up for each calendar year and hold certification of inscription in form of a "General Permit" (valid for one year) Applications for inscription to be made in November or December (Art.77) -Each vessel also required to hold "Special Permit" issued by Directorate General, (valid for up to 90 days) (Art. 78) -Foreign companies holding special permits subject to pertinent provisions of the law and regulations (Art. 80) (General Law on Fisheries Activities, Decree No. 799 of 14 September 1981)	

TABLE C
COASTAL STATE REQUIREMENTS FOR FOREIGN FISHING

STATE	Foreign fishing vessel licence conditions (other than reporting requirements) [including observers, bonds, etc.]	Logbook and reporting requirements for foreign fishing
EQUATORIAL GUINEA	LEGISLATION No mention in legislative texts. AGREEMENTS *Agreement with Spain of 31 October 1979. Freezer trawler licence (Type "A") restricted to 10 vessels of 170 to 425 G.R.T. each. Type "B" restricted to 40 vessels of 170 to 425 G.R.T. each. Tuna freezers restricted to 50 vessels of up to 1 600 G.R.T. each; Fresh fish restricted to 10 vessels of up to 250 G.R.T. each Freeezer trawlers (licence type "A") and fresh fish vessels to employ at least 30% Guinean crew. *Agreement with Nigeria of 27 November 1981 -"Request" for fishing to mention: overall length of the vessel, construction date and flag, gross registered tonnage; characteristics of the engine; kind of fishing and equipments used, the composition of the crew; - 20 vessels allowed, made up of 10 trawlers less than 1 000 GRT and 10 purse seiners; - Minimum mesh size; - Each vessel to take on board 3 Guinean citizens; - Designated officer of Equatorial Guinea to board any vessel at liberty. *Agreement with Cameroon, of 26 November 1981 - Guinean vessels to hold permit from state of origin - Operations forbidden in estuaries and within 2-mile zone reserved for artisanal fishing - Each vessel less than 500 GRT. Landing of catch only in ports of flag state. *Agreement with Nigeria of 27 November 1981 - Nigerian vessels to provide technical information in relation to fishing operations.	

TABLE C

COASTAL STATE REQUIREMENTS FOR FOREIGN FISHING

STATE	Foreign fishing vessel licence conditions (other than reporting requirements) [including observers, bonds, etc.]	Logbook and reporting requirements for foreign fishing
EQUATORIAL GUINEA (Cont'd)	*Agreement with the EEC, 1983 valid thru' 1986 -Community to take necessary measures to ensure compliance by its vessels with terms of agreement and regulations -Community authorities to notify list of vessels to carry out fishing operations for next 12 months, 3 months before commencement of fishing operations -Vessels to take on observers on request of local authorities. Presence of observers not to exceed time required to carry out verification of catch. (Text published in EC Official Journal No. L 237/13 of 26/8/1983)	*Agreement with the EEC, 1983 valid thru' 1986 -Vessels to report results of each seining operation to the Annobon radio station.
ETHIOPIA	No mention in legislative texts.	
EUROPEAN COMMUNITY	LEGISLATION For Spanish fishing vessels: Quotas established for catches for each species. Limits on permitted by-catches (catch on board controlled) Fishing operations excluded from 12 mile limits except where otherwise specified. Vessels to hold licence on board and comply with conservation and supervisory measures. Number of licences to be issued limited; each vessel may hold only 1 licence. Information to be given on licence application specified Licence valid for 1 vessel only, unless licence authorizes Periodic programmes and lists of vessels to which licences may be issued required for certain fishing operations Licence for some fishing operations may be invalidated if	LEGISLATION For Spanish fishing vessels: -Vessels to keep logbook detailing quantity of each species caught, date and time of beginning and end of fishing, position of catches(ICES statistical square) fishing method used, radio reports made. -Entries to be made after each fishing operation Vessels licensed for hake, sardines, or anchovies to notify EC Commission, Brussels, (via authorized radio station) on entering and leaving 200 mile community fishing zone, and in the case of vessels licensed for hake or sardines: (i) when moving from one ICES sub-area to another, (ii) on entering or leaving a Community port, and (iii) daily while within the zone.

TABLE C
COASTAL STATE REQUIREMENTS FOR FOREIGN FISHING

STATE	Foreign fishing vessel licence conditions (other than reporting requirements) [including observers, bonds, etc.]	Logbook and reporting requirements for foreign fishing
EUROPEAN COMMUNITY (cont'd)	information on catches not received from flag state authorities by specified deadlines Technical measures specified (prohibition gillnets, mesh sizes, limitations on fishing effort etc.) Periods of validity of licences specified; licences to expire when quotas filled Fishing boxes and windows established Licences shall be withdrawn for infringement of conditions Where vessel fishes without valid licence, licence may be withdrawn from another licensed vessel belonging to same owner Licences not to be issued for specified periods where conditions infringed. Licences subject to following special conditions: -Licence to be held on board -Registration letters and numbers to be clearly marked on bow and on each side of superstructure where best seen, in contrasting colours and not effaced, altered, obscured (Council Regulation (EEC) No 7/85 laying down for 1985 certain measures for the conservation and management of fishery resources applicable to vessels flying the flag of Spain 19 December 1984)	-Reports to include :- -date, time, geographical position, ICES statistical square -quantity of each species in holds (using code) -quantity of each species caught since last transmission -ICES statistical square in which catches taken; -quantity of each species transferred since last transmission -(Name, call sign and licence number of vessel to which transferred) (Council Regulation (EEC) No 7/85 laying down for 1985 certain measures for the conservation and management of fishery resources applicable to vessels flying the flag of Spain 19 December 1984)
	For fishing vessels from Norway, Faroes -Quotas established for each country, by area and species -Number of licences issued limited by area and species Fishing operations allowed only outside 12 mi zone except as expressly authorized under regulation. -By-catches of species under quota counted against quota	For fishing vessels from Norway, Faroes -Vessels to maintain logbook in prescribed form to be completed after each fishing operation and detailing: (i) quantity of each species caught; (ii) date and time of each fishing operation; (iii) geographical position of catch;

TABLE C
COASTAL STATE REQUIREMENTS FOR FOREIGN FISHING

STATE	Foreign fishing vessel licence conditions (other than reporting requirements) [including observers, bonds, etc.]	Logbook and reporting requirements for foreign fishing
EUROPEAN COMMUNITY (cont'd)	-Vessels fishing under quotas to comply with conservation and control measures. -Registration letters and numbers to be clearly marked on both sides of the bow of the vessel. -For fishing in certain areas under quota management (and in other areas by vessels over specified size) must hold licence on board and comply with licence conditions -Licences valid for 1 vessel only. -Licences may be withdrawn for infringement of regulation -No new licence to be issued to vessel committing infringe ment for up to 12 months (not applicable to Sweden). -Information to be given on licence application specified -Technical measures established for specified fisheries. (Council Regulations (EEC) Nos 4/85 & 5/85 of 19 December 1984 laying down for 1985 certain measures for the conservation and management of fishery resources applicable to vessels flying the flags of Norway and Faroes, (as amended)	(iv) method of fishing; (v) each radio report made. -Vessels unless fishing in exempted zones, to report to EC Commission: (i) on entry EEC 200 mi zone or specified sub-areas with details of vessel and vessel position (name, call sign identification marking, name of master, licence number, type of message, date, time and position,) quantity of fish by species in the holds, time and place of commencement of fishing operations; (ii) on departure from EEC 200 mile zone giving details of vessel and vessel position etc., quantity of fish by species in the holds, catch since last report, position of catch (by ICES statistical square), details of transhipments and landings, and number of discarded fish where leaving specified subarea; (iii) 48 hours prior to departure from specified areas; (iv) every 3 days where fishing for herring/ every week for other species, giving details of vessel and vessel, position, catch since last report, location of catch, (for herring fishing in North Sea by Swedish vessels only, number of active fishing days). Form of radio message and codes specified. (Council Regulation (EEC) Nos 4/85 & 5/85 of 19 December 1984 laying down for 1985 certain measures for the conservation and management of fishery resources applicable to vessels flying the flags of Norway and Faroes, (as amended)

TABLE C
COASTAL STATE REQUIREMENTS FOR FOREIGN FISHING

STATE	Foreign fishing vessel licence conditions (other than reporting requirements) [including observers, bonds, etc.]	Logbook and reporting requirements for foreign fishing
EUROPEAN COMMUNITY (cont'd)	For fishing off the coast of French Dept of Guyana Fishing Vessels from USA, Japan, Barbados, Guyana, Surinam Trinidad and Tobago, Korea and Venezuela authorized to catch listed species 1 Jan 1985 to 31 Dec. 1985 within 200-mile Zone of the French department of Guyana. Limits on number of licences and catches. Vessels to hold licence on board and comply with conditions, control measures and other regulatory provisions. -Registration letters and numbers to be clearly marked on prow and on each side of superstructure where most visible in contrasting colours and not effaced, altered, obscured. Licences for shrimp fishing issued to US and Japanese vessels if under contract to land all their catches in French Guyana (max no. specified-proof contract required) Licences for shrimp fishing issued to vessels from Barbados, Guyana, Surinam, Trinidad and Tobagosubject to specified limits and on basis of fishing plan submitted by the flag state authorities and approved by the Commission- Validity of licences limited to fishing period as in plan -Licences for tuna fishing issued to vessels from Japan and Korea, subject to undertaking to permit observers, and for snapper and other species for vessels from Barbados and Venezuela. Licences for snapper subject to condition that owner lands 50% of catches in French Guyana or 75% if larger number of licences issued.(Proof contract required) Information to be given on licence application specified Licences valid for 1 vessel only. -Applications to be submitted at least 1 month in advance -Shrimp fishing prohibited in waters less than 30 metres -Only long-lining permitted for species other than shrimp -Licences may be withdrawn for infringement of conditions Where vessel fishes without valid licence, licence may be withdrawn from another licensed vessel belonging to same owner	For fishing off the coast of French Dept of Guyana -Licensed vessel to complete fishing return (logbook) after each fishing operation in specifed form. -Copy of fishing return to be sent to Commission within 30 days of last day of each fishing trip. -Master of each licensed vessel to notify EC Commission, Brussels, (via authorized radio station) (i) on entering and leaving 200 mile zone; (ii) on entering or leaving a Community port, and (iv) every week in respect of previous week. -Transmissions to include:- -name of vessel -radio call sign -licence number -number of transmission -type of transmission -date, time and geographical position -where licensed for shrimp fishing under contract to local company, activity of vessel during period covered by report -quantity of each species caught (using code) -quantity of each species caught since last transmission -quantity of each species transferred since last transmission -Name, call sign and licence number of vessel to which transferred -name of master; (Council Regulation (EEC) No 8/85 of 19/12 1984 laying down certain measures for the conservation and management of fishery resources applicable to vessels flying the flag of certain non-member countries in the 200 nautical mile Zone off the Coast of the French Department of Guyana

TABLE C
COASTAL STATE REQUIREMENTS FOR FOREIGN FISHING

STATE	Foreign fishing vessel licence conditions (other than reporting requirements) [including observers, bonds, etc.]	Logbook and reporting requirements for foreign fishing
EUROPEAN COMMUNITY (cont'd)	Licences not to be issued for specified periods where conditions infringed. (Council Regulation (EEC) No 8/85 of 19/12 1984 laying down certain measures for the conservation and management of fishery resources applicable to vessels flying the flag of certain non-member countries in the 200 nautical mile Zone off the Coast of the French Department of Guyana	
FIJI	LEGISLATION Licence conditions may include: - determination of fishing area, periods and type and method of fishing; - requirements concerning local landing and processing; - acceptance on board of Fiji trainees; - acceptance of Fiji observers on the vessel; - vessel to carry specified identification marks and position fixing equipment. (Marine Spaces Act 1977 S. 12) - Flag State to appoint national fisheries representatives through whom all communications to be made (R. 4) - National Fisheries representative to submit fishing plan covering proposed operations of boats flying his country's flag, including proposed fishing areas, estimated times of arrival and departure from zone, duration of plan, likely calls into port, proposed transhipments, proposed landings of catch, proposed support operations (R. 5) - Minister may require proportion of catch to be landed for processing at a port in Fiji; [R. 10(3)] - where licence conditions varied licence to be delivered for endorsement where required within 72 hours of entry	LEGISLATION Licence conditions may require reporting of catch and effort and vessel position reports. (Marine Spaces Act, 1977 S. 12) - Notification of proposed entry into zone to be given to Permanent Secretary at least 24 hours in advance (R. 18) - Notification to include details of vessel including name, call sign and country of registration, location of entry, port to which will proceed for inspection; fish on board (species, quantity and condition) (R. 18) Notification of proposed port calls to be given to Permanent Secretary at least 24 hours in advance (R. 21) - Vessel to maintain ship's log and separate fishing log in English in form supplied or approved by Permanent Secretary with daily entries of effort, method of fishing, areas, catch (R. 25) - Fishing log to be forwarded to Permanent Secretary within 72 hours of arrival in Fiji port (R. 25) - Vessel to report daily to Permanent Secretary, details of vessel and position; (R. 28)

TABLE C
COASTAL STATE REQUIREMENTS FOR FOREIGN FISHING

STATE	Foreign fishing vessel licence conditions (other than reporting requirements) [including observers, bonds, etc.]	Logbook and reporting requirements for foreign fishing
FIJI (cont'd)	of vessel into a Fiji port (R. 12) - Suspended or cancelled licences to be surrendered within 72 hours of receipt of notice (RR. 13,14) - Licence to be produced on demand (R. 15) - Licence to be maintained in good condition on board vessel (R. 16) - Compulsory port inspection on entry to zone and before departure, unless exempted by Permanent Secretary (R. 19,20) - No vessel to be used for fishing until clearance to fish given by Fisheries officer (R. 19) - Vessel to fly the flag of country of registration (R. 22) - Vessel to display call sign in specified form to be legible from sea and air (R. 23) - Vessel to display lights and shapes required by international Regulations for Preventing Collisions at Sea (R. 24) - Vessel to carry interpreter into English (R. 26) - Vessel to carry latest edition of International Code of Signals (R. 27) - Vessel to stow gear when in area not authorized to fish (R. 30) - Transhipment of catch at sea prohibited without prior authorization (R. 31) - Prohibition on discharge, etc. of substances liable to cause harm to fish or marine mammals, obstruct fishery equipment or become hazard to navigation (R. 32) - Vessel to allow boarding by observers and enforcement officers and to put into port on request for such purpose. Vessel to allow observers or Fisheries Officers full access to equipment, records and fish, allow observer to make tests, etc. provide assistance, food and accomodation. (R. 34)	- Vessel to report weekly quantity of each species of fish taken during previous week and area of catch (R. 28) - National Fisheries Representative to notify filling of quota (R. 29) (Marine Spaces (Foreign Fishing Vessels) Regulations 1979)

TABLE C
COASTAL STATE REQUIREMENTS FOR FOREIGN FISHING

STATE	Foreign fishing vessel licence conditions (other than reporting requirements) [including observers, bonds, etc.]	Logbook and reporting requirements for foreign fishing
FIJI (Cont'd)	- Vessel to comply with instructions of enforcement officers (R. 36) (Marine Spaces (Foreign Fishing Vessels) Regulations 1979) Note: -In accordance with the decision of the South Pacific Forum in August 1982 and as from 1 September 1983, no member of the Forum Fisheries Agency will licence a foreign vessel to fish for tuna in their fishing zone unless it is listed in good standing on the regional register maintained by the Forum Fisheries Agency. (Source: AFZ Information Bulletin Canberra May-July 1983)	
FINLAND	NO INFORMATION	
FRANCE	Conditions specified in measures for foreign fishing adopted by EEC. 12-mile coastal zone reserved in principle for local fishermen. Limited fishing by Belgium, Germany, Netherlands and UK in specified areas within the 6-12 mile coastal zone. (Council Regulation (EEC) No 170/83 of 25 January 1983)	Specified in measures for foreign fishing boats adopted by EEC.
FRENCH DEPENDENT TERRITORIES - NEW CALEDONIA	LEGISLATION -Licence to be carried on board. Conservation measures and other Regulations imposed as conditions of licence. (Resolution No. 163, 21 February 1979)	LEGISLATION Logbooks to be maintained recording catch per species, date and time of commencement and end of fishing operation, geographical position of catch, and fishing methods used. -Reports to be made on entering and departing Zone, at

TABLE C
COASTAL STATE REQUIREMENTS FOR FOREIGN FISHING

STATE	Foreign fishing vessel licence conditions (other than reporting requirements) [including observers, bonds, etc.]	Logbook and reporting requirements for foreign fishing
FRENCH DEPENDENT TERRITORIES - NEW CALEDONIA (Cont'd)		the time of any transhipment to another vessel and on arriving and leaving a port within the Zone. Reports to be address to Avispeche, Noumea and to include: name of vessel, call sign, licence number and date, time and geographical position. (Resolution No. 163, 21 February 1979)
GABON	LEGISLATION Trawl fishing regulated for all vessels in terms of maximum number of vessels, horsepower and fishing areas. (Decree No. 290 of 12 February 1979 Art. 1) Fishing in rivers, lagoons, estuaries and within 3 miles of coasts reserved to artisanal fisheries (Law No. 1/82 of 22 July 1982, Framework Law on Water and Forests, Art. 74)	LEGISLATION Vessel owner or operator to communicate statistical data on fishing operations to Water and Forest Administration in accordance with prescribed conditions. (Law No. 1/82 of 22 July 1982, Framework Law on Water and Forests, Art. 72)
GAMBIA	LEGISLATION Licence conditions may include: - conditions concerning location, method and conduct of fishing operations, size of catch allowed and conservation measures to be adopted; - requirements concerning landing, marketing and processing of catch; - requirements concerning construction of shore based facilities; - requirements concerning transfer of technology, carrying out of research or survey programmes and employment and training of local fishermen;	LEGISLATION Master of vessel to make such returns of catch at such times and in such form as Director may require. Master of vessel to make statistical returns as required. (Fisheries Act 1977 S. 15 and Fisheries Regulations, 1978, Reg. 10)

TABLE C

COASTAL STATE REQUIREMENTS FOR FOREIGN FISHING

STATE	Foreign fishing vessel licence conditions (other than reporting requirements) [including observers, bonds, etc.]	Logbook and reporting requirements for foreign fishing
GAMBIA (cont'd)	- protection of local and traditional fisheries; - no fish to be transhipped at sea unless expressly authorized by the Director; - fish to be landed only at authorized landing places. (Fisheries Act 1977 S. 21)	
GERMAN DEMOCRATIC REPUBLIC	NO INFORMATION	
GERMAN FEDERAL REPUBLIC	Licence conditions specified in measures for foreign foreign fishing adopted by EEC. 12-mile coastal zone reserved in principle for local fishermen. Limited fishing by Denmark, Netherlands and UK in specified areas within the 3-12 mile coastal zone. (Council Regulation (EEC) No 170/83 of 25 January 1983)	Specified in measures for foreign fishing boats adopted by EEC.
GHANA	LEGISLATION Catch required to be landed and/or processed locally. Fishing by foreign vessels prohibited except for tuna fishery. Licences may be issued in respect of tuna fishing vessels where vessel is: (a) at least 50% locally owned; or (b) owned by company having at least 50% share owned by nationals; or (c) on charter to local person or company and charter agreement confers option to purchase within 3 years	LEGISLATION Written returns to be submitted concerning the operations of the vessel as required by the licencing officer. (Fisheries Decree 1979 S. 8)

TABLE C
COASTAL STATE REQUIREMENTS FOR FOREIGN FISHING

STATE	Foreign fishing vessel licence conditions (other than reporting requirements) [including observers, bonds, etc.]	Logbook and reporting requirements for foreign fishing
GHANA (cont'd)	and adequate provisions made for training and transfer of skills and expertise, and adequate arrangements made for supply of ice that will not prejudice supply to local fleet. All catch and fish load of licensed tuna vessels must be landed in Ghana before any transhipment or export thereof. No black skipjack tuna to be transhipped or exported. Permission to export required for all species of tuna from licensed vessels. At least 10% of designated species of tuna landed in Ghana to be offered for sale to local canneries (skipjack; yellow fin; big eye; albacore). Vessels to observe requirements concerning identification marking. (Fisheries Decree 1979 S. 7)	
GREECE	Licence conditions specified in measures for foreign foreign fishing adopted by EEC. 12-mile coastal zone reserved in principle for local fishermen. (Council Regulation (EEC) No 170/83 of 25 January 1983)	Specified in measures for foreign fishing boats adopted by EEC.
GRENADA	LEGISLATION Permit may contain conditions concerning fishing areas, quantities of fish permitted to be taken, method of fishing, periods of time, conditions respecting the landing of fish, permitted ports for landing catch, permitted use of catch etc. (Marine Boundaries Act 1978) (New Legislation under consideration)	

TABLE C

COASTAL STATE REQUIREMENTS FOR FOREIGN FISHING

STATE	Foreign fishing vessel licence conditions (other than reporting requirements) [including observers, bonds, etc.]	Logbook and reporting requirements for foreign fishing
GUATEMALA	LEGISLATION -Vessels operating under licence types A or B must be registered in Guatemalan port within period prescribed. -Foreign vessels may be chartered for fishing for a maximum period of 6 months. -Encouragement is given to landings and processing through the level of fees and royalty payments. -Vessels operating under licence types A or B to land all catch at base port and process when at their own plants. -Vessels operating under licence types A or B to distribute by sale in the country 60% of fish caught and 10% of shrimp caught. -Vessels operating under licence type C may operate to mother ships, provided these are registered in Guatemala subject to increased charges for dockage. -Legal agents or representatives of the owner to be maintained in the State during the period of the fishing operations for vessels operating under licence types B or C. -Bonds to be deposited to guarantee performance of legal obligations for vessels operating under licence types B or C (Q. 2 000 - 5 000). (Decree 1470 of 1961) -By-catch from shrimp operations to be landed in accordance with prescribed percentages for vessels operating under licence types A or B. (Decree No. 1470 of 1961)	LEGISLATION Notice to be given of dates of sailing to Port Captain who will telegraph Department of Fisheries for vessels operating under licence types B or C. Vessel owners to notify Port Captain on sailing whether will be fishing for shrimp of other species. Inspectors to inform Department of Fisheries of sailings and landings of each boat, giving details of the capacity of the boat and quantities of fish taken. Persons or enterprises operating under licence types A or B to inform municipality and Department of Fisheries monthly of quantity of products received and processed. (Decree No. 1470 of 1961)

TABLE C

COASTAL STATE REQUIREMENTS FOR FOREIGN FISHING

STATE	Foreign fishing vessel licence conditions (other than reporting requirements) [including observers, bonds, etc.]	Logbook and reporting requirements for foreign fishing
GUINEA	LEGISLATION (Code de la pêche maritime, 1985, et Règlement général d'application, 1985) -Access agreements to include provision establishing responsibility of foreign country or other entity to take necessary measures to ensure compliance by its vessels with agreement and fishing laws (CPM, art. 12) -Apart from general conditions provided for in Fishing Code and regulations, conditions which may be specified in a licence may include (CPM, art. 26): -type and fishing methods and related authorized activities; -authorized fishing areas; -species, size and quantities of fish and restrictions regarding incidental catch. -Industrial fishing vessels prohibited from operating within 12-mile limit (CPM, art. 31). -Gear to be stowed when vessels in areas where not authorized to fish (CPM, art. 37 and RGA, art. 19) -Vessels may be required to call at Conakry for prefishing inspection (RGA, art. 11). -Transshipments and support operations to be specially authorized by Minister (CPM, art. 30 and RGA art. 12). -Vessels may be required to display identification marks (CPM, art. 36 and RGA, art. 18). -Vessels may be required to take observers on board and provide food, accommodation and working facilities (CPM, art. 18 and RGA, 20). -Catch of any marine mammal forbidden (CPM, art. 34). -Minimum mesh size for demersal trawling of 60 mm (RGA, arts. 13 and 14).	LEGISLATION (Code de la pêche maritime, 1985, et Règlement général d'application, 1985) -Foreign vessels may be required : -to fill in logbooks (CPM, art. 39 et RGP art. 17); -to report location and time of entry into EEZ limits and position at intervals as required (CPM, art. 40). -All vessels obliged to supply monthly returns of catch (CPM, art. 38 and RGA, art. 16).

TABLE C
COASTAL STATE REQUIREMENTS FOR FOREIGN FISHING

STATE	Foreign fishing vessel licence conditions (other than reporting requirements) [including observers, bonds, etc.]	Logbook and reporting requirements for foreign fishing
GUINEA (Cont'd)	-Foreign shipowners may be obliged to subscribe an insurance or contribute to a special fund to compensate artisanal fishermen for damages caused during fishing operations (CPM, art. 35) -Foreign shipowners may be required to have a permanent agent in Guinea (RGA, art. 3). AGREEMENTS *Agreement with AMOPESCA, 1 April 1980 - 6 vessels of a global tonnage of 4 518 allowed to operate; - fishing zones and minimum mesh size; - fishing vessels to embark at least 25 per cent Guinean crew (financial charges to be born by Amopesca) AGREEMENTS *Agreement with Spain, 1982 (Effective 1 November 1982 to 1 November 1983) A Spanish freezer trawler to undertake exploratory voyage in Guinea Waters for one month to determine state of marine resources, present levels and potentials for exploitation of Cephalopods and Crustacea. A Guinean scientist to be on board. (Source: La Pêche maritime November 1982 and January 1983)	
GUINEA BISSAU	LEGISLATION Licence required (Act No. 3-78 of 19 May 1978, Art. 4) Annual licences may be issued to foreigners if nationals not able to meet market demand. (Decree No. 209 of 1913 Art. 182)	AGREEMENTS *Agreement with EEC, 1980 (as extended 28 March 1983, valid until March 1986) Reports Vessel to send, at least once every three months, statement of catch to the national fisheries authorities; it

TABLE C
COASTAL STATE REQUIREMENTS FOR FOREIGN FISHING

STATE	Foreign fishing vessel licence conditions (other than reporting requirements) [including observers, bonds, etc.]	Logbook and reporting requirements for foreign fishing
GUINEA BISSAU (cont'd)	AGREEMENTS *Agreement with EEC, 27 Feb 1980 (as extended 28 Mar 1983, valid until March 1986) Licence not transferable. Vessels may be obliged to land a proportion of catch at ports in Guinea Bissau. Trawlers may be obliged to employ nationals up to 25 per cent of the crew. Nationals to be employed either on board the tuna boats or in suitable positions ashore. Training grants to be given to nationals of Guinea Bissau in the Member States establishments. (Council Regulations (EEC) Nos. 2213/80 & 707/83)	should include date, name of vessel, nationality of vessel tonnage (G.R.T.) engine rating, fishing methods used, area, number of fishing operations, number of fishing hours, species caucht and port of landing Logbook Master to keep logbook on board vessel and supply following information to the national fisheries authorities on monthly basis: month, name of vessel, nationality of vessel, engine rating in H.P., gross registered tonnage, fishing methods used, port of landing, statistical table of catches. (Council Regulation (EEC) No. 2213/80) (Council Regulation (EEC) No. 707/83)
GUYANA	LEGISLATION Encouragement given to landings and processing through the level of licence fees. Minister may designate countries allowed to fish and areas and quantities to be fished. (Maritime Boundaries Act 1977, S. 25) AGREEMENTS *Agreement with Barbados of 2 October 1978 - Establishment of fishing zones and fishing seasons - Each vessel to land 4 000 pounds of by-catch, 50 per cent of shrimp and 50 per cent of fin fish at Georgetown - Maximum of 20 vessels allowed; Vessels not to exceed 26 metres in length; - Minimum weight of shrimp specified (no more than 8 % of shrimp over 51 to the pound and no more than 1% over 70 to the pound); - Specified documents and information to be produced in	AGREEMENTS *Agreement with Barbados of 20 October 1978 -Each Barbados vessel to record in a fishing log book to be furnished by the Government of the Republic of Guyana information on the catch, the fishing operations and biological data relating to the catching of shrimp in the fishing areas. -Each Barbados vessel to submit, at the end of 3 month period, to the authorities of Guyana, information relating to the shrimp processed at the end of each trip. *Agreement with Suriname, April 1979 Vessels required to report when entering and leaving the fishery zone, and to report daily position. Fishing log to be completed; information to be compiled for each trip and to be submitted to Guyanese authorities at the end of each period of 3 months.

TABLE C
COASTAL STATE REQUIREMENTS FOR FOREIGN FISHING

STATE	Foreign fishing vessel licence conditions (other than reporting requirements) [including observers, bonds, etc.]	Logbook and reporting requirements for foreign fishing
GUYANA (Cont'd)	English or in a certified English translation, including registration certificate, certificate of seaworthiness, insurance certificate, 5 recent photographs of the vessel in profile, port of registry, port where operations are based, maximum speed of vessel in knots, navigational equipment, radio types and frequencies; - Detailed provisions relating to the display of identification code numbers. *Agreement with Suriname, April 1979 - Fishing for shrimp stocks by Surinamese vessels seawards of the 19 fathoms isobath. - Up to 30 Surinamese trawlers allowed to catch 625 metric tons of shrimp; by-catch to be retained by fishing vessels. - Surinamese authorities to provide specified information on vessel and owner/operator, including photographs of the vessel, port of registry, maximum speed, capacity, navigational equipment, etc. - Vessels to display identification numbers according to detailed provisions laid down in Annex. - Minimum mesh size laid down. *Agreement with Jamaica, 1982 Jamaican fleet issued licence to fish in Guyana waters. Part of catches to be sold to local processing factories. (Source: Eurofish Report, 24 February 1983 & Government Reply 21 February 1983)	
HAITI	LEGISLATION Foreign flag vessels operating in national waters must: -obtain concession contract; -hold permit or licence; -present documents of registration, nationality, sanitation, identification of vessel, health of crew. (Art 17)	LEGISLATION Log books to be maintained specifying quantities of fish taken, description of species and fishing areas. Six monthly report to be made on catch landed. (Decree of 27 October 1978 (Art. 69).

TABLE C
COASTAL STATE REQUIREMENTS FOR FOREIGN FISHING

STATE	Foreign fishing vessel licence conditions (other than reporting requirements) [including observers, bonds, etc.]	Logbook and reporting requirements for foreign fishing
HAITI (Cont'd)	-Owner to hold fishing permit. (art. 19, 20) -products of fishing to be landed first in Haiti even if destined for export; (Art. 24) -No vessel over 3 tons to fish within 3 miles of coast(34) -Only locals have right to fish in territorial waters (12 miles) and internal waters (Art. 36) -Concessions ans permits may only be issued to companies formed under laws of Haiti and having head office there, with at least 51% voting capital subscribed by Haitiens, bank guarantee of 25% of value of investment. (Art 64) -Persons fishing in territorial waters must take only authoized species in determined zones, respect quotas, accept Haitiens as trainees on board, submit to any control measures deemed useful by authorized fisheries officers. (Art 69) (Decree of 27 October 1978 Art. 69)	
HONDURAS	LEGISLATION State to determine under sovereign powers allowable catch taking into account objective of optimum utilization. Priority to requirements of Honduran people. Surplus available for foreign fishing under licence or permit. Legislation to be issued regarding issue of licence, payment of fees and other matters listed in Art. 62 of Draft Convention on the Law of the Sea (Informal Text) (Decree No. 921 of 28 April 1980). No foreign fishing for commercial purposes in territorial sea. (Fisheries Law, Decree No 154 of 9 June 1959 Art. 20, 29) Note: New legislation under consideration	

TABLE C
COASTAL STATE REQUIREMENTS FOR FOREIGN FISHING

STATE	Foreign fishing vessel licence conditions (other than reporting requirements) [including observers, bonds, etc.]	Logbook and reporting requirements for foreign fishing
ICELAND	LEGISLATION General prohibition on fishing by foreign vessels within the fishery limits except under bilateral agreement. (Regulations concerning the fishery limits off Iceland of July 15, 1975 Art. 2; and Law No. 41 of 1 June 1979 concerning the territorial sea, the Economic Zone and the Continental Shelf)	LEGISLATION Daily reports to be made on position. (1975 agreement with German Federal Republic 1976 agreement with Norway). Fisheries statistics to be forwarded to Fisheries Association of Iceland in form and manner prescribed. (Regulations concerning the fishery limits off Iceland, 1975 Art. 5; Law No. 55 of 27 June 1941 concerning catch and fisheries reports).
INDIA	LEGISLATION -Licence application details specified (R. 3) -Licences issued for any of following activities; commercial fishing, transshipping fish or supplies, processing fish, transporting fish from grounds, landing fish, purchasing bait, supplies, fuel etc. (R. 3) -Licence for foreign vessel valid for period specified(R.4 -Licensee to pay fees at time of delivery of licence.(R.5) -Vessel to engage only in activities authorized by licence -Activities to be carried out only within authorized areas and during authorized periods; (R. 5) -Foreign members of crew to be employed only after clearance by Central Government (R. 5) -Vessel to fish only for authorized stocks and authorized quantities; no fishing for catches listed as prohibited. -Crew not to discard substantial quantities caught in excess of authorized quantities, but retain on board, record and surrender as directed by authorized officer (R. 5) -crew not to fish except with fishing equipment and gear authorized in licence (R. 5)	LEGISLATION Master of vessel to give 24 hours prior notice to the authorised officer of entry into zone, location of entry, approximate schedule of activities to be conducted. (R. 5) Notification to be given of time and location of commencement of fishing, time and location of any temporary departure from the fishing grounds for the purpose of embarking or disembarking observer or for call at an Indian port or any other temporary departure from the fishing grounds, time and position of return to the fishing grounds following temporary departure; time and position at which vessel leaves the zone and ceases fishing. (R.5) Written records to be maintained on daily basis of fishing effort, catch, species size and weight, transshipment and processing. (R.5) -Data to be kept on quantity of fish caught in excess of permitted quantity. (R.5) Written records to be kept of any other information that

TABLE C
COASTAL STATE REQUIREMENTS FOR FOREIGN FISHING

STATE	Foreign fishing vessel licence conditions (other than reporting requirements) [including observers, bonds, etc.]	Logbook and reporting requirements for foreign fishing
INDIA (Cont'd)	-Transporting of fish allowed only as specified in licence -Vessel to have on board equipment and fishing gear, including communications equipment described in licence as "required equipment" (R. 5) -Where not authorized to fish, vessel to stow gear (R. 5) -Where vessel required to carry out programmes of sampling observation, research, master to comply with instructions. -Master to take observers on board if required, (R. 5) -master to take all reasonable precautions for safety of observers boarding or leaving ship. (R. 5) -observers to be provided with food and accomodation if on board for more than 4 hours. (R. 5) -master to arrange communication facilities for observer and provide other assistance, including access to position -fixing equipment (R. 5) -master of vessel to proceed to port or place at sea for inspection if required. (R. 5) -master to comply with directions given by authorized officer; international code of signals to be used (R. 5) -vessel to fly flag of flag state (R. 5) -Identifying letters and numbers to be displayed in place clearly visible from air and sea in white markings on black at least 1 metre in height for vessels over 20 mteres or otherwise half metre in height to be maintained legible -Licensee when so required to make arrangements for training of Indian crew and personnel on board vessel (R. 5) -additional conditions may be specified in licence.(R. 5) -Licence to be displayed on board (R. 9) -Vessel not to cause damage to Indian fishing vessels, gear, etc, wilfully or through gross negligence (R.10) -Vessel not to commence fishing operations before cleared by Coast Guard (R.11)	may be prescribed. (<u>Maritime Zones of India (Regulation of Fishing by Foreign Vessels) Rules, 1982.</u>)

TABLE C
COASTAL STATE REQUIREMENTS FOR FOREIGN FISHING

STATE	Foreign fishing vessel licence conditions (other than reporting requirements) [including observers, bonds, etc.]	Logbook and reporting requirements for foreign fishing
INDIA (Cont'd)	-Vessel not to fish in territorial waters unless permitted -Vessel not to carry explosives, poisonous substances, etc -Vessel not to destroy or abondon gear to avoid detection -Application to include name and adress of person resident in India who is authorized to represent licensee for purpose of providing liaison with Government .(R.3) (Maritime Zones of India (Regulation of Fishing by Foreign Vessels) Rules, 1982. CONTROLS OVER TRANSIT BY UNLICENSED VESSELS -Fishing gear of unlicensed vessels to be kept stowed in prescribed manner when transitting zone. (S. 7) Where any foreign vessel found in maritime zone and fish-gear not properly stowed, or fish is found on board, it shall be presumed unless the contrary is proved, that the vessel was used for fishing within the zone. (S. 22) (Maritime Zones of India (Regulation of Fishing by Foreign Vessels) Act 1981) -Method of stowage of gear includes stowage below deck of all gear, or otherwise moved from where normally and rend-not readily available for fishing, disconnecting of nets, lines, trawlboards, etc. from towing lines. (R. 14) (Maritime Zones of India (Regulation of Fishing by Foreign Vessels) Rules, 1982.	
INDONESIA	LEGISLATION Licence required. Conditions may include restrictions regarding fishing regions and types of tish or other marine products	LEGISLATION Owner of vessel given fishing permit to submit a quarterly report to Directorate General of Fisheries as result of fishing operation including total catch,

TABLE C
COASTAL STATE REQUIREMENTS FOR FOREIGN FISHING

STATE	Foreign fishing vessel licence conditions (other than reporting requirements) [including observers, bonds, etc.]	Logbook and reporting requirements for foreign fishing
INDONESIA (Cont'd)	authorized. Special conditions may be made regarding e.g. employment of foreigners in crew. Foreign licence holder must have local representative in Indonesia. (Coastal Fishery Ordinance, 1927) Permit required (valid 3 months) (Circular note No. 1187/80/29) Note: New legislation enacted dealing with licensing of foreign fishing operations, but texts not yet received. Government Regulation No. 15/1984 - Management of Living Resources in Indonesia's EEZ; Ministererial Decree No 473a 1985 relating to the total allowable catch in the Indonesian EEZ; Ministerial Decree No 475/1985 on licensing for foreign individual or foreign legal bodies engaged in fishing in the Indonesian EEZ; Ministerial Decree No. 477/1985 on fees charged to foreign individual or foreign legal bodies engaged in fishing in the Indonesian EEZ; Ministerial Decree No. 476/1985 on the check points for fishing vessels having licence to engage in fishing in the Indonesian EEZ; Law No 9/1985 - The Fisheries Law.	species, area, trip) within 1 month after the expiration the fishing permit. (Form A1 - Application for fishing permit. Declaration of the President of the Republic concerning the Exclusive Economic Zone of Indonesia, March 1980)
IRAN	LEGISLATION Fishing by foreign vessels prohibited except under contract or agreement already signed. Requirements concerning refrigeration equipment and handling of fish. Mesh size and species size limitations for shrimp and finfish (Arts. 14-26) closed seasons and areas (Arts. 27-31) (Temporary regulations for catching fish, shrimp and other sea animals, of 2 December 1973)	

TABLE C

COASTAL STATE REQUIREMENTS FOR FOREIGN FISHING

STATE	Foreign fishing vessel licence conditions (other than reporting requirements) [including observers, bonds, etc.]	Logbook and reporting requirements for foreign fishing
IRAQ	NO INFORMATION	
IRELAND	Licence conditions specified in measures for foreign fishing operations adopted by EEC. 12-mile coastal zone reserved in principle for local fishermen. Limited fishing by Belgium, France, Germany, Netherlands and UK in specified areas within the 6-12 mile coastal zone. (Council Regulation (EEC) No 170/83 of 25 January 1983)	Specified in measures for foreign fishing boats adopted by EEC.
ISRAEL	NO INFORMATION	
ITALY	Licence conditions specified in measures for foreign fishing operations adopted by EEC. 12-mile coastal zone reserved in principle for local fishermen. (Council Regulation (EEC) No 170/83 of 25 January 1983)	Specified in measures for foreign fishing boats adopted by EEC.
IVORY COAST	LEGISLATION - Number of foreign vessels authorized to fish in territorial sea limited to 25. (Order No. 720 of 17 April 1968 Art. 1) - Ministerial authorization required for sardine boats and longlines which must be less than 7 years old (Order No. 720, Art. 4) - Special authorization required for shrimps trawlers (Order No. 1067 of 13 May 1970, Art. 1)	

TABLE C
COASTAL STATE REQUIREMENTS FOR FOREIGN FISHING

STATE	Foreign fishing vessel licence conditions (other than reporting requirements) [including observers, bonds, etc.]	Logbook and reporting requirements for foreign fishing
JAMAICA	No licensed foreign fishing at present: New legislation for EEZ now under consideration	
JAPAN	LEGISLATION Allowable catch by foreign fishing limited on the basis of resource trends supported by proper scientific evidence, overall catch limits and actual situation with respect to local and foreign fishing. Legislation excludes highly migratory species from the exclusive management authority of Japan but includes anadromous species spawning in national waters throughout their migratory range. Vessel to bear identification marks. Permit to be kept on board of vessel. (Law on Provisional Measures relating to the Fishing Zone, 1977)	
JORDAN	Fishing forbidden without an authorization. Details of granting authorizations to be dealt with by decision of the Minister. (Agrarian Law No 20 of 1973, Art 182; 184) NO FURTHER INFORMATION	
KAMPUCHEA	NO INFORMATION	
KENYA	LEGISLATION Unspecified at the discretion of the Director of Fisheries. (Fish Protection (Fishing by non-Kenya Citizens) Rules L.N. 360/1964) Note: New legislation under consideration	

TABLE C
COASTAL STATE REQUIREMENTS FOR FOREIGN FISHING

STATE	Foreign fishing vessel licence conditions (other than reporting requirements) [including observers, bonds, etc.]	Logbook and reporting requirements for foreign fishing
KIRIBATI	LEGISLATION -Foreign fishing permits subject to conditions prescribed or endorsed on permit by Chief Fisheries Officer.(S. 5(4)) -Fishing gear to be stowed where vessel not authorised to fish (S. 5(6)) (Fisheries Ordinance 1977) AGREEMENTS *Agreement with Japan, (Federation of Japan Tuna Fisheries Cooperative Associations), August 1984, valid 1 Sept 1984 thru 31 Aug 1985) (longline and pole and line) Members of association to comply with Kiribati fishery law Gov. may exclude areas to protect local fishery operations Procedures for application for registration specified Vessels holding registration can submit applcation for licences. Licences valid for one trip. Licence to be carried on board and produced on demand, where issued when at sea, number of licence sufficient -Purse-seine prohibited unless notice to contrary given -Fishing in 12 mile territorial sea prohibited -Fishing within 1.5 miles of any Fish Aggregating Device installed by Government prohibited -All vessels to display radio call signs or signal letters on top and both sides amidships where clearly discernible from air and sea; letters and numbers at least 1 metre high x 40 cms wide in contrasting colours; registration number if no radio call sign; name in English on bow and stern of vessel -Observers authorized by Government to be permitted on board at ports where voyage commences or in fishery limits -Observers to be provided with normal rations accomodation and medical care equal to vessel officers, at vessels cost -Observers to be given access to communications and position fixing equipment, charts, other facilities and catch	AGREEMENTS **Agreement with Japan, (Federation of Japan Tuna Fisheries Cooperative Associations) 1984, -Vessel to keep on board up-to-date catch reports (catch Report Form) maintained on a daily basis; -Must produce catch reports for inspection on demand; -Signed catch report forms to be sent to Chief Fisheries Officer no later than 45 days after completion of trip -Vessel to report by telex entry into and departure from zone; Weekly position and catch report to be made each Wednesday while in fishery limits in specified form -Vessel to report within 48 hours of completion of trip

TABLE C
COASTAL STATE REQUIREMENTS FOR FOREIGN FISHING

STATE	Foreign fishing vessel licence conditions (other than reporting requirements) [including observers, bonds, etc.]	Logbook and reporting requirements for foreign fishing
KIRIBATI (Cont'd)	-An agent to be maintained by Organizations in Kiribati, authorized to receive and respond to any legal process concerning licensed vessels *Agreement with Sobryflot (USSR) 1985 valid for 1 year -Vessels authorized to fish for tuna and tuna-like species by purse-seine and longlining only -Only vessels listed in good standing on FFA regional register eligible to apply for permit -Application procedures specified -Company to ensure that permitted vessels comply with provisions of Agreement, permit and Ordinance -Permit to be displayed in wheelhouse and produced on demand; number suffices where vessel at sea at time issue -All vessels to display radio call signs or signal letters on top and both sides amidships where clearly discernible from air and sea; letters and numbers at least 1 metre high x 40 cms wide in contrasting colours; registration number if no radio call sign; name in English on bow and stern of vessel -Observers authorized by Government to be permitted on board at ports where voyage commences or in fishery limits -Observers to be provided with normal rations accomodation and medical care equal to vessel officers, at vessels cost -Observers to be given access to communications and position fixing equipment, charts, other facilities and catch -Fishing in 12 mile terrritorial sea prohibited -Fishing within 1.5 miles of any Fish Aggregating Device installed by Government prohibited -Permit issued subject to provisions of Fisheries Ordinance and regulations made thereunder Note: -In accordance with the decision of the South Pacific Forum in August 1982 and as from 1 September 1983, no	*Agreement with Sobryflot (USSR) 1985 -Vessel to report by telex entry into and departure from zone; Weekly position and catch report to be made each Thursday while in fishery limits in specified form -Vessel to keep on board up-to-date catch reports (catch Report Form) maintained on a daily basis; -Must produce catch reports for inspection on demand; -Signed catch report forms to be sent to Chief Fisheries Officer no later than 45 days after completion of trip -On completion landing, discharge or transhipment of catch, master to adise Government of total weight and value of catch by species, within 45 days

TABLE C
COASTAL STATE REQUIREMENTS FOR FOREIGN FISHING

STATE	Foreign fishing vessel licence conditions (other than reporting requirements) [including observers, bonds, etc.]	Logbook and reporting requirements for foreign fishing
KIRIBATI (Cont'd)	member of the Forum Fisheries Agency will licence a foreign vessel to fish for tuna in their fishing zone unless it is listed in good standing on the regional register maintained by the Forum Fisheries Agency. (Source: AFZ Information Bulletin Canberra May-July 1983)	
KOREA DEMOCRATIC REPUBLIC	NO INFORMATION	
REPUBLIC OF KOREA	LEGISLATION Prohibition of foreign fishing activities within a 12-mile zone (territorial sea). Licence required for foreign fishing activities in the fishing resource protection zone. Authorization by National Assembly required for issue of licences for foreign fishing boats even if companies constituted under Korean laws. Limitation of fishing areas, fishing seasons and species which may be fished. Regulations concerning gear. Catch to be landed in Korean ports. Foreign vessels to post bonds to guarantee performance of licence conditions. (Fisheries Law and Enforcement Decree) NO FOREIGN FISHING IN PRACTICE	LEGISLATION Periodical reports to be made to Administrator of the Fisheries Office.

TABLE C
COASTAL STATE REQUIREMENTS FOR FOREIGN FISHING

STATE	Foreign fishing vessel licence conditions (other than reporting requirements) [including observers, bonds, etc.]	Logbook and reporting requirements for foreign fishing
KUWAIT	LEGISLATION Licence from Directorate of Fisheries Resources required No conditions specified (Ministerial Decree No 19/1980 on Foreign Fishing Vessels)	LEGISLATION
LEBANON	NO INFORMATION	
LIBERIA	LEGISLATION -Licence required -Licenced vessels to be marked with official registration number issued by Division of Fisheries under supervision. -Fishing areas and effort liable to be restricted. -Observers may be placed on board licenced vessels; -All catch to be landed in Liberia and vessels must be physically based in Liberia. -Life saving gear to be carried (Revised Fishing Rules and regulations, 1973 as amended)	LEGISLATION -Commercial fishermen to submit quarterly report on monthly basis of catch and landing to Division of Fisheries on 28th day of last month of each quarter. -Reports to indicate tonnage (boxes) of fish landed; place where caught; species; type of gear; approx. value of catch. -Processors to submit reports on similar basis indicating method of processing; kind, quantity and value of fish processed. (Revised Fishing Rules and regulations, 1973 as amended)
LIBYA	LEGISLATION Application to be submitted through Consul of flag State. Conditions concerning safety of vessel, crew conditions, etc. (Law No. 8 of 1962 regulating fishing).	
MADAGASCAR	LEGISLATION Same general requirements and system of licensing as national fishing. Restriction on number of trawlers authorized to operate in the same area.	LEGISLATION Monthly reports to be made of catch and effort (if not, licence may be suspended for 6 months) (Decree No. 71-238 of 18 May 1971 Art. 9-10)

TABLE C
COASTAL STATE REQUIREMENTS FOR FOREIGN FISHING

STATE	Foreign fishing vessel licence conditions (other than reporting requirements) [including observers, bonds, etc.]	Logbook and reporting requirements for foreign fishing
MADAGASCAR (Cont'd)	For large vessels, licenses are issued on the advice of a technical commission. For smaller vessels: quota for the total number of licences to be issued. Controls over fishing vessels and gear. (Decree No. 71-238 of 18 May 1971) Note: New Legislation under preparation AGREEMENTS *Agreement with EEC 1985 valid 3yrs renewable automatically for periods 2 years unless notice denunciation -Tuna boats to take on board observers at request Government; as general rule, observer not to be present for longer than time required to make spot checks on catches -Shipowners to be represented by agent in Madagascar -At request Government, vessels fishing deep-water crustaceans to sign on Malagasy scientist capable of analyzing results of reconnassance campaigns for first 18 months; thereafter a Malagasy fisherman to carry out role over and above his seaman's duties: Seaman to have access to places and documents necessary for his observer duties. -Shipowners to make payment of 10 ECU to Government for each observer/day: If ship leaves zone with observer, every step to be taken to ensure observer returns to Madagascar as soon as possible -Each vessel fishing for deepwater crustaceans to employ 1 Malagasy seaman; -Ocean-going tuna fleet to sign on 2 Malagasy seamen If Government has no applicants to propose, payment 50% wages to be used for training -Community vesssels to have access to all waters outside 2 nautical miles from coast -Vessels fishing for deepwater crustaceans not to fish at depths less than 200 m isobath. -Government and shipowners to lay down conditions for use of port facilities	AGREEMENTS *Agreement with EEC 1985 valid 3yrs -Vessels to communicate to Antsiranana radio station every 3 days while engaged in fishing activities in Madagascar fishing zone, giving position and catches -vessels to communicate at end of each trip the result of their catches -Government to forward to EEC delegate in Madagascar data on state of catches twice a year

TABLE C
COASTAL STATE REQUIREMENTS FOR FOREIGN FISHING

STATE	Foreign fishing vessel licence conditions (other than reporting requirements) [including observers, bonds, etc.]	Logbook and reporting requirements for foreign fishing
MALAYSIA	LEGISLATION Every international fishery agreement (access agreement) to include undertaking by government of contracting party to comply or ensure compliance by its fishing vessels with provisions of Fisheries Act. (S. 17) Application for foreign fishing vessel permit to be made to Director General through Malaysian agent who is to undertake legal and financial responsibility for activities to be carried out by vessel. (S.19) Director General may require payment of security (bond) which may be utilized to defray fine or claim resulting from activities of vessel. Conditions that may be imposed by Director General include authorized areas and periods; species, age, weight, quantity of fish to be retained on board, landed or transhipped; methods of fishing; types, numbers etc. of gear and mode of stowage; transfer, transhipment, landing and processing of fish; entry into ports for inspection or other purposes; statistical and reporting requirements (catch and position); conduct of research, sampling etc.; training and employment of Malaysians; keeping and displaying of permit on board; permanent marking of vessel; compliance with directions of Government craft; placing of observers; installation of transponders and navigational equipment; construction of shore-facilities; carriage of communications equipment, charts, etc.; protection of local fisheries and compensation for loss or damage; landing of all or part of catch in Malaysia; composition and nationality of crew; inspection of vessel and seaworthiness; fees royalties and other payments; maintainance of log and	LEGISLATION Permit conditions that may be imposed by Director General include statistical and reporting requirements (catch and position); (Fisheries Act, 1984 S. 19) CONTROLS OVER TRANSIT BY UNLICENSED VESSELS Master of foreign fishing vessel entering Malaysian fisheries waters for purpose of exercising right of innocent passage to notify entry by radio to an authorized officer giving name, flag state, location, route and destination of vessel, types and amount of fish on board and circumstances under which entering Malaysian fisheries waters. (S. 16) -Any fish or fishing gear found on board a foreign fishing vessel in Malaysian fishery waters is presumed to have been caught or used in those waters without a permit. -Radio call before entry into waters notifying that vessel exercising right of innocent passage, notifying route and quantity of fish on board, and showing proof that fish held in sealed hold, gear properly stowed and vessel traveeling through waters by shortest practicable route, sufficient to constitute defence. (S. 56) (Fisheries Act, 1984

TABLE C
COASTAL STATE REQUIREMENTS FOR FOREIGN FISHING

STATE	Foreign fishing vessel licence conditions (other than reporting requirements) [including observers, bonds, etc.]	Logbook and reporting requirements for foreign fishing
MALAYSIA (Cont'd)	sales records; other matters as considered necessary(S.19) CONTROLS OVER TRANSIT BY UNLICENSED VESSELS Foreign fishing vessel may enter Malaysian fisheries waters for purpose of exercising right of innocent passage in course of voyage to destination outside waters; passage includes stopping and anchoring only if vessel is in dis tress, for purpose of obtaining emergency medical assistance or to render assitance to persons, ships etc in danger or distress. Master entering Malaysian waters for such purposes to notify entry by radio. While in Malaysian waters, vessel to observe stowage of gear regulations, and return outside waters as soon as purpose of entry fulfilled. (S.16) (Fisheries Act, 1984) Trawl licences not issued to any wholly or partially foreign owned fishing boat which is less than 70 tons. They must fish in waters beyond 30 miles from coast. The use of beam trawl net is prohibited. (Regulation 4 (4), Term and Conditions of Licence for Trawl Fishing, 1982.	
MALDIVE ISLANDS	No foreign fishing allowed at present: New Legislation under consideration	
MALTA	LEGISLATION No landing of fresh fish in Malta without prior permission of Controller of Fisheries. Permit to land fish valid one day. Fish to be landed at wholesale fish market. (Fish Industry Act. 1953 S. 5)	LEGISLATION Holder of permit to land fish to furnish Controller of Fisheries with all information regarding origins, sale and disposal of fish. (Fish Industry Act, 1953 S. 5)

TABLE C
COASTAL STATE REQUIREMENTS FOR FOREIGN FISHING

STATE	Foreign fishing vessel licence conditions (other than reporting requirements) [including observers, bonds, etc.]	Logbook and reporting requirements for foreign fishing
MAURITANIA	LEGISLATION - Same conditions with respect to conservation measures, mesh sizes etc. as for national vessels AGREEMENTS *Many bilateral agreements concluded in the 1970's and early 1980's included provisions under which: -permitted fishing areas were assigned to foreign vessels on basis of their size; -certain proportion of catch was required to be landed and or processed; * Agreement with Senegal of 11 August 1983 with protocol -Senegalese vessels to take 35% of Mauritanian crews. * Agreement with the Republic of Korea of 1981, implementing procès-verbal of 3 May 1983 - All the catch landed in Nouhadibou but transshipment may take place in bay on certain conditions. - A number of Mauritanian nationals, varying according to size of vessles to be taken on board. -local fishermen to be trained on board foreign vessels; -scholarships to be granted to Mauritanian citizens; -observers to be taken on board. *Procès Verbal of 17 April 1980 -Tuna vessels allowed to operate only beyond 30 miles; but may "pursue" fish beyond this line; -Vessels to take on board 5 Mauritanian crew-members and one observer; -minimum mesh size specified. *Agreement with Spain, 1982 (effective 1 March 1982, valid 1 year) Up to 25 Spanish vessels to fish for octopus in Mauritania waters beyond 6-mile from coast. Nets to be used must be 60 mm mesh. Vessels to have on board two Mauritanians as crew members.	AGREEMENTS *Many bilateral agreements concluded in the 1970's required foreign fishing vessels to submit catch reports. * Agreement with Senegal of 11 August 1983 with protocol -Monthly returns of catch to be provided.

TABLE C
COASTAL STATE REQUIREMENTS FOR FOREIGN FISHING

STATE	Foreign fishing vessel licence conditions (other than reporting requirements) [including observers, bonds, etc.]	Logbook and reporting requirements for foreign fishing
MAURITIUS	LEGISLATION Licence conditions may include specifications regarding target species, size, weight fish, etc; the vessel, the fishing gear and fishing methods and the areas and amounts to be fished, closed seasons, and requiring local landing and processing of catch and training and employment of local nationals. (Maritime Zones (Fishing Licences) Regulations 1978 S. 5) Note: New legislation under consideration	
MEXICO	LEGISLATION Certain fisheries are reserved for national (cooperatives (sardines, shrimp, lobster). (Federal Law 1972, Art. 25) -Foreign fishing allowed only when total allowable catch for a species is greater than the capacity of national vessels (Decree in order to establish an EEZ, 1976, Art.8) -Permits granted valid for one trip. (Federal law 1972) -Fishing quotas - Restriction on catches. (Art. 13). -Local landing of catch by foreign fishing vessels prohibited. (Art. 37) -Foreign tuna fishing operations must maintain accredited representative in Mexico. (Source NMFS:IFR/81/69) -Vessel must leave zone within specified time limits. -Fishing of marine mammals not allowed. (Art. 37) -Technology used in fishing and processing to be made available to nationals free (Art. 37) -Bonds (cash deposits) must be posted to guarantee performance of legal obligations and payment of any fees (not to exceed 100 000 pesos [US$2 058]). (Art. 42) At least 50% of crew must be nationals (Art. 37) -Crew must be hired in Mexico, with wages and benefits	LEGISLATION Periodical reports to be made to the Fisheries Department (Federal Law on Fisheries Development, 1972)

TABLE C
COASTAL STATE REQUIREMENTS FOR FOREIGN FISHING

STATE	Foreign fishing vessel licence conditions (other than reporting requirements) [including observers, bonds, etc.]	Logbook and reporting requirements for foreign fishing
MEXICO (Cont'd)	equal to those of foreign crew if higher than national wages and benefits. (Art. 37) -No fishing of sardines for live bait in prohibited zone (Art. 37) -No commercial fishing in reserved zones. (Art. 37) (Vessels from countries granting equal conditions of reciprocity to Mexican vessels may be exempted from any of above requirements when national interests justify. (Federal Law on Fisheries Development, 1972)	
MONACO	NO INFORMATION	
MOROCCO	LEGISLATION Fishing in Moroccan waters reserved for vessels under Moroccan flag or operated by nationals or Moroccan companies (e.g.under Charter). (Act No. 1-73-211 of 2 March 1973, Art. 5) Trawl fishing for sardines permitted only beyond 3 miles in Mediterranean sea and beyond 12 miles in Atlantic. Fishing quotas closed seasons and gear limitations fixed under bilateral agreement. AGREEMENTS *Agreement with Spain 1977 contains provisions requiring moroccanization of "joint venture" fleet (50% after 5 years)].	

TABLE C
COASTAL STATE REQUIREMENTS FOR FOREIGN FISHING

STATE	Foreign fishing vessel licence conditions (other than reporting requirements) [including observers, bonds, etc.]	Logbook and reporting requirements for foreign fishing
MOZAMBIQUE	LEGISLATION -Minister of Industry and Energy empowered to establish conditions for licensed fishing operations. (Art. 2) -Every foreign vessel authorized to fish in jurisdictional waters must fly national flag and display registration number and must comply with the regulations laid down for fishing by national vessels. (Art. 4) -Any foreign vessel found fishing, preparing to fish or transshipping fish products is subject to inspection and control by the competent maritime authorities, which may cover fishing gear, fish caught, sonar records and logbooks. (Art. 5) CONTROLS OVER TRANSIT BY UNLICENSED FISHING VESSELS -Offence characterized as "fishing or preparing to fish" in jurisdictional waters without authorization. (Art. 2) -"Preparing to fish" defined as any activities of anchoring, mooring, stopping, laying to or following a zig-zag course in jurisdictional waters, where this is not motivatered by *force majeure*, such as damage, bad weather, strong currents, or other cause independent of the will of the owner, chartere, captain or other person responsible for the fishing vessel. Equally any vessel will be considered to be preparing to fish if signs are shown of recent or future use of its fishing gear. (Art. 1) (Law No. 8/78 of 22 April 1978)	LEGISLATION
NAMIBIA	-	

TABLE C
COASTAL STATE REQUIREMENTS FOR FOREIGN FISHING

STATE	Foreign fishing vessel licence conditions (other than reporting requirements) [including observers, bonds, etc.]	Logbook and reporting requirements for foreign fishing
NAURU	LEGISLATION Licence conditions may include: - determination of fishing area, periods and type and method of fishing; - requirements concerning local landing and processing; - acceptance on board of Nauruan trainees; - vessel to carry specified identification marks and position fixing equipment. (Marine Resources Act 1978, S. 7) Note: -In accordance with the decision of the South Pacific Forum in August 1982 and as from 1 September 1983, no member of the Forum Fisheries Agency will licence a foreign vessel to fish for tuna in their fishing zone unless it is listed in good standing on the regional register maintained by the Forum Fisheries Agency. (Source: AFZ Information Bulletin Canberra May-July 1983)	LEGISLATION Licence conditions may require reporting of catch and effort and vessel position reports. (Marine Resources Act 1978, S. 7)
NETHERLANDS	Licence conditions specified in measures for foreign fishing operations adopted by EEC. 12-mile coastal zone reserved in principle for local fishermen. Limited fishing by Belgium, Denmark, France, Germany and UK in specified areas within the 3-12 mile coastal zone. (Council Regulation (EEC) No 170/83 of 25 January 1983)	Specified in measures for foreign fishing boats adopted by EEC.
NETHERLANDS ANTILLES	NO INFORMATION	

TABLE C
COASTAL STATE REQUIREMENTS FOR FOREIGN FISHING

STATE	Foreign fishing vessel licence conditions (other than reporting requirements) [including observers, bonds, etc.]	Logbook and reporting requirements for foreign fishing
NEW ZEALAND	LEGISLATION Flag State to appoint national fisheries representatives through whom all communications to be made. (R. 4) National Fisheries representative to submit fishing plan covering proposed operations of boats flying his country's flag, including proposed fishing areas, estimated number of boats, estimated times of arrival and departure from zone, duration of plan, likely calls into port, proposed transhipments, proposed landings of catch, proposed support operations. (R. 5) Licences to be delivered for endorsement within 72 hours where conditions varied (R. 11) or surrendered within 72 hours where suspended or cancelled (R. 12, 13); Licence to be maintained in good condition on craft (R.16) Compulsory port inspection on entry to zone and before departure, unless exempted by D.G.,; no vessel to be used for fishing until clearance to fish given by an enforcement officer at port of inspection (R.19); Craft to fly the flag of country of registration. (R. 23) Craft to display call sign in specified form to be legible from sea and air. (R. 24) Licensed craft to display lights and shapes required by International Regs for Preventing Collisions at Sea (R.25) Craft to carry interpreters into English. (R. 27) Licensed craft to carry latest edition of International Code of Signals (R. 28) Restrictions on trawling and bottom lining in certain areas. (R. 31) Craft to stow gear when in area not authorized to fish. (R. 32)	LEGISLATION Notification of proposed entry into zone to be given to Director General at least 24 hours in advance. (R. 18) Notification to include details of craft, including name, call sign and country of registration, location of entry, port to which will proceed for inspection; fish on board (species, quantity and condition).(R. 18) Notification of proposed port calls to be given to D.G. at least 24 hours in advance. (R. 22) Craft to maintain ship's log and separate fishing log in English with daily entries of effort, method of fishing, areas, catch, by-catch discards. (R. 29) Fishing log to be forwarded to D.G. within 72 hours of arrival in N.Z. port. (R. 29) Licensed craft to report position daily (trawling, purse-seining and longlining) or weekly (others)(R.29) Catch (species, quantity and area) to be reported weekly (R. 29) National Fisheries Representative to report filling of country quota. (R. 30) (Exclusive Economic Zone (Foreign Fishing Craft) Regulations, 1978)

TABLE C

COASTAL STATE REQUIREMENTS FOR FOREIGN FISHING

STATE	Foreign fishing vessel licence conditions (other than reporting requirements) [including observers, bonds, etc.]	Logbook and reporting requirements for foreign fishing
NEW ZEALAND (cont'd)	Licensed foreign craft to steer at least 1/2 mile clear of set and marked gear (R. 33); Transhipment of catch at sea prohibited without prior authorization. (R. 34) Landing of catch in New Zealand prohibited without authorizations of D.G. (R. 35) Prohibition on discharge, etc. of substances, liable to cause harm to fish or marine mammals, obstruct fishing equipment or become hazard to navigation (R. 36) Craft to allow boarding by observers and enforcement officers, and to put into port for such purpose (R. 38); Craft to allow observers full access to equipment and records and fish on board, allow observers to make tests, observations and records as required, provide assistance and food and accomodation equivalent to that provided for officers (R. 38); Craft to comply with instructions of enforcement officers. (R. 40) (Exclusive Economic Zone (Foreign Fishing Craft) Regs 1978) Note: -In accordance with the decision of the South Pacific Forum in August 1982 and as from 1 September 1983, no member of the Forum Fisheries Agency will licence a foreign vessel to fish for tuna in their fishing zone unless it is listed in good standing on the regional register maintained by the Forum Fisheries Agency. (Source: AFZ Information Bulletin Canberra May-July 1983)	

TABLE C
COASTAL STATE REQUIREMENTS FOR FOREIGN FISHING

STATE	Foreign fishing vessel licence conditions (other than reporting requirements) [including observers, bonds, etc.]	Logbook and reporting requirements for foreign fishing
NEW ZEALAND DEPENDENT TERRITORIES - TOKELAU	LEGISLATION Conditions to be prescribed. (Territorial Sea and Exclusive Economic Zone, Act 1977, S.8 AGREEMENTS Note: Agreement between New Zealand (for Tokelau), Niue, Tuvalu and Western Samoa and the American Tuna Boat Association, 1983, AGREEMENT NO LONGER IN FORCE Note: -In accordance with the decision of the South Pacific Forum in August 1982 and as from 1 September 1983, no member of the Forum Fisheries Agency will licence a foreign vessel to fish for tuna in their fishing zone unless it is listed in good standing on the regional register maintained by the Forum Fisheries Agency. (Source: AFZ Information Bulletin Canberra May-July 1983)	
NEW ZEALAND ASSOCIATED STATES -COOK ISLANDS	LEGISLATION Licence conditions may include conditions relating to: - fishing areas; - authorized season, times, voyages for fishing; - species, size, age and quantities of fish; - fishing methods; - authorized fishing gear and storage requirements; - use, transfer, transhipment, landing, processing of catch; -entry into Cook Island ports;	LEGISLATION Licence conditions may include conditions relating to statistical and other information required to be given by foreign fishing craft to Ministry of Economic Services and natural Resources, including statistics relating to catch and effort and reports as to positions of the craft. Territorial Sea and Exclusive Economic Zone, 1977, S. 13

TABLE C

COASTAL STATE REQUIREMENTS FOR FOREIGN FISHING

STATE	Foreign fishing vessel licence conditions (other than reporting requirements) [including observers, bonds, etc.]	Logbook and reporting requirements for foreign fishing
NEW ZEALAND ASSOCIATED STATES -COOK ISLANDS (Cont'd)	-compensation for damage to local craft, gear or fish stocks; -fisheries research; -training and transfer of technology; -display of licence and marking of craft; -compliance with enforcement institutions; -observers; -carriage of transponders or other position fixing equipment and charts; etc. Territorial Sea and Exclusive Economic Zone Act 1977, S.13	
	Flag State to appoint national fisheries representatives through whom all communications to be made. (R. 4) National Fisheries representative to submit fishing plan covering proposed operations of boats flying his country's flag, including proposed fishing areas, estimated number of boats, estimated times of arrival and departure from zone, duration of plan, likely calls into port, proposed transhipments, proposed landings of catch, proposed support operations. (R. 5) Licences to be delivered for endorsement within 72 hours where conditions varied (R. 11) or surrendered within 72 hours where suspended or cancelled (R. 12, 13); Licence to be maintained in good condition on craft (R.16) Compulsory port inspection on entry to zone and before departure, unless exempted by D.G.,; no vessel to be used for fishing until clearance to fish given by an enforcement officer at port of inspection (R.19); Craft to fly the flag of country of registration. (R. 23) Craft to display call sign in specified form to be legible from sea and air. (R. 24) Licensed craft to display lights and shapes required by	Notification of proposed entry into zone to be given to Director General at least 24 hours in advance. (R. 18) Notification to include details of craft, including name, call sign and country of registration, location of entry, port to which will proceed for inspection; fish on board (species, quantity and condition).(R. 18) Notification of proposed port calls to be given to D.G. at least 24 hours in advance. (R. 22) Craft to maintain ship's log and separate fishing log in English with daily entries of effort, method of fishing, areas, catch, by-catch discards. (R. 29) Fishing log to be forwarded to D.G. within 72 hours of arrival in N.Z. port. (R. 29) Licensed craft to report position daily (trawling, purse-seining and longlining) or weekly (others)(R.29) Catch (species, quantity and area) to be reported weekly (R. 29) National Fisheries Representative to report filling of country quota. (R. 30) (Exclusive Economic Zone(Foreign Fishing Craft)Regs1979)

TABLE C

COASTAL STATE REQUIREMENTS FOR FOREIGN FISHING

STATE	Foreign fishing vessel licence conditions (other than reporting requirements) [including observers, bonds, etc.]	Logbook and reporting requirements for foreign fishing
NEW ZEALAND ASSOCIATED STATES -COOK ISLANDS (cont'd)	International Regs for Preventing Collisions at Sea (R.25) Craft to carry interpreters into English. (R. 27) Licensed craft to carry latest edition of International Code of Signals (R. 28) Restrictions on trawling and bottom lining in certain areas. (R. 31) Craft to stow gear when in area not authorized to fish. (R. 32) Licensed foreign craft to steer at least 1/2 mile clear of set and marked gear (R. 33); Transhipment of catch at sea prohibited without prior authorization. (R. 34) Landing of catch in New Zealand prohibited without authorizations of D.G. (R. 35) Prohibition on discharge, etc. of substances, liable to cause harm to fish or marine mammals, obstruct fishing equipment or become hazard to navigation (R. 36) Craft to allow boarding by observers and enforcement officers, and to put into port for such purpose (R. 38); Craft to allow observers full access to equipment and records and fish on board, allow observers to make tests, observations and records as required, provide assistance and food and accomodation equivalent to that provided for officers (R. 38); Craft to comply with instructions of enforcement officers. (R. 40) Exclusive Economic Zone (Foreign Fishing Craft) Regs 1979) Note: Agreement between New Zealand (for Tokelau), Niue, Tuvalu and Western Samoa and the American Tuna Boat Association, 1983, AGREEMENT NO LONGER IN FORCE	

TABLE C
COASTAL STATE REQUIREMENTS FOR FOREIGN FISHING

STATE	Foreign fishing vessel licence conditions (other than reporting requirements) [including observers, bonds, etc.]	Logbook and reporting requirements for foreign fishing
NEW ZEALAND ASSOCIATED STATES -COOK ISLANDS (cont'd)	Note: -In accordance with the decision of the South Pacific Forum in August 1982 and as from 1 September 1983, no member of the Forum Fisheries Agency will licence a foreign vessel to fish for tuna in their fishing zone unless it is listed in good standing on the regional register maintained by the Forum Fisheries Agency. (Source: AFZ Information Bulletin Canberra May-July 1983)	
NEW ZEALAND ASSOCIATED STATES - NIUE	LEGISLATION In granting licences, the Cabinet may attach such conditions as are provided for in the regulations. Territorial Sea and Exclusive Economic Zone, Act 1978, S 13 AGREEMENTS Note: Agreement between New Zealand (for Tokelau), Niue, Tuvalu and Western Samoa and the American Tuna Boat Association, 1983, AGREEMENT NO LONGER IN FORCE Note: -In accordance with the decision of the South Pacific Forum in August 1982 and as from 1 September 1983, no member of the Forum Fisheries Agency will licence a foreign vessel to fish for tuna in their fishing zone unless it is listed in good standing on the regional register maintained by the Forum Fisheries Agency. (Source: AFZ Information Bulletin Canberra May-July 1983)	

TABLE C

COASTAL STATE REQUIREMENTS FOR FOREIGN FISHING

STATE	Foreign fishing vessel licence conditions (other than reporting requirements) [including observers, bonds, etc.]	Logbook and reporting requirements for foreign fishing
NICARAGUA	LEGISLATION Total catch to be landed locally. No interference with domestic fishing. (Art. 12) Prohibition on commercial turtle fishing. Guarantee deposit of US$ 1 000 - 10 000 (Art. 22) (Special law on fishery exploitation, 1961).	
NIGERIA	LEGISLATION Fishing in territorial waters and exclusive economic zone reserved to Nigerian flag vessels. Foreign fishing allowed only under joint venture by vessels owned by the joint venture company. -Policy of Fisheries Department to licence only vessels not longer than 83 feet (25.3 meters) L.O.A. and not larger than 150 GRT Shrimp trawlers ideally not to be above 76 ft L.O.A. and not more than 100 GRT. If shrimp catch to be exported, necessary processing grading, packaging, freezing and storage while awaiting exportation should be land-based. Shrimps only need to be chilled on board for land-based processing. (Conditions under which a vessel may be granted permission or licence to fish in Nigerian Territorial Waters.) -Licence issued quarterly or yearly (Sea Fisheries Decree 1971 S. 3) -Prohibition on industrial fishing within 2 miles of coast -Provisions relating to the use of nets, trawls. -All the catch must be landed in port and no part of it may be exported or transhipped at sea. Vessels not to dump edible and marketable sea products at sea. Fish landed by shrimp trawlers must be at least 75% by weight of total landings. (Sea Fisheries (Fishing) Regulations 1972)	LEGISLATION Periodical returns to be made. (Sea Fisheries Decree, 1971 S. 6)

TABLE C
COASTAL STATE REQUIREMENTS FOR FOREIGN FISHING

STATE	Foreign fishing vessel licence conditions (other than reporting requirements) [including observers, bonds, etc.]	Logbook and reporting requirements for foreign fishing
NORWAY	LEGISLATION Foreign fishing (apart from Swedish and Danish) only in 12-200 mile zone. S.1 Licence shall apply to one specific vessel and is not transferable; licence to be carried on board vessel. (S. 4) Applications to be submitted for each individual vessel together with fishing plan in manner prescribed for each country. (S. 5) Rules for fishing by Norwegian vessels to apply to foreign vessels. (S. 6) Conditions may include vessel quotas, permitted fishing areas and gear, period of validity of the licence, species of fish for which the licence is valid. (S. 7) Licence to lapse when fishing quota for flag state harvested. (S. 7) Vessels to bear identification marks and fly national flag. (S. 12) Local landing of catch prohibited. -Vessel shall receive Norwegian inspectors and allow to remain during fishing operations and provide food, accommodation, assistance, information, access to storage space, radio or telex facilities, etc. at vessel's expense (S. 12). -Applications to be submitted for each individual vessel, together with fishing plan, in manner prescribed for each country. (S.6) (Regulations relating to foreign fishing, 13 May 1977). AGREEMENTS *Agreement with German Democratic Republic (of 28 January 1977) and with Poland (of 24 May 1977) valid through 1 Jan January 1987	LEGISLATION Notification to be made to Bergen office by telegram or telex (24 hours before commencement and ending of fishing. S. 9. Vessels fishing south of 62° N latitude to notify each time temporarily leaves or enters zone. S.9 Vessels assisting fishing fleet to notify Directorate of Fisheries each time they enter or leave zone. S.9 Director may require notification of when vessel crossing boundary lines for statistical areas. S. 9. Vessels to submit catch reports on catches brought on board in the zone: (a) weekly on days prescribed for flag state; (b) monthly through flag state authorities. Reports to contain number of fishing days, volume of catch in metric tons, live weight according to species and prescribed statistical areas (S. 10) Support vessels also to submit reports on quantities of different species received from each fishing vessel. (S. 10) (Regulations relating to foreign fishing; 13 May 1977) AGREEMENTS *Agreement with German Democratic Republic (of 28 Jan. 1977) and with Poland (May 1977) valid through Jan. 1987 -Foreign fishing vessels to enter daily data concerning fishing places, fishing effort and catch in logbooks that will be available for inspection at any time. -Each vessel to report arrival at the fishing area, to send at the end of the week a detailed report on catch, fishing time and other relevant information as further plan of operations.

TABLE C
COASTAL STATE REQUIREMENTS FOR FOREIGN FISHING

STATE	Foreign fishing vessel licence conditions (other than reporting requirements) [including observers, bonds, etc.]	Logbook and reporting requirements for foreign fishing
NORWAY (cont'd)	-German and Polish authorities to advise Norwegian authorities of names, registration numbers, fishing gear to be used and to provide other relevant information. Such information also to be given with regard to eventual provision and auxiliary vessels which accompany fishing vessels. -Foreign governments to ensure that vessels flying their flag comply with the provisions of the Agreement. AGREEMENTS *Agreement with EEC and Denmark on the Regulation of Fisheries in the Skagerrak and the Kattegat in 1983 Valid from 1 January to 31 December 1983. Total catches for Cod, Haddock, Whiting, Plaice and Herring is Skagerrak and Kattegat specified and allocated. Directed fishing for Herring permitted only for human consumption. The period of fishing, size of vessels, use of trawls, purse seines and pair trawls specified. (Council Regulation (EEC) No. 621/83)	
OMAN	LEGISLATION Minister to issue regulations prescribing, *inter alia*, conditions and terms of licences. (Art. 4) Foreign fishing boats entering harbour not to selll fish without licence from competent authority. (Art. 24) (Sultanic Decree No 53/81 promulgating the Law on Marine Fisheries and Conservation of Living Aquatic Resources) Fishing boats to affix serial number plates on both sides of vessel (Art. 25) (Ministerial Decree No. 3/82 on the Executive Regulations for the Marine Fisheries and Protection of Living Resources Law)	LEGISLATION Owners of fishing boats to maintain on board a fishing operations logbook. (Art. 29) Fishing professionals to provide competent authority with required data and statistics. (Art. 33) (Ministerial Decree No. 3/82 on the Executive Regulations for the Marine Fisheries and Protection of Living Resources Law)

TABLE C
COASTAL STATE REQUIREMENTS FOR FOREIGN FISHING

STATE	Foreign fishing vessel licence conditions (other than reporting requirements) [including observers, bonds, etc.]	Logbook and reporting requirements for foreign fishing
PAKISTAN	LEGISLATION Licence may be limited to a certain area. (S. 6) All fish taken in the zone shall be landed at ports having customs check post. (S. 16) Same rules and conditions apply to both local and foreign vessels. (S. 1) Conditions include conservation measures, closed seasons, etc. (S. 6) Vessels subject to navigational regulations. (Exclusive Fishery Zone (Regulation of Fishing) Act, 1975)	LEGISLATION Information on catch to be given. (S. 12) (Exclusive Fishery Zone - Regulation of Fishing Act, 1975.)
PANAMA	LEGISLATION Conditions subject to negotiation with boat owner. Catch quotas. No fishing for shrimp, pearl, mother pearl, anchovies or herring by non-domiciled foreigners. Local agent to be maintained.	LEGISLATION Periodical returns to be made. (Decree Law No. 17 of 1959, Art. 55)
PAPUA-NEW GUINEA	LEGISLATION - Licence may contain a condition that an officer shall be allowed to be on board and shall be provided with reasonable board and accomodation free of charge at all times or at any time while the boat is operating under the licence; (Fisheries Act, 1974 S. 7) - Vessel to bear designated identification marks on stern, on each side of bow and on top of wheel-house; - Fish taken on board a licensed boat not to be delivered or trans-shipped to any other boat without prior permission in writing from the licensing authority; - Licensee not to interfere with traditional fishing. (Fisheries Regulations 1975)	LEGISLATION - Minister empowered to make regulations providing for the furnishing of returns on fish catches and sales or disposal of catches. (Fisheries Act 1974, S. 22) - Licensed vessels to report entry into and departure from PNG waters and give periodic position reports while within PNG waters.

TABLE C

COASTAL STATE REQUIREMENTS FOR FOREIGN FISHING

STATE	Foreign fishing vessel licence conditions (other than reporting requirements) [including observers, bonds, etc.]	Logbook and reporting requirements for foreign fishing
PAPUA-NEW GUINEA (Cont'd)	AGREEMENTS *(Agreements with Federation of Japan Tuna Fisheries Cooperative Association, the National Federation of Fisheries Cooperative Association, the Japan Far Seas Purse-Seine Fishing Association, and the Federation of North Pacific District Purse-Seine Fisheries Cooperative Association (1981) - identification marks to be displayed on top of vessel where clearly discernible from air; - vessel name to be clearly printed; - technical observers to be placed; - authorized officers to be permitted to board; - association shall appoint and maintain agent in Port Moresby; - permitted to fish for all types of tuna and billfish. Note: -In accordance with the decision of the South Pacific Forum in August 1982 and as from 1 September 1983, no member of the Forum Fisheries Agency will licence a foreign vessel to fish for tuna in their fishing zone unless it is listed in good standing on the regional register maintained by the Forum Fisheries Agency. (Source: AFZ Information Bulletin Canberra May-July 1983)	AGREEMENTS *Agreements with Federation of Japán Tuna Association, National Federation of Fisheries Cooperative Association, Japan Far Seas Purse-Seine Fishing Association, Federation of North Pacific District Purse-Seine Fisheries Cooperative Association of Japan - 1981 - Entry to be notified 24 hours prior; - position of fishing vessel to be reported every Wednesday together with daily catch report for previous seven days; - daily catch record to be kept on board at all times; - departure to be notified 24 hours prior; - at time of departure, the vessel's position, amount of catch on board, the total amount of fish caught in the zone to be reported by telex; - 24 hours prior notice to transit prohibited area; - 24 hours notice for first entry where repeated entry and departure necessary on boundary and 24 hours of notice of final departure; - completed catch data form to be forwarded with 45 days of completion of trip.

TABLE C
COASTAL STATE REQUIREMENTS FOR FOREIGN FISHING

STATE	Foreign fishing vessel licence conditions (other than reporting requirements) [including observers, bonds, etc.]	Logbook and reporting requirements for foreign fishing
PERU	LEGISLATION Trawlers: -Foreign flag trawlers may operate in Peruvian waters under agreements concluded with the State through its public enterprises, under charter contracts or through joint ventures with Peruvian persons or enterprises or under the authority of a fishing permit and the payment of fees -Registration, navigation permits and fishing permits all valid for periods of 1 year. -Owners or charterers of trawlers must request the presence of an inspector to inspect the vessel before commencing fishing operations. -Vessels to display on both sides amidships international radio call signs. -Owner or charterer to post irrevocable bond or security valid for a period of at least 180 days. The amount of the bond is to be US$100 per nrt of the vessel -Vessels to comply with written conservation measures (Supreme-Decree No. 012-84-PE of 19 September 1984)	LEGISLATION Trawlers: -Vessels over 150 nrt must report position and size of catch each day. -At the end of each trip, the owner or charterer must submit a report on catches, fishing effort, etc. (Supreme-Decree No. 012-84-PE of 19 September 1984)
	Freezer Tuna vessels -Freezer tuna vessels may operate in Peruvian waters under the authority of fishing permits or under approved charter contracts with Peruvian companies. -Registration, navigation permits and fishing permits for tuna fishing vessels all valid for periods of 180 days. -Owners or charterers of trawlers must request the presence of an inspector to inspect the vessel before commencing fishing operations. -Vessels to display on both sides amidships international radio call signs.	Freezer Tuna vessels -Licensed vessels must must report each day position, size of catches by species, the water temperature in the fishing grounds, and any other infromation requested. (Supreme-Decree No. 008-84-PE of 6 July 1984)

TABLE C
COASTAL STATE REQUIREMENTS FOR FOREIGN FISHING

STATE	Foreign fishing vessel licence conditions (other than reporting requirements) [including observers, bonds, etc.]	Logbook and reporting requirements for foreign fishing
PERU (Cont'd)	-Owner or charterer to post irrevocable bond or security valid for a period of at least 180 days. The amount of the bond is to be US$160 per nrt of the vessel -Vessels to comply with written conservation measures (Supreme-Decree No. 008-84-PE of 6 July 1984)	
PHILIPPINES	LEGISLATION No provision made for fishing by foreign vessel except under charter to majority (70%) owned Philippine Company. Charters must be for 5 years, payment to be made in kind and no more than 75% of crew may be foreign nationals. Filippino crew to be given on-the-job training. Foreign crew to be replaced by Filippino crew after 2 years.(S. 6) -Fishing boat under charter to be given temporary certificate fo Philippine registry; -Foreign crew members to register with Immigration, seek clearance coastguard and obtain fishermen's licences; -Charterer etc. to obtain special commecial fishing boat licence (S. 9) -Charterer to comply with fishery laws, rules, regulations -Charterer to assume responsibility for acts of agents, employees, etc. (Fisheries Administrative Order No. 121 of 1976) Licence conditions include: -Compliance with all legal requirements; -Life-saving, firefighting, medical equipment etc. -Employment only licenced fishermen; -Allow observers to board - notify departure for grounds; -Assume responsibility for acts of agents, employees etc.;	LEGISLATION Special commercial fishing boat licence conditions include: -Licensee to keep fishing log-book on daily basis giving catch, species, fishing ground, time of set and haul; and position, in English or vernacular on form provided -Report on catch to be submitted monthy in first 10 days on ensuing month; -Copies of reports on all payments made to foreign persons, whether in cash or kind, to be made to BFAR, together with monetary value of products.

TABLE C

COASTAL STATE REQUIREMENTS FOR FOREIGN FISHING

STATE	Foreign fishing vessel licence conditions (other than reporting requirements) [including observers, bonds, etc.]	Logbook and reporting requirements for foreign fishing
PHILIPPINES (cont'd)	-Land catch only at designated landing places; -Certificates of clearance (fisheries) and military clear ance if required before departure for grounds; -Contracts and licences and consitions may be varied when national interest requires; -President may suspend licence on recommendation of govt. agency for violations of conditions prescribed in rules and regulations pending conduct of hearing; -BFAR to be consulted if significant change in venture; -Licence may be suspended/cancelled if not used within 3 months, sub-letting of vessel, violation of conditions, laws etc., misrepresentation or in public interest; -Renewal subject to review of compliance.	
POLAND	LEGISLATION The Minister may determine: - partial or total prohibition of the fishing of certain species of fish; (S. 24) - fishing seasons and minimum dimensions; (S. 24) - fishing quotas; (S. 24) - prohibited areas and restrictions relative in fishing methods and gear; (S. 24) - identification marks to be borne by the vessel. (S. 16) (Sea Fishing Act of 21 May 1963).	
PORTUGAL	LEGISLATION -Except in maritime frontier areas and within the framework of reciprocal agreements of local application, foreign fishing operations may only be authorized in areas of the EEZ not declared protection zones, within the framework of specific agreements.	LEGISLATION -All vessels operating in fisheries regions to maintain fishing logbook in prescribed form (Art. 15) -All vessels to maintain and submit a report of fish landings (Art. 16) -All vessels to maintain and submit a report of fish

TABLE C
COASTAL STATE REQUIREMENTS FOR FOREIGN FISHING

STATE	Foreign fishing vessel licence conditions (other than reporting requirements) [including observers, bonds, etc.]	Logbook and reporting requirements for foreign fishing
PORTUGAL (Cont'd)	-Authorizations of foreign fishing must take into account national interests and be subject to system of licences- -For foreign fishing in subareas 2 (Madeira) or 3 (Azores) regional governments must be consulted on agreements -Licence conditions to be set by regulatory decree(Art 14) (Decree-Law No 52/85 of 1 March 1985) - Fishing quotas, fishing areas to be determined for each country within the limits of the total allowable catch in the fishery (Act. 33/77 of 1977, Art. 5) - Vessels required to fly national flag while in Portuguese waters; - Vessels required to display painted identification marks on either side of bridge and on top of superstructure; - Vessels required to report radio frequencies to authorities before entry into zone; - Licence required for each vessel; (Regulation No. 41-79 of 24 January 1979)	transhipments (Art. 17) (Decree-Law No 52/85 of 1 March 1985) - Notification to be given of the date and the location of entry into and departure from the exclusive economic zone; - Vessels to maintain fishing log book and record of catch and effort; -Record of catches and effort to be prepared in duplicate weekly covering period midnight Sunday to midnight Sunday. - Record of catches and effort to be maintained up-to-date and submitted: - on request to fisheries or control authorites; - within 60 days of expiry of licence to fisheries authorities. (Art. 24) (Regulation No. 41-79 of 24 January 1979)
QATAR	LEGISLATION Minister to issue regulations prescribing terms and conditions of licences (Art 5) -Licence for foreign fishing operations to indicate duration of licence, locations and seasons of fishing, species and quantities of living aquatic resources to be caught, fishing techniques and gear to be employed. (Art. 14) -Foreign vessels entering harbour not to sell fish without first obtaining required licence. (Art. 25) (Law No. 4 of 1983 on Exploitation and Conservation of Living Aquatic Resources in Qatar)	LEGISLATION -Any person engaged in fishing or marketing living aquatic resources or related industries to submit data specified by the competent authority. (Art. 6) (Law No. 4 of 1983 on Exploitation and Conservation of Living Aquatic Resources in Qatar)

TABLE C
COASTAL STATE REQUIREMENTS FOR FOREIGN FISHING

STATE	Foreign fishing vessel licence conditions (other than reporting requirements) [including observers, bonds, etc.]	Logbook and reporting requirements for foreign fishing
QATAR (Cont'd)	-Vessel licences valid 1 year and renewable (Art. 7) -Name and number of vessel to be well displayed on vessel and same name and number clearly written in Arabic on both sides of vessel -Vessel to have navigational lights during night fishing plus necessary safety and salvage equipment (Art. 15) -Conservation measures prescribed -Fishing trawlers not to be used for depths under 25 m. (Executive Regulations of the Law on Exploitation and Conservation of Living Aquatic Resources in Qatar)	
ROMANIA	NO INFORMATION	NO INFORMATION
ST. CHRISTOPHER & NEVIS	LEGISLATION Access agreements to include provision establishing responsibility of foreign country or association to take nec essary measures to ensure compliance by its vessels with agreement and fishing laws. (S. 7(3)) -Fishing gear to be stowed except where authorized to fish -licences subject to general conditions to be prescribed, or specified by notice published in the Gazette and to special conditions specified by the Minister. (The Fisheries Act, No. 10 of 1984 S. 9 & 13) Note: New regulations specifying general conditions including reporting now under consideration	

TABLE C
COASTAL STATE REQUIREMENTS FOR FOREIGN FISHING

STATE	Foreign fishing vessel licence conditions (other than reporting requirements) [including observers, bonds, etc.]	Logbook and reporting requirements for foreign fishing
ST. LUCIA	LEGISLATION Access agreements to include provision establishing responsibility of foreign country or association to take necessary measures to ensure compliance by its vessels with agreement and fishing laws. (S. 7(3)) -Fishing gear to be stowed except where authorized to fish -licences subject to general conditions to be prescribed, or specified by notice published in the Gazette and to special conditions specified by the Minister. (The Fisheries Act, No. 10 of 1984 S. 9 & 13) Note: New regulations specifying general conditions including reporting now under consideration	
ST. VINCENT & GRENADINES	New legislation under consideration	
SAO TOME & PRINCIPE	LEGISLATION For promoting optimum utilization of the biological resources of the EEZ, the State of Sao Tome shall authorize foreign countries to exploit the surplus catch (under bilateral agreements). (Art. 6) (Decree No. 15-78 of 16 June 1978) Foreign vessels not permitted to fish in 12 mile territorial sea except with permission of Government to be given only in cases of special interest to State.(Art. 3) Fishing permitted only in areas, seasons and hours legally established. (Art. 10) All vessels must be licensed. Fishing vessel licences valid 1 year renewable (Arts. 18, 21) (Decree Law no. 68/81 of 31 December 1981)	LEGISLATION -Vessels required to report by radio on entering and leaving the EEZ; Daily reports required of position and catch. (Decree Law No. 68/81 of 31 December 1981 (Art. 22))

TABLE C
COASTAL STATE REQUIREMENTS FOR FOREIGN FISHING

STATE	Foreign fishing vessel licence conditions (other than reporting requirements) [including observers, bonds, etc.]	Logbook and reporting requirements for foreign fishing
SAO TOME & PRINCIPE (Cont'd)	AGREEMENTS *Agreement of October 1979 with Portugal -Portuguese vessels to take Sao Tome citizens on board. -Portugal to grant scholarships to Sao Tome citizens. *Agreement with the EEC, 1983 valid thru' 1986 -Community to take necessary measures to ensure compliance by its vessels with terms of agreement and regulations -Community authorities to notify list of vessels to carry out fishing operations for next 12 months, 3 months before commencement of fishing operations -Vessels to take on observers on request of local authorities. Presence of observers not to exceed time required to carry out verification of catch. (Text published in EC Official Journal No. L 282/57 of 14/10/1983)	*Agreement with the EEC, 1983 valid thru' 1986 -Vessels to report entry and departure from zone to the Sao Tome & Principe radio station, giving details of quantities of fish on board.
SAUDI ARABIA	LEGISLATION Fishing in territorial waters by foreign fishing vessels not allowed without permit issued by Minister of Agriculture and Water with the approval of the Prime Minister. Permit to specify species and periods for fishing. Foreign fishing vessels operating for national companies exempt from permit requirement. (Art. 9) (Fishing Regulation, Exploitation and Conservation of Living Aquatic Resources Scheme)	LEGISLATION Companies and institutions engaged in fishing, extracting, processing or marketing living aquatic products to maintain books to record production according to weight, species, and quantities exported or marketed in Saudi Arabia, and furnish Ministry of Agriculture and Water and Ministry of Commerce with copies of these records. (Art. 10) (Fishing Regulation, Exploitation and Conservation of Living Aquatic Resources Scheme)

TABLE C

COASTAL STATE REQUIREMENTS FOR FOREIGN FISHING

STATE	Foreign fishing vessel licence conditions (other than reporting requirements) [including observers, bonds, etc.]	Logbook and reporting requirements for foreign fishing
SENEGAL	LEGISLATION - Zones reserved for national fishermen and for different types of fishery (sardine boats, purse seiners (fresh) up to 3 miles from the coast; freezer boats (Senegalese and countries with fishing agreement) outside 12 miles; where no agreement, outside 50 miles. Trawlers (fresh) and small freezer boats allowed outside 6 miles; big freezer trawlers: outside 12 miles; tuna boats allowed to fish for tuna and bait anywhere. (Arts. 18 and 20) - Prescription of the gross tonnage and/or the horse-power of the vessels allowed to fish in Senegalese waters (1500 GRT or less, in the case of refrigerated vessels fishing outside the 12-mile limit). (Art. 4) - Encouragement is given to landings and processing through the level of licence fees (double for catches not landed locally). (Arts. 19-23) - Bonds must be posted to guarantee performance obligations where no bilateral agreement is in force. Amount ranges from 1 500 000 CFA for vessels under 50 GT and less than 5 years old to 28 000 000 CFA for vessels over 200 GT and more than 10 years old. (Art. 24) (Act No. 76-89 of 2 July 1976 as amended 1979)	LEGISLATION All licensed vessels to submit return of catch in form set out in Annex IV to the Act. Returns to be made to Dept. of Oceanography and Maritime Fisheries within 24 hours of arrival in port. (Act No. 76-89 of 2 July 1976 as amended 1979, Art. 15)
	AGREEMENTS *Agreement with Spain, 16 February 1982 - Freezer trawlers and fresh fish vessels allowed to operate outside 12 miles from northern boundary until 14 27' N. latitude and beyond 25 miles from this point up to the Guinea Bissau boundary. Tuna freezer vessels allowed to operate in the whole Senegalese zone. - 60 mm minimum mesh size for fresh fish vessels. - Spanish vessels to embark up to 33% Senegalese crew. For freezer tuna vessels, Senegal will take into account	AGREEMENTS *Agreement with Ivory Coast, 11 June 1979 Ivory Coast administration to send to Senegalese authorities declaration of catch of authorized vessels of Ivory Coast.

TABLE C
COASTAL STATE REQUIREMENTS FOR FOREIGN FISHING

STATE	Foreign fishing vessel licence conditions (other than reporting requirements) [including observers, bonds, etc.]	Logbook and reporting requirements for foreign fishing
SENEGAL (Cont'd)	the number of nationals of other countries that Spanish vessels operating in the same region have to take on board. - Vessels to carry one Senegalese observer. - Tuna vessels to land an average of 123 tons per year per vessel according to a pre-established schedule and a set of prices both to be agreed upon every 3 months. *Agreement with EEC - with Protocol - 21 January 1982 valid through 15 November 1983 - Vessels to take one observer on board. (Vessel owners to reimburse the Senegalese Government at a flat rate of CFA 8 000 per day spent by the observer on board the vessel. Captain of the vessel to facilitate his work.) - EEC to provide 10 study and training grants for a five-year period in disciplines connected with fisheries. - Wet trawlers and tuna boats obliged to land their entire catch in Senegal. *Agreement with Ivory Coast, 11 June 1979 - Permits to be granted to 12 fishing vessels of less than 1 500 tonnes each. - Fishing vessels to take up to 30% Senegalese crew. *Agreement with Poland, 17 March 1976 - Polish vessels to embark up to 30% Senegalese crew.	
SEYCHELLES	LEGISLATION - Gear to be stowed when in area where not authorized to fish; - Vessel to fly flag of country where registered; - Master to comply with instructions of authorized officers; - Vessels to have on board required communication and position fixing equipment;	LEGISLATION - Master or agent to notify Minister of estimated time and location of entry into zone and give approximate fishing plan, date of arrival in port for inspection unless exempted, and fish on board (species, quantity, condition). - written record to be maintained on daily basis of fishing effort and catch in prescribed for;

TABLE C
COASTAL STATE REQUIREMENTS FOR FOREIGN FISHING

STATE	Foreign fishing vessel licence conditions (other than reporting requirements) [including observers, bonds, etc.]	Logbook and reporting requirements for foreign fishing
SEYCHELLES (Cont'd)	- Records and communications to be maintained or made in English or French languages. International Code of signals to be used; - Vessel owner to maintain local agents or representatives undertaking legal and financial responsibility for the proposed operations; - Vessel owner or agent may be required to post bond to guarantee performance obligations; - Vessel to bear specified identification markes; - Vessel may be required to accept observers on board and provide facilities; - Compulsory inspection in Port Voctoria on entry and before departure from zone unless exempted; - Restriction concerning species, areas to be fished, gears, methods of fishing, etc. - By-catch not to exceed specified percentage; - Transhipment only in Port Victoria, under supervision unless otherwise authorized. (Foreign Fishing Vessel Regulations 1979, Reg. 6) -Holder to comply with and ensure vessel is used in conformity with the provisions of the Control of Foreign Fishing Vessels Decree, 1979 and Foreign Fishing Vessels Regulations 1979. Conditions for Tuna Long-line Fishing Vessels: - Vessels licenced for more than 2 months requested to call at Port Victoria for inspection within 6 months period; -Transshipment of fish inside EEZ only in Victoria. Vessel to give advance notice of intention to transship 72 hours before ETA.	- written records to be sent to Minister monthly, or at request of fisheries officer, and not later than 30 days after expiry licence; radio reports of position every 3rd day, and reports of fish held on board or caught or - transhipped weekly; notification of entry into Port Victoria at least 24 - hours in advance; notification of time and location of departure at least 48 hours in advance. (Foreign Fishing Vessel Regulations 1979 Reg. 6) CONTROLS OVER TRANSIT BY UNLICENSED FISHING VESSELS -Fishing gear to be stowed in prescribed manner. (S. 13) -Any fish found on board any foreign fishing vessel within the exclusive economic zone shall be presumed until the contrary is proved to have been taken within the exclusive economic zone by such vessel. -A radio call made by a foreign fishing vessel before entering the exclusive economic zone and notifying its proposed route and the quantity of fish on board shall suffice to rebut the presemption. S. (15) (Control of Foreign Fishing Vessels Decree, 1979) -Form of message prescribed. (Foreign Fishing Vessels (Radio Calls) Regs. 1979) Conditions for Tuna Long-line Fishing Vessels: -Master to radio Cable and Wireless (Mahe) every 3 days giving vessel's name position by latitude and longitude, total catch of each species inside EEZ and total fish volume on board.

TABLE C

COASTAL STATE REQUIREMENTS FOR FOREIGN FISHING

STATE	Foreign fishing vessel licence conditions (other than reporting requirements) [including observers, bonds, etc.]	Logbook and reporting requirements for foreign fishing
SEYCHELLES (Cont'd)	-Agent to inform Captain of vessels licence number if licence deposited with agent. -Vessel's number to be displayed visibly on starboard side of vessel. (Licence conditions on Foreign Fishing Vessel Licence)	-Completed Catch and Effort Form to be deposited directly with Chief Fisheries Officer at the finishing time. (Licence conditions on Foreign Fishing Vessel Licence)
	AGREEMENTS *Agreement with EEC (Valid from 11.1.1984 to 10.1.1987) -On request of Seychelles authorities, vessels to take on board an observer. Presence of observer should not exceed time necessary to make spot checks on catches. -On request of Seychelles authorities, vessels may board a Seychelles fisherman to carry out role of observer over and above his seaman's duties: Seaman to have access to places and documents necessary for his observer duties. -Government and shipowners to lay down conditions for use of port facilities -In order to avoid harming Seychellois artisanal fisheries, purse-seining operations not to be authorized in the continental shelf zone bounded by the 200 m. isobath and within 3 nautical miles of fish aggregating devices placed by Seychelles.	AGREEMENTS *Agreement with EEC (Valid from 11.1.1984 to 10.1.1987) -While fishing in Sechelles zone, vessels to report to Victoria radio station every 3 days their position, and catches and at the end of each trip the state of their catches.
	*Agreement with Spain, I June 1984 valid for 5 years. Spain undetakes to take all necessary measures to ensure that its vessels comply with the provisions of the agreement and the regulations on fishing in the Seychelles zone -Joint Venture Company established Seychelles =80% capital Spanish = 20% capital. Licences to be given to up to 15 tuna purse-seiners -Permits valid for 12 months and non-transferable -vessels to board Seychelles scientists on request of Seychelles authorities,	*Agreement with Spain, I June 1984 valid for 5 years. -Vessels to report 3 monthly to Seychelles Fishing Authority complete statistics on catches using the ICCAT data-forms -Vessels to report to Victoria radio station at time of entry into and departure from Seychelles zone, giving quantities of fish on board

TABLE C
COASTAL STATE REQUIREMENTS FOR FOREIGN FISHING

STATE	Foreign fishing vessel licence conditions (other than reporting requirements) [including observers, bonds, etc.]	Logbook and reporting requirements for foreign fishing
SEYCHELLES (Cont'd)	-Victoria to be the preferred port for the Spanish tuna fleet in the Western Indian Ocean -Vessel captain to be represented by agent designated by Seychelles Fishing Authority *Agreement with 2 private fishing companies 1984 valid 5yr -Permits valid for 5 years and non-transferable -vessels to board Seychelles scientists on request of Seychelles authorities, -In order to avoid harming Seychellois artisanal fisheries, purse-seining operations not to be authorized in the continental shelf zone bounded by the 200 m. isobath and within 3 nautical miles of fish aggregating devices placed by Seychelles. -Where companies place fish aggregating devices, they must report pósitions to and have approval of Seychelles FA	*Agreement with 2 private fishing companies 1984 -Vessels to report 3 monthly to Seychelles Fishing Authority complete statistics on catches using the ICCAT data-forms -Vessels to report to Victoria radio station at time of entry into and departure from Seychelles zone, giving quantities of fish on board
SIERRA LEONE	Fishing by motor vessels within 2 miles from coast or within 200 metres of canoe or other fishing vessel prohibited (Fisheries Regs. 1974, Reg. 7) - Yearly or half yearly licences; - Vessel to bear specified identification marks; (Fisheries Act, (Cap. 195), S. 6)	- Written returns to be made concerning the operations undertaken by the vessel. (Fisheries Act, (Cap. 195), S. 8)
SINGAPORE	NO INFORMATION	NO INFORMATION

TABLE C
COASTAL STATE REQUIREMENTS FOR FOREIGN FISHING

STATE	Foreign fishing vessel licence conditions (other than reporting requirements) [including observers, bonds, etc.]	Logbook and reporting requirements for foreign fishing
SOLOMON ISLANDS	LEGISLATION - Fishing in certain areas and use of gear liable to be limited; - Vessels to bear specified identification marks letters- - Restrictions on transhipment of fish. (Fisheries Regulations, 1972-77) -Issuance of permit conditional on vessel having good standing on the regional register; permit valid only while vessel remains on good dstanding on the register -Master of foreign fishing vessel in respect of which permit issued, must: -comply with Fisheries Act and Regulations; -comply with lawful instructions of an authorized officer; -permit authorized officer to inspect vessel, catch, gear and navigational and catch records; -carry the permit on board and produce it on demand, or where not received, produce number of current permit; -carry observer on board as required, and permit him to board and leave vessel at times and places required; and provide maintenance, food and accomodation as for officers allow him to observe and record all aspects of operations and allow access to catch on board and at unloading, daily catch records, charts etc.,communication channels etc.; -except for vessels chartered by Solomon Islands companies not fish within internal waters or the territorial sea or any area endorsed on the permit; -paint identifying marks on the vessel as shown on permit. -For foreign fishing vessels chartered by Solomon Islands companies: -not, save for baitfishing, fish within 500 metres of low water mark or within one nautical mile of any village or local fishing area specified by the Principal Licensing	LEGISLATION For all Vessels -Keep daily catch record; For Vessels chartered by local Company -report weekly position as required to Principal Licensing Officer position, summary of catch on board etc.; -Submit daily catch record of bait and other fishing operations or statement of no operations not more than 14 days after end of voyage and as required; For Vessels not chartered by local Company -Report location and time of entry into fishery limits 24 hours in advance with catch on board; -Report entry and departure with time, position and catch on board; -Report position, and weight of catch by species on board at intervals as required; -Submit catch and effort report to Principal Licensing Officer or regional fisheries agency as required, not more than 7 days after end of voyage; Submit statement of no operations within 7 days of end of voyage if no operations when authorized to fish. (Fisheries (Foreign Fishing Vessels) Regulations 1981-3)

TABLE C
COASTAL STATE REQUIREMENTS FOR FOREIGN FISHING

STATE	Foreign fishing vessel licence conditions (other than reporting requirements) [including observers, bonds, etc.]	Logbook and reporting requirements for foreign fishing
SOLOMON ISLANDS (cont'd)	officer and shown on approved local fishing maps or in any manner not authorized by the permit; -if vessel permitted to fish by pole and line: -not baitfish in area unless shown on baitground maps; -carry on board latest baitground maps; -keep daily record of baitfishing; -carry on board approved local fishing area maps; -erase all foreign fishing registration markings and paint approved identifying marks at turn of bow and on both sides of bridge superstructure or other part of vessel as required in contrasting colours, at least one metre high; and name of vessel in English in large letters at bow and stern; -clearly exhibit the identifying marks on all baitfishing boats and fixed fishing gear; Not fish on submerged reef outside 500 metre limits except with written permission, pursuant to agreement on terms with customary owners, area councils, provincial governments of area; -For foreign fishing vessels not chartered by Solomon Islands companies: -Not fish in territorial sea limits -Paint identifying mark (International Radio Call Sign) shown on permit on hull amidships on both sides and elsewhere as required in contrasting colours at least one metre high and name of vessel in English in large letters on bows and stern of vessel. (Fisheries (Foreign Fishing Vessels) Regulations, 1981-3)	
	AGREEMENTS	
	*Agreement with Japanese Tuna Fisheries Co-operative Associations (Jan. 1984 valid thru' Dec.1984 & extended -Associations to make best efforts to ensure members and vessels comply with Fisheries Act. -Associations to appoint and maintain agent in Honiara	*Agreement with Japanese Tuna Fisheries Co-operative -Reports to be made on entry into and departure from zone in prescribed form giving catch on board by species -Weekly position and catch report to be made each Wednesday in prescribed form

TABLE C

COASTAL STATE REQUIREMENTS FOR FOREIGN FISHING

STATE	Foreign fishing vessel licence conditions (other than reporting requirements) [including observers, bonds, etc.]	Logbook and reporting requirements for foreign fishing
SOLOMON ISLANDS (cont'd)	-Vessel applying to fish must first submit Fishing Vessel Register Application Form, then eligible to apply permit -Permits valid for calendar year but must be activated for period to be fished. Permit activation may be by telex -Permitted vessels to display radio call sign or signal letters on top and both sides amidships of vessel where it is clearly discernible from air, in contrasting colours, with letters at least 1 metre high and 40 cms wide. -Observers to be carried as mutually agreed. Observers to be given food and accomdation at no less standard than that of the vessel's crew. Observers not to intervene in lawful operation of the vessels. -Vessels not required to enter port unless specifically instructed to do so -Permission required for transhipment of catch or entry into port for purposes of loading or unloading catch etc. Note: -In accordance with the decision of the South Pacific Forum in August 1982 and as from 1 September 1983, no member of the Forum Fisheries Agency will licence a foreign vessel to fish for tuna in their fishing zone unless it is listed in good standing on the regional register maintained by the Forum Fisheries Agency. (Source: AFZ Information Bulletin Canberra May-July 1983)	-Permit holder to report by telex within 7 days completion of each trip, in prescribed form if vessel has obtained a permit activation for that trip. If not, permit holder to send statement of no operation stating he has not entered fishery limits during trip. -Captain of vessel to maintain on board a daily record of catch, in prescribed form -Catch report form to be kept current and produced on demand: completed form to be forwarded to Principal Licensing Officer within 45 days of completion of each fishing trip. -Communications with patrol vessels by means of international code of signals
SOMALIA	AGREEMENTS - Exploratory fishing agreements have normally included the following conditions: - Somali officials to be put on board vessel for duration survey at foreign company's expense; - proportion of value of catch to be transferred to Government;	AGREEMENTS - Exploratory fishing agreements have normally included following conditions: - vessel to inform Ministry of daily movements; - foreign operator to make full scientific report at end of exploratory fishing operations.

TABLE C

COASTAL STATE REQUIREMENTS FOR FOREIGN FISHING

STATE	Foreign fishing vessel licence conditions (other than reporting requirements) [including observers, bonds, etc.]	Logbook and reporting requirements for foreign fishing
SOMALIA (Cont'd)	- reporting requirements; - vessels not to be operated in such way as to damage marine resources or engage in indiscriminate fishing.	
SOUTH AFRICA	LEGISLATION Vessels to bear specified identification marks. (Regulations, Sea Fisheries Act, 1973, S. 16)	AGREEMENTS *Agreement with Japan of 6 December 1977 - Ship's record of operations to be kept.
SPAIN	LEGISLATION - Fishing of certain species liable to be restricted: (Act No. 20 of 8 April 1967, Art. 1) - Conditions may include conservation measures, closed seasons, reserved areas etc.; (Art. 1) - vessel to respect national laws and regulations applicable to foreign fishing vessels. (Crown Decree No. 3327 of 9 December 1977, Art. 12) -Fishing by foreign fishing vessels prohibited within 12 miles territorial sea unless different arrangements are made on reciprocal basis. -Licences issued to vessels belonging to States which have negotiated catch quotas in Spanish EEZ with Spain. Information to be given on licence application specified. (Order No. 6640 of 2 March 1982) CONTROLS OVER TRANSIT BY UNLICENSED FISHING VESSELS Foreign fishing vessels to stow fishing gear so that it cannot be used. Authorized officers may board vessel. (Law 53/1982 on fishing offences, art. 6-3)	LEGISLATION Vessels to maintain logbook to be completed after each fishing operation, entering the time, position, methods used and quantity of fish caught. Vessels to report to Under Secretary for Marine Fishing each week giving details of quantities of fish transshipped. Vessels to report to Under Secretary for Marine Fishing on entering and leaving Spanish EEZ, giving details of location and time of entry or departure and quantities of fish of each species on board. (Order No. 6640 of 2 March 1982)

TABLE C
COASTAL STATE REQUIREMENTS FOR FOREIGN FISHING

STATE	Foreign fishing vessel licence conditions (other than reporting requirements) [including observers, bonds, etc.]	Logbook and reporting requirements for foreign fishing
SRI LANKA	LEGISLATION Areas may be reserved for national fishermen; - Licence conditions to be prescribed may include: - requirements concerning appointment of local representatives or agents; - maintenance of bonds; - maintenance of log books and other records of position, catch and effort; - requirements concerning statistical returns; - marking of boat and installation of transponders, etc. - facilities for trainees; - employment of local citizens; - placing of observers on board; - compliance with instructions of authorized officers. (Fisheries (Regulation of Foreign Fishing Boats) Act 1979) -Foreign fishing vessels to stow gear if prohibited from fishing according to specified criteria. (Reg. 2) -Information to be given on permit application specified, (includes call sign, fishing operations plan, name and address of local representative and evidence of legal authorization to undertake legal and financial obligations on behalf of owner/charterer (Reg. 3) -Area up to 24 miles from coast reserved local fishermen; area from 24 to 35 miles reserved local fishermen and approved joint ventures. (Reg. 6) -No joint ventures to be approved if of type or in area already adequately developed by local fishermen or if would conflict with local operations. (Reg. 7) -Owner or chartere to appoint and maintain local legal representative, authorized to accept legal and financial responsibility on behaf of owner/charterer for fishing operations. (Reg 8)	LEGISLATION Licence conditions may include requirements concerning maintenance of fishing records and reports as to position, catch and effort of foreign fishing boats. (Fisheries (Regulation of Foreign Fishing Boats) Act 1979) - master or local representative to notify Director of estimated time and location of entry into and departure from Sri lankan waters at least 24 hours in advance, giving fishing plan (on entry only) and catch on board (Reg. 8) -Master to maintain written records of catch, effort and transhipments, processing, on daily basis. (Reg. 8) -Records to be transmitted to Director on request or not later than 30 days after expiry of permit. (Reg. 8) -Position reports to be made and catch statistics given as specified in permit or required by Director.(Reg. 8) - Records reports notifications to be in English(Reg. 8) (The Foreign Fishing Boats Regulations 1981)

TABLE C
COASTAL STATE REQUIREMENTS FOR FOREIGN FISHING

STATE	Foreign fishing vessel licence conditions (other than reporting requirements) [including observers, bonds, etc.]	Logbook and reporting requirements for foreign fishing
SRI LANKA (Cont'd)	-Port inspection required unless exempted on entry and departure from zone. (Reg. 8) -Master to bring boat to port for inspection when required -Boat to stow gear when in area not authorized to fish. --Boat to fly flag and display assigned number. -Master to permit boarding of observers and provide suitable food, accomodation and facilities including communications facilities. (Reg. 8) -Master to comply with instructions of authorized officer and enforcement vessels. (Reg. 8) (The Foreign Fishing Boats Regulations 1981)	
SUDAN	LEGISLATION -Vessels to be marked. (S. 2) -Local landing of catch prohibited (S. 4) (The Marine Fisheries Regulations 1960) -Foreign vessels must land their catch in Port Sudan only -Priority in marketing of fish to meeting local demand -Observers, deposits may be required. (Government reply)	
SURINAME	LEGISLATION Licence conditions may include restrictions concerning species, methods of fishing, (Art. 14) Identification marks, (Art. 9) (Regulations under the law extending Suriname jurisdiction, 7 May 1978) Foreign fishing vessels classified into "foreign fishing vessels permitted to enter Suriname" (FFVPES) and "alien fishing vessels" (AFV). (Art. 4 and 5) FFVPES defined as vessels mooring or intending to moor	

TABLE C
COASTAL STATE REQUIREMENTS FOR FOREIGN FISHING

STATE	Foreign fishing vessel licence conditions (other than reporting requirements) [including observers, bonds, etc.]	Logbook and reporting requirements for foreign fishing
SURINAME (Cont'd)	regularly in Suriname, whose operator has offices in Suriname and is registered with Chamber of Commerce and Factories and whose operator ensures that the catch is largely processed in Suriname. (Art. 4) FFVPES must be registered on Central Fishery Register Part C, maintained by Harbour Master. (Art. 6) Owner or operator of FFVPES to inform Harbor Master of changes likely to result in modifications to register entry. (Art. 12) Minister to announce in January each year maximum number of licences to be issued to Surinamese vessels and to FFVPES and AFV's, and general conditions of licences, including allowable means and methods of fishing, mesh sizes, seasons, zones, minimum fish size catch maxima and reporting requirements, and any applicable special conditions. (Art. 17) Licences valid for maximum 1 year and non-transferable. Copy of licence to be carried on board. (Art 22) Alien Fishing Vessels present in zone to fly flag of registry. (Art 11) CONTROLS OVER TRANSIT BY UNLICENSED FISHING VESSELS Persons present with AFV in fishery zone or alien vessel from which fishing could be done without a licence guilty of offence unless prove that in direct transit or that there for some other purpose related to navigation or communication recognized by international law.(Art.28) (Decree of 31 December 1980 regulating Sea Fishery) AGREEMENTS *Agreement with Guyana of April 1979 - 18 Guyanese trawlers allowed to catch 375 metric tons of shrimp; 2 Guyanese trawlers to harvest 500 metric tons of fin fish. - Fishing for shrimp seawards the 19 fathoms isobath and for fin-fish seawards the 12 fathoms isobath.	AGREEMENTS *Agreement with Guyana, April 1979 Vessels required to report when entering and leaving the economic zone; reporting of daily position; Fishing log to be completed; information to be compiled for each trip and to be submitted to Guayanese authorities at the end of every 3 month period.

TABLE C

COASTAL STATE REQUIREMENTS FOR FOREIGN FISHING

STATE	Foreign fishing vessel licence conditions (other than reporting requirements) [including observers, bonds, etc.]	Logbook and reporting requirements for foreign fishing
SURINAME (Cont'd)	- Practices inimical to the well being of the resources prohibited (such as chemical, toxic or explosive substances). - Special provisions applying to artisanal fishermen whose vessels (55 vessels under one metric ton and 30 vessels under 6 metric tons) may harvest 1250 metric tons of fin fish. - Guyana authorities to provide information, including name, documents and photographs of vessels, name of operators, port of registry; maximum speed;capacity in tons; navigational equipment, facilities for preserving catch; types of fish processing equipment, etc. - Vessels to dispaly identification numbers according to detailed provisions relating inter alia to size and position. - Minimum mesh size.	
SWEDEN	LEGISLATION - Fishing quotas may be allocated for foreign vessels. - Vessels to fly national flag and bear visible identification marks. (S. 5) (Provisional Regulations for fishing activities by foreign vessels of 22 December 1977)	LEGISLATION - Vessels to inform coastaguard of commencement and completion of fishing operations; (S. 4) - Daily radio position reports and periodical catch and efforts reports to be made; (S. 4) - Vessels to maintain log books giving position, effort, catch and other relevant data including transhipments; (S. 4) Reports to be made to the Coast Guard Service. (S. 4) (Provisional Regulations etc. 1977)
SYRIAN ARAB REPUBLIC	LEGISLATION - Conditions to be fixed by Minister of Agriculture; May include requirements to undertake research, to develop and strengthen means of exploitation of acquatic resources (Decree Law 25/8/1964 - S. 8)	

TABLE C

COASTAL STATE REQUIREMENTS FOR FOREIGN FISHING

STATE	Foreign fishing vessel licence conditions (other than reporting requirements) [including observers, bonds, etc.]	Logbook and reporting requirements for foreign fishing
TANZANIA	LEGISLATION -Same general requirements and system of licences as national fishermen; -Controls over methods of fishing, use of gears, nets, etc., closed seasons, minimum length or size of any species, etc., (S. 18) -Vessels to bear visible identification marks. (S. 6) (The Fisheries (General) Regulations, 1973)	
THAILAND	NO FOREIGN FISHING IN PRACTICE AT PRESENT	
TOGO	LEGISLATION - Fishing reserved to national fishermen except under bilateral or regional agreement. (Ordinance No. 24 of 16 August 1977 Art. 4)	
TONGA	LEGISLATION Prohibition on entry of foreign fishing vessels into territorial waters not to prohibit fishing in areas where special provision made for such fishing by any arrangement between Govenment of Tonga and of flag state. No conditions specified. (Fisheries Protection Act, 1973, S. 3) [Licence conditions may include: -determination of fishing areas, seasons, times and voyages during which fishing authorized; -species, size, age and quantities of fish to be taken; -methods of taking fish, and types, size and amounts of fishing gear; -requirements concerning use, transfer, landing and ; -processing;	LEGISLATION [Licence conditions may require reporting of catch and effort and vessel position reports.] [Territorial Sea and Exclusive Economic Zone Act 1978 S. 5](Not yet in force)

TABLE C
COASTAL STATE REQUIREMENTS FOR FOREIGN FISHING

STATE	Foreign fishing vessel licence conditions (other than reporting requirements) [including observers, bonds, etc.]	Logbook and reporting requirements for foreign fishing
TONGA (Cont'd)	-requirements concerning entry into port for inspection; -compensation payable for damage to local gear catch or fish stocks; -conduct of research; -acceptance on board of Tongan trainees; -display of licence, marking of the craft; -directions of authorized officers to be complied with -placing of observers on the vessel and reimbursement of costs to the Government; -installation of transponders or other position fixing position fixing equipment; -carriage of specified nautical charts.] [Territorial Sea and Exclusive Economic Zone Act 1978, S. 14] (Not yet in force) Note: In practice no licensed foreign fishing at present Note: -In accordance with the decision of the South Pacific Forum in August 1982 and as from 1 September 1983, no member of the Forum Fisheries Agency will licence a foreign vessel to fish for tuna in their fishing zone unless it is listed in good standing on the regional register maintained by the Forum Fisheries Agency. (Source: AFZ Information Bulletin Canberra May-July 1983)	
TRINIDAD AND TOBAGO	LEGISLATION Legislation on EEZ and foreign fishing under consideration AGREEMENTS *Agreement of 12 December 1977 with Venezuela - Artisanal fishing vessels allowed - Controls over general and special fishing areas, methods of fishing, minimum mesh size, closed seasons. - Percentage of catch to be sold in Trinidad and Tobago - Other conditions to be prescribed by a mixed fishing commission.	

TABLE C
COASTAL STATE REQUIREMENTS FOR FOREIGN FISHING

STATE	Foreign fishing vessel licence conditions (other than reporting requirements) [including observers, bonds, etc.]	Logbook and reporting requirements for foreign fishing
TUNISIA	LEGISLATION Permit rquired for fishery operations. Permit to specify the period of validity, the type of fishing authorized and the areas to be fished. (Decree of 26 July 1951 revising the legislation on the policing of marine fisheries, Art. 5)	LEGISLATION Fishermen required to furnish statistical or technical information as required by Administration. (Decree of 26 July 1951 revising the legislation on the policing of marine fisheries, Art. 18)
TURKEY	Foreigners or companies whose share holders are foreigners are not allowed to fish in Turkish waters. (Fisheries Law, N° 1380)	
TUVALU	LEGISLATION - Vessel to bear specified identification marks (S. 3) - Such permit conditions as may be prescribed or endorsed on the permit by the Fisheries officer. (S. 5) - Permits to enter limits, fish, load and unload or tranship fish, load or unload fish and supplies. (S. 5) (Fisheries Ordinance, 1978)	
(Cont'd)	LEGISLATION -Licence to be displayed;- vessel to fly flag of registry and call sign or other specified system of recognition; -Vessel to have on board person speaking English and copy of International Code of Signals; -Vessel to stow gear when not authorized to fish; - Vessel to avoid set gear; -vessel not to place fish aggregating devices (FADS) without permission and in accordance conditions set; -No transshipments without prior authorization; -No landing of fish without prior authorization; -Discharge of polluting substances prohibited.	LEGISLATION Foreign vessels authorized to fish in Tuvalu Fishery Limits required to give 24 hours notice of intention to enter or depart fishery limits, reporting details of vessel, position and catch on board; -Vessel to report, by telex to Fisheries Officer: -on entry to and departure from limits; every 7th day while within limits; - reports to give details of vessel (call sign/permit number etc) position and quantity of fish on board.

TABLE C
COASTAL STATE REQUIREMENTS FOR FOREIGN FISHING

STATE	Foreign fishing vessel licence conditions (other than reporting requirements) [including observers, bonds, etc.]	Logbook and reporting requirements for foreign fishing
TUVALU (Cont'd)	-Directions of authorized officers to be obeyed; -Observers to be allowed on board and given full access and facilities; -Master and crew to take reasonable precautions for safety of authorized officers. -Permit holders to give telegraphic address at which all notices may be served -vessel not to fish in territorial waters; -vessel not to call at any Tuvalu port other than port of Funafuti except in case of emergency. (Fisheries (Foreign Fishing Vessel) Regulations, 1982)	-Vessel to maintain logbook of fishing activities in English and forward original unaltered logbook to Fisheries Officer within 45 days of completion of voyage. (Fisheries (Foreign Fishing Vessel) Regulations, 1982)
	AGREEMENTS	AGREEMENTS
	*Agreement with Republic of Korea, 1980 Government of Korea to ensure in accordance with relevant law of Korea, that fishing vessels of Republic of Korea shall not fish in the fishery limits unless licensed under the agreement, and that nationals and vesselsfishing under the agreement comply with provisions of the Agreement	
	*Agreement with Deep-Sea Fisheries Association of Republic of Korea (Dec 1982 - valid thru' Dec 1983) -Captain of licensed vessel to carry copy of permit on board and to produce it on demand by authorized officer if vessel at sea at time of issue, quotation of permit number sufficient -Transfer of permit prohibited -Only long-line fishing authorized -Fishing in territorial waters prohibited -permit may be cancelled or withdrawn if vessel contravenes provisions of agreement, permit or laws. Government to provide statement of offence and supporting evidence, and give Association or vessel owner opportunity to appeal	*Agreement with Deep-Sea Fisheries Association of Republic of Korea 1982 -Licensed vessels to maintain and complete log book in prescribed form -Association to ensure that copies of log books relating to fishing in fishery limits sent to Government as soon as possible and not later than 45 days after completion of voyage.

TABLE C
COASTAL STATE REQUIREMENTS FOR FOREIGN FISHING

STATE	Foreign fishing vessel licence conditions (other than reporting requirements) [including observers, bonds, etc.]	Logbook and reporting requirements for foreign fishing
TUVALU (Cont'd)	Note: Agreement renewed 31 Jan 1984 valid thru' 31 Jan. 1986. Changes to terms unknown. Note: Agreement between New Zealand (for Tokelau), Niue, Tuvalu and Western Samoa and the American Tuna Boat Association, 1983, AGREEMENT NO LONGER IN FORCE Note: -In accordance with the decision of the South Pacific Forum in August 1982 and as from 1 September 1983, no member of the Forum Fisheries Agency will licence a foreign vessel to fish for tuna in their fishing zone unless it is listed in good standing on the regional register maintained by the Forum Fisheries Agency. (Source: AFZ Information Bulletin Canberra May-July 1983)	
USSR	LEGISLATION - Certain fishing areas reserved for nationals; (Decree of the Presidium of the Supreme Soviet of 10 December 1976 S. 2) - Licence conditions may include closed seasons, prohibition of fishing of certain species, use of certain gear, etc.; S. 3) (Decision No. 174 of 25 February 1977) AGREEMENTS *Agreement with Japan Concerning Salmon quotas in Northwest Pacific, 1983 Four Soviet controllers to be on board each vessel (Source: Eurofish Report, May 1983)	

TABLE C
COASTAL STATE REQUIREMENTS FOR FOREIGN FISHING

STATE	Foreign fishing vessel licence conditions (other than reporting requirements) [including observers, bonds, etc.]	Logbook and reporting requirements for foreign fishing
UNITED ARAB EMIRATES	LEGISLATION -Vessels must be duly licensed by competent authorities. Licence to include details regarding compensation due in return for licence, species for which fishing permitted, fishing methods to be used, area covered by leave and permitted quota of catch. Licences only to be issued in respect of "surplus living resources" in Zone (Declaration on the Exclusive Economic Zone and its Delimitation) Minister to issue regulations prescribing terms and conditions of licences (Art 4) -Licence for foreign fishing operations to indicate details of vessel, number of crew, locations and seasons of fishing, species and quantities of living aquatic resources to be caught, fishing techniques and gear to be employed. (Art. 6) -Fishing vessels to carry licence on board and produce to authorized officers on demand (Art. 7) -Vessel to comply with navigational regulations, and have the necessary safety and salvage equipment (Art. 9) -Foreign vessels entering harbour not to sell fish without first obtaining required licence. (Art. 24) (Federal Law of 1982 on Exploitation and Conservation of Living Aquatic Resources)	-Any person engaged in fishing or marketing living aquatic resources or related industries to submit data specified by the competent authority. (Art. 6) (Federal Law of 1982 on Exploitation and Conservation of Living Aquatic Resources)

TABLE C

COASTAL STATE REQUIREMENTS FOR FOREIGN FISHING

STATE	Foreign fishing vessel licence conditions (other than reporting requirements) [including observers, bonds, etc.]	Logbook and reporting requirements for foreign fishing
UNITED KINGDOM	Licence conditions specified in measures for foreign fishing adopted by EEC. 12-mile coastal zone reserved in principle for local fishermen. Limited fishing by Belgium, France, Germany, Ireland and Netherlands in sepcified areas within the 6-12 mile coastal zone. (Council Regulation (EEC) No 170/83 of 25 January 1983)	Specified in measures for foreign fishing adopted by EEC.
UNITED KINGDOM DEPENDENT TERRITORIES - Bermuda	LEGISLATION -Identification marks to be displayed on sides and cabin top or deck so as to be visible from above in characters -Owner or operator to keep log of catch and effort statistics. Statistics required for each line set. -Foreign fishing vessels not to fish within 50 nautical miles of baselines. -Master not to fish in contravention of Fisheries Act. etc. -Transponders or other appropriate position fixing and identifying equipment as Minister determines appropriate or necessary to be installed and maintained in working order on the boat. -Authorized observers to be permitted on board and Government to be reimbursed for the cost. -Agents to be appointed and maintained in Bermuda to receive and respond to any legal process. -When possible, owner/master to train Bermudians on board and hire qualified Bermudians. -failure to comply with conditions may result in suspension or revocation of licence. (Licence conditions pursuant to Fisheries Act 1972,S.7-(2).	LEGISLATION - Master of boat to report to Bermuda through Harbour Radio service before entering EEZ and on leaving EEZ. - Minister may require boat to put into Bermuda to submit statistics and declare catch on completion of each voyage. - Master to report to Bermuda Harbour radio presence of any unlicenced boat fishing in EEZ. - Statistics on catch and effort required for each line set to be submitted to Department of Agriculture and Fisheries at end of fishing activities. (Licence conditions pursuant to Fisheries Act 1972, S. 7 (2))

TABLE C
COASTAL STATE REQUIREMENTS FOR FOREIGN FISHING

STATE	Foreign fishing vessel licence conditions (other than reporting requirements) [including observers, bonds, etc.]	Logbook and reporting requirements for foreign fishing
UNITED KINGDOM DEPENDENT TERRITORIES		
- British Virgin Islands	LEGISLATION Foreign fishing prohibited under the law except for scientific research.	
- Cayman Island	NEW LEGISLATION UNDER CONSIDERATION.	
- Pitcairn Islands	LEGISLATION Governor may by Order prohibit all or specified fishing in Zone except under licence. Licence may contain conditions relating to area, periods, times, quantity of fish, methods, type of gear, training o of Pitcairn Islanders, unse, transfer, transhipment, landing and processing of catch, effort and position of vessel, fisheries research programme, installation and maintenance of equipment, information on fishing operation and identification marks. (Fisheries Zone Ordinance, 1980 S. 5)	
- Turks and Caicos	LEGISLATION - Vessel to display licence number in a prominent place. - Such other conditions as the Governor may consider desirable. (Fisheries Protection Regulations 1976 Reg. 5).	

TABLE C
COASTAL STATE REQUIREMENTS FOR FOREIGN FISHING

STATE	Foreign fishing vessel licence conditions (other than reporting requirements) [including observers, bonds, etc.]	Logbook and reporting requirements for foreign fishing
UNITED STATES OF AMERICA	<u>LEGISLATION</u> -Each Governing International Fishery Agreement to include binding commitment on part of foreign nation and its fishing vessels to comply with specified terms and conditions. -Permit conditions and restrictions to include : -requirements of applicable fisheries management plan; -permit non-transferable; -no transhipment of fish from US vessels unless authorized <u>Magnusson Fishery Conservation and Management Act S201/204</u> -Tunas excluded from exclusive management authority of the USA, but billfishes and anadromous species spawning in national waters are included: (S. 601-11) -vessels to display international radio call sign (IRCS) on both sides of deck house in letters/numbers at least 1 m. high (1/2 m. for vessels 20 metres or less;(S. 611-5) -Operators of vessels to comply with enforcement instructions to facilitate boarding and inspection; (S. 611-6) -vessels to accept observers and provide facilities and access to communication facilities; (S. 611-8) -Vessels to take care to avoid fixed gear if using mobile gear; (S. 611-11) -vessels to maintain plots of location of fixed gear broadcast by coastguard; (S.611-11 -gear conflicts to be reported to coastguard; (S. 611-11) -fishing authorization to lapse when national catch quota reached; (S. 611-15) -incidental catch of prohibited species to be minimized, incidental catch of regulated species must be authorized on permit if to be retained; (S. 611-13-14)	<u>LEGISLATION</u> -Vessel to notify regional office of National Marine Fisheries Service and coastguard of time and location of commencement and ceasing of operations at least 24 hours in advance; (S. 611-4) -Vessel to notify temporary departures from fishing grounds and return to grounds, shifts in fishing area (S. 611-4) -Vessel to maintain log book of catch and effort information, and daily cumulative log; (S. 611-9) -Transfers of fish to be recorded; (S. 611-9) -Records to be available for inspection; (S. 611-9) -Records to be maintained on daily basis of position, amount of catch, date, type of gear, effort; S. 611-9 -Weekly report to be submitted by country representatives showing effort and yield; (S. 611-9) -Weekly reports normally to be submitted by 4th day following end of reporting week (S. 611-9) -Weekly reports required of receipts of US harvested fish and marine mammals incidental catch (S. 611-9) - Other information may be required. <u>(Code of Federal Regulations, 1984)</u>

TABLE C
COASTAL STATE REQUIREMENTS FOR FOREIGN FISHING

STATE	Foreign fishing vessel licence conditions (other than reporting requirements) [including observers, bonds, etc.]	Logbook and reporting requirements for foreign fishing
UNITED STATES OF AMERICA (Cont'd)	-unattended gear to be conspicuously marked; (S. 611-5) -catch quotas, closed seasons, gear (mesh), restrictions specified for each target fishery; -vessels must have special permit to receive US - caught fish. (S. 611-10) (Code of Federal Regulations 1984) AGREEMENTS *Agreement with Panama and Costa Rica, 14 March 1983 (not in force) Covers tuna species in Eastern Pacific Ocean. Area covered includes waters under national jurisdiction of Contracting Parties as well as high seas adjacent to them (Art. II (B). Note: A Council to be established whose functions include: to issue licences in respect of fishing in Agreement Area, to appoint national authority to issue licences for Agreement Area and to establish licence fee according to Protocol to the Agreement. Coastal States defined in Art. II (B) and member States of IATTC may become parties to the Agreement (Art. VII). Other States may adhere to the Agreement by unanimous approval of the Council (Art. VIII)	All licenced vessels to provide written reports on size of the catches taken in Agreement Area and where the catches were made. These details must be entered in logbook of each licensed fishing vessel.
U.S. TRUST TERRIT. - Federated States of Micronesia	LEGISLATION -In negotiating foreign fishing agreement, the Authority shall seek substantial agreement that the foreign party and owners and operators of vessels fishing under agreement to: -abide by all regulations issued; -permit authorized officers to board, search, inspect any vessel at any time and make arrests and seizures where	

TABLE C
COASTAL STATE REQUIREMENTS FOR FOREIGN FISHING

STATE	Foreign fishing vessel licence conditions (other than reporting requirements) [including observers, bonds, etc.]	Logbook and reporting requirements for foreign fishing
U.S. TRUST TERRIT. - Federated States of Micronesia (Cont'd)	reasonable cause to believe offence committed; -prominently display permit in wheelhouse; -cause appropriate position fixing and identification equipment to be installed and maintained; -permit observers on board vessels and reimburse Govt. for costs incurred; -appoint and maintian agents authorized to receive and respond to legal process; -not in any year exceed such party's allocation of TAC. (Title 52, Trust Territory Code)	
	AGREEMENTS	
	*Agreement with Japanese Fishing Associations, 1984 -Organizations to use best efforts to ensure that their members comply with Act and terms of Agreement and to ensure that all judgments and orders concerning violations entered by courts are satisfied. -Only fishing for tuna and tuna-like fishes, billfish and incidental catches by long-line, pole and line and purse-seine methods allowed -No fishing permitted within 3 mile territorial sea or 12 mile exclusive fishing zone, except with approval state -No catch quotas established; number of vessels limited to maximum of 650 -Permits to be prominently displayed in wheelhouses -permits may be applied for and issued (permit number)by telegram -Permits non-transferable -Permits may be cancelled or withdrawn for contraventions Authority to notify Organizations and permit appeals -Authorized officers to be permitted to board and inspect and make arrests and seizures on reasonable grounds	*Agreement with Japanese Fishing Associations, 1984 -Each vessel to maintain daily catch records in annexed form Certified copy of original of catch records to be dis-patched through Organizations to Authority within 45 days of end of trip -Statements of No Operation for licensed veesels which have not fished in FSM waters during any quarter to be dispatched to Authority within 45 days of end of quarter -Vessel failing to submit catch records or statement of no operation must pay penalty of Y500 000 to the Authority for each failure

TABLE C
COASTAL STATE REQUIREMENTS FOR FOREIGN FISHING

STATE	Foreign fishing vessel licence conditions (other than reporting requirements) [including observers, bonds, etc.]	Logbook and reporting requirements for foreign fishing
U.S. TRUST TERRIT. - Federated States of Micronesia (Cont'd)	-Observers may be boarded; maximum of 2 observer trips for single purse seine vessels, and 2 for group purse seiners Normal food and accomodation to be provided, observer not to intervene in lawful operation of vessel -Position fixing/identification equipment to be installed -Agent or agents to be maintained in FSM authorized to receive and respond to any legal process issued in respect of any vessel owned by members of Organization. Note: -In accordance with the decision of the South Pacific Forum in August 1982 and as from 1 September 1983, no member of the Forum Fisheries Agency will licence a foreign vessel to fish for tuna in their fishing zone unless it is listed in good standing on the regional register maintained by the Forum Fisheries Agency. (Source: AFZ Information Bulletin Canberra May-July 1983)	
U.S. TRUST TERRIT. - Marshall Islands	LEGISLATION -In negotiating foreign fishing agreement, the Authority shall seek substantial agreement that the foreign party and owners and operators of vessels fishing under agreement will fulfill following conditions: -abide by all regulations issued; -not exceed such party's allocation of TAC; -permit authorized officers to board, search, inspect any vessel at any time and make arrests an seizures where reasonable cause to believe offence committed; -permit authorized officers to examine and make notations on permit; -prominently display permit in wheelhouse;	

TABLE C

COASTAL STATE REQUIREMENTS FOR FOREIGN FISHING

STATE	Foreign fishing vessel licence conditions (other than reporting requirements) [including observers, bonds, etc.]	Logbook and reporting requirements for foreign fishing
U.S. TRUST TERRIT. - Marshall Islands (Cont'd)	-cause appropriate position fixing and identification equipment to be installed and maintained; -permit observers on board vessels and reimburse Govt. for costs incurred; -appoint and maintain agents authorized to receive and respond to legal process; Marshall Islands Marine Resources Jurisdiction Act of 1978 AGREEMENTS *Agreement with Japan, 1981 (current Head Agreement) -Government of Japan to take necessary measures to ensure, in accordance with relevant laws and regulations of Japan, that fishing vessels of Japan shall not fish in Zone unless licensed and if licensed shall comply with Agreement and terms and conditions of licenses *Agreement with Federation of Japanese Tuna Fisheries Cooperative Associations and National Off-Shore Tuna Fisheries Association, valid from 1 May 1985 thru' 30 April 1986 and thereafter until 6 months after notice of termination by either party)(under 1981 Head Agreement) -Only fishing for tuna and tuna-like fishes, billfish and incidental catches by long-line, pole and line and hand-lining allowed. No purse-seining without Govt. approval. -Organizations shall undertake best efforts to ensure that members comply with laws of Republic and terms of agreement and that no fishing by members in zone except in accordance with permit conditions -Vessels required to be registered with Authority before can apply for permit. Form of reg. application specified. -Permits to be applied for by cable or telex for each fishing trip. Permits valid 1 trip only and non-transferable -No fishing permitted within 12 mile territorial sea or a radius of 2 miles from any fish aggregating device. -Permits to be prominently displayed in wheelhouses and produced on demand -Position fixing and identification equipment to be installed and maintained in working order on vessels in zone	AGREEMENTS *Agreement with Federation of Japanese Tuna Fisheries Cooperative Associations etc. of 1 May 1985 -Vessels to report on entry into and departure from zone in annexed form. Reports to be telexed not later than 48 hours after entry or departure -Vessel to report to Authority in specified format after completion fishing trip (within 48 hours) -Vessel to give weekly position and catch reports while in zone in annexed form -All reports to be made by telex, radio or cable. -Vessel to maintain daily catch records in annexed form -Daily catch records to be produced on demand -Copy of catch records to be submitted to Authority within 45 days of completion of voyage -Authority may refuse to grant permits to vessels failing to submit catch records as required.

TABLE C
COASTAL STATE REQUIREMENTS FOR FOREIGN FISHING

STATE	Foreign fishing vessel licence conditions (other than reporting requirements) [including observers, bonds, etc.]	Logbook and reporting requirements for foreign fishing
U.S. TRUST TERRIT. - Marshall Islands (Cont'd)	-Observers to be permitted to board, to be provided with food, accomodation and medical care equivalent to officers -Observers to be allowed access to facilities and catch. -Vessels to be appropriately and adequately insured for general liability and oil pollution damage. -Organizations to ensure that judgments entered against members are satisfied -Agent or agents to be maintained in Marshalls authorized to receive and respond to any legal process issued in respect of any vessel owned by members of Organization. -Vessels to display Radio Call Sign or Signal Letters on top and both sides amidships of vessel where clearly discernible from air and sea, in letters and numbers at least 1 metre high by 40 cms wide on contrasting background if no radio call sign, vessel registration number. -Name of vessel to be printed in English on bow and stern. Note: In accordance with the decision of the South Pacific Forum in August 1982 and as from 1 September 1983, no member of the Forum Fisheries Agency will licence a foreign vessel to fish for tuna in their fishing zone unless it is listed in good standing on the regional register maintained by the Forum Fisheries Agency. (Source: AFZ Information Bulletin Canberra May-July 1983)	
U.S. TRUST TERRIT. - Palau	LEGISLATION -In negotiating foreign fishing agreement, the Authority to seek substantial agreement that the foreign party and owners and operators of vessels fishing under agreement to: -abide by all regulations issued; -permit authorized officers to board, search, inspect any vessel at any time and make arrests and seizures where reasonable cause to believe offence committed; -permit authorized officers to examine and make notations on permit;	

TABLE C
COASTAL STATE REQUIREMENTS FOR FOREIGN FISHING

STATE	Foreign fishing vessel licence conditions (other than reporting requirements) [including observers, bonds, etc.]	Logbook and reporting requirements for foreign fishing
U.S. TRUST TERRIT. - Palau (Cont'd)	-prominently display permit in wheelhouse; -cause appropriate position fixing and identification equipment to be installed and maintained; -permit observers on board vessels and reimburse Govt. for costs incurred; -appoint and maintain agents authorized to receive and respond to legal process; -not in any year exceed such party's allocation of TAC. (Public Law No. 6-7-14)	
	AGREEMENTS -*Agreement with Fisheries Associations of Japan, 1983 -Associations to ensure that their members do not fish without permit and comply with fisheries laws and to use best efforts to ensure that any judgments for violations entered by courts are satisfied. -Only fishing for living resources normally taken by tuna long-line, skipjack pole and line or purse seine methods -Permits to be prominently displayed in wheelhouses -Permits non-transferable 12 mile exclusive fishing zone, except with approval state -Number of vessels limited to 290; no catch limits -vessels to display radio call sign pained in conspicuous location on side of vessel in contrasting colours, with letters at least 1 metre high and 40 cms wide. -Authorized officers to be permitted to board and inspect and make arrests and seizures on reasonable grounds -Observers may be boarded; to be assisted in performance of duties; acceptable procedures to be agreed upon -Observers not to interfere in lawful operation of vessel -Observers to be given access to facilities and equipment -Agent or agents to be maintained in Palau authorized to receive and respond to any legal process issued in respect of any vessel owned by members of Organization.	AGREEMENTS -*Agreement with Fisheries Associations of Japan, 1983 -Each vessel to maintain current fishing logs, listing inter alia, date, position, time and catch -Vessels to complete catch reports in annexed form. -Associations to ensure catch reports dispatched to Authority within 45 days of end of trip -Associations to airmail, in timely manner, monthly summaries from selected markets of weight and value of species landed

TABLE C
COASTAL STATE REQUIREMENTS FOR FOREIGN FISHING

STATE	Foreign fishing vessel licence conditions (other than reporting requirements) [including observers, bonds, etc.]	Logbook and reporting requirements for foreign fishing
U.S. TRUST TERRIT. Palau (Cont'd)	-Associations to use best efforts to ensure that vessels have appropriate and adequate insurance *Agreement with Sino-Palau Fishing Co. Ltd. 1982 -Fishing for tuna, sharks and other fishes taken by long-line and seine methods -No fishing within 50 miles of Malakal Harbour -Fishing by small seiners and/or net trawlers in territorial sea and exclusive fishery zone prohibited -Capture and retention of reef and lagoon fish prohibited -Vessels to board observers and provide food/accomodation -Vessels to allow authorized officers to board and inspect -Company vessels to have adequate insurance to compensate local parties for damage, including to fishing gear -Permit to be prominently displayed in wheelhouse -Permits non-transferable -Company to satisfy legal judgments -Company to designate local agent, to receive service of process and other legal purposes Note: -In accordance with the decision of the South Pacific Forum in August 1982 and as from 1 September 1983, no member of the Forum Fisheries Agency will licence a foreign vessel to fish for tuna in their fishing zone unless it is listed in good standing on the regional register maintained by the Forum Fisheries Agency. (Source: AFZ Information Bulletin Canberra May-July 1983)	*Agreement with Sino-Palau Fishing Co. Ltd. 1982 -Company to complete and file catch reports in annexed form; reports to be submitted to Authority within 15 days of end of each calendar month Catch reports to contain record of each day's activities

TABLE C
COASTAL STATE REQUIREMENTS FOR FOREIGN FISHING

STATE	Foreign fishing vessel licence conditions (other than reporting requirements) [including observers, bonds, etc.]	Logbook and reporting requirements for foreign fishing
URUGUAY	LEGISLATION -12 mile area reserved for national vessels. (Art. 1) -generally vessels fishing for national industries and landing catch in Uruguayan port must hold Uruguayan registration; (Art. 4) -exceptionally on recommendation SOYP foreign vessels may be allowed for limited period (up to 5 years) and revocable for reasons of the special nature of fishing operations to be undertaken; (Art. 14) -foreign vessels subject to laws and conservation controls; (Art. 9) -permits to foreign boats must be recorded in special SOYP register; (Art. 8) -May require as licence condition that all catch be landed and totally or partially processed in Uruguay -transhipment of catch in port or zone prohibited except for export in which case must be in port and under supervision of authorities; (Art. 12) -permission for transhipment required; (Art. 12) -licences transferable only with permission of authorities (Decree No. 540/971 of 26 August 1971)	LEGISLATION - Must notify General Maritime Prefecture of entry and departure from Territorial Seas. (Art. 10) - Must report to SOYP daily at midday position and catch by species. (Art. 10) (Decree No. 540/971 of 26 August 1971)
VANUATU	LEGISLATION Access agreements to include provision establishing responsibility of foreign country or association to take necessary measures to ensure compliance by its vessels with agreement and fishing laws. (S. 3(3)) -Fishing gear to be stowed except where authorized to fish -licences subject to general conditions to be prescribed, and to special conditions specified by the Minister. (The Fisheries Act, No. 37 of 1982, S. 5 & 13) Only species specified in licence may be caught.	LEGISLATION LOGBOOK A logbook to be kept on board recording on a daily basis the details of the fishing operation. Logbook to be transmitted to the Director of Fisheries or other authorized person in its original form within 45 days of completion of voyage or at any time requested by the Director of Fisheries or any authorized officer. Vessels required to report to the Director of Fishery or person authorized by him immediately after entering and

TABLE C
COASTAL STATE REQUIREMENTS FOR FOREIGN FISHING

STATE	Foreign fishing vessel licence conditions (other than reporting requirements) [including observers, bonds, etc.]	Logbook and reporting requirements for foreign fishing
VANUATU (Cont'd)	No fish may be transhipped from or onto the vessel while in Vanatu Waters. -Vessel to fly the flag of its State, display identification marks and its international radio call or the number assigned to it. -Change in information to be notified within 7 days -No fishing to be undertaken except authorized by licence -Vessel to allow observers to board and give full access and facilities; -Vessel to take precautions to avoid damage to local fishing operations. (The Fisheries Regulations, 1983) Note: -In accordance with the decision of the South Pacific Forum in August 1982 and as from 1 September 1983, no member of the Forum Fisheries Agency will licence a foreign vessel to fish for tuna in their fishing zone unless it is listed in good standing on the regional register maintained by the Forum Fisheries Agency. (Source: AFZ Information Bulletin Canberra May-July 1983)	leaving and once a week while in Vanatu Waters the following information: international radio call sign or number assigned to it, position of vessel at the time of report and total catch by species on board at the time of the report. (The Fisheries Regulations, 1983)
VENEZUELA	LEGISLATION -fishery resources of the EEZ reserved for nationals or foreigners of States which have negotiated bilateral agreements; (Exclusive Economic Zone Act of 26 July 1978)	

TABLE C
COASTAL STATE REQUIREMENTS FOR FOREIGN FISHING

STATE	Foreign fishing vessel licence conditions (other than reporting requirements) [including observers, bonds, etc.]	Logbook and reporting requirements for foreign fishing
VENEZUELA (cont'd)	-Permits to specify area to be fished, authorized methods and gear, species to be fished, identification of fishing boats to be used, person under whose responsibility fishing to be carried out and period of validity of permit (Decree No. 829 of 1 April 1975 Art. 3) AGREEMENTS *Agreement with Trinidad and Tobago of 12 December 1977 -foreign fishing under agreement only beyond 2 miles from coast except in special areas (Art. 4) In special areas -only vessels under 12 meters of artisanal construction and maximum capacity of 1 ton to be used; (Art. 7) -mesh size limitation; maximum of 4 crew members;(Art. 7) -50% of the catch to be sold in Venezuela. (Art. 7) Other conditions to be set by mixed fishing Commission	
VIETNAM	LEGISLATION Fishing licence required; valid one year (Enactment No. 31 of 29 Jan. 1980 Art. 4) Foreign fishing ships navigating in EEZ to stow gear, fish finders and alluring devices etc. (Art. 12) Vessel to compensate state enterprises and nationals for damage to resources or property. (Enactment No. 30 of January 29 1980 Art. 10)	LEGISLATION Licensed vessels to notify Ministry of place from which vessels to start their trips at least 1 week before coming to fishing grounds. (Art. 6) Licensed vessels to report annually to Ministry of Marine Products on operation of vessels and to report results of each fishing trip in prescribed form.(Art. 8) (Enactment No. 30 of January 29 1980)
WESTERN SAMOA	LEGISLATION Licence conditions may include: -determination of fishing areas, seasons, times and voyages during which fishing authorized; -species, size, age and quantities of fish to be taken; -methods of taking fish, types, size, and amounts of gear;	LEGISLATION Licence conditions may require reporting of catch and effort and vessel position reports. (Exclusive Economic Zone Act 1977, S. 5)

TABLE C
COASTAL STATE REQUIREMENTS FOR FOREIGN FISHING

STATE	Foreign fishing vessel licence conditions (other than reporting requirements) [including observers, bonds, etc.]	Logbook and reporting requirements for foreign fishing
WESTERN SAMOA (Cont'd)	-requirements concerning use, transfer, landing and ; -processing; -requirements concerning entry into port for inspection; -compensation payable for damage to local gear catch or fish stocks; -conduct of research; -acceptance on board of Samoan trainees; -display of licence, marking of the craft; -directions of authorized officers to be complied with -placing of observers on the vessel and reimbursement of costs to the Government; -installation of transponders or other position fixing position fixing equipment; -carriage of specified nautical charts. (Exclusive Economic Zone Act 1977, S. 5) AGREEMENTS Note: Agreement between New Zealand (for Tokelau), Niue, Tuvalu and Western Samoa and the American Tuna Boat Association, 1983, AGREEMENT NO LONGER IN FORCE Note: -In accordance with the decision of the South Pacific Forum in August 1982 and as from 1 September 1983, no member of the Forum Fisheries Agency will licence a foreign vessel to fish for tuna in their fishing zone unless it is listed in good standing on the regional register maintained by the Forum Fisheries Agency. (Source: AFZ Information Bulletin Canberra May-July 1983)	

TABLE C

COASTAL STATE REQUIREMENTS FOR FOREIGN FISHING

STATE	Foreign fishing vessel licence conditions (other than reporting requirements) [including observers, bonds, etc.]	Logbook and reporting requirements for foreign fishing
YEMEN ARAB REPUBLIC	LEGISLATION -Each licensed boat to have letters and numbers of licence painted on it (Fisheries Law No 20 of 1978 Art 3)	LEGISLATION
YEMEN DEM. REPUBLIC	LEGISLATION Minister to regulate by resolution issue of permits (Law No 24 of 1979 Concerning the Organization of the Catches of Marine Resources and their Exploitation and Protection Art. 11) AGREEMENTS Conditions include specification of target species, areas. -Percentage of crew of each vessel to be local; -Observers permanently on board; -Provision made for compensation for local gear damaged; -Use of by-catch specified; -Transhipment of catch only in local ports; -Percentage of catch to be supplied to local markets; -Licence duration not more than 2 years renewable.	LEGISLATION AGREEMENTS Reports to be made daily and weekly. Data required includes information for calculation of royalty payments as well as for biological analysis.
YUGOSLAVIA		
ZAIRE	LEGISLATION Licences may be issued to industrial fishing vessels. Industrial fishing vessels defined as to have capacity to catch over 300 tons of fish. (Ordinnance No. 79-244 Oct. 1979 Art. 23)	

TABLE D

COMPLIANCE CONTROL AND REPORTING CONDITIONS

COMPLIANCE CONTROL AND OTHER CONDITIONS

*. Provisions contained in legislation or agreements regarding flag state responsibility for compliance control
A. Vessel to bear specified identification markings
B. Licence/permit to be carried on board
C. Vessel to board observers as required
D. Vessel to submit fishing plan
E. Vessel to put in for port inspections on entry/departure from zone
F. Vessel to carry specified position fixing equipment/transponders
G. Vessel owners to appoint local legal agents
H. Flag state to appoint national representative
I. Vessel to post performance bond/guarantee/deposit
J. Vessel to carry interpreters
K. Vessel to seek prior authorization for transhipments
L. Vessel to stow gear while in area where not authorized to fish
M. Requirements concerning local landing/processing of catch
N. Requirements concerning protection of local fisheries/gear
O. Requirements concerning employment/training of coastal state nationals in crew

REPORTING REQUIREMENTS

P. Reporting on or prior to entry into the zone
Q. Reporting on or prior to departure from the zone
R. Reporting on commencement or cessation of fishing operations
S. Reporting on or prior to entry into coastal state ports
T. Timely reporting on position
U. Timely reporting on catch and effort
V. Maintenance of fishing logs.
W. Submission logbooks/catch reports: - on request/as required/at specified intervals
X. Submission logbooks/catch reports: - on entry into port
Y. Submission logbooks/catch reports: - on/after completion voyage/end of permit
Z. Controls over transitting of zone by unlicensed foreign fishing vessels

TABLE D

COMPLIANCE CONTROL AND REPORTING CONDITIONS

COASTAL COUNTRIES	*	A	B	C	D	E	F	G	H	I	J	K	L	M	N	O	P	Q	R	S	T	U	V	W	X	Y	Z
ALBANIA																											
ALGERIA																											
ANGOLA		X	X	X	X							X		X		X	X							X90			
ANTIGUA & BARBUDA	X												X														
ARGENTINA																											
AUSTRALIA *	X	X		X		X							X	X	X		X	X	X	X	XD2	X6	XD	X	X	X	X
BAHAMAS																											X
BAHREIN																											
BANGLADESH		X		X	X	X	X	X		XR		X	X		X	X	X24	X48			XWR	XWR	XD	XMR			
BARBADOS																											
BELGIUM		X	X												X		X	X		X	X%	X%	XO				
BELIZE																											
BENIN										X				X	X	X											
BRAZIL				X				X				X		X	X	X	X	X			XD		X	XR			
BULGARIA																											
BURMA																											
CAMEROON														X	X												
CANADA		X		X	X		X	X					X		X		X24	X72		X24	XW	XW	XD	XR		X60	
CAPE VERDE															X									XM			
CHILE				X								X		X	X		X	X						X			
CHINA																											
COLOMBIA					X					X				X	X									X			
COMORO ISLANDS															X												

\- For key to alphabetical code see page preceding this table.

\- Numbers represent periodicity of reports (in days/hours) or deadlines for submission of reports; W = weekly; D = daily; M = monthly; R = on request.

% = Reports to be made daily for Spanish vessels, every 3 days for vessels from Norway, Sweden and Faroes when fishing for herring, weekly when fishing for other species.

0 = Logbook to be filled out (radio report to be made) after every fishing operation.

* = Country is a party to the South Pacific FFA arrangement that licences will not be issued to foreign fishing vessels unless those vessels are listed in good standing on the regional register of fishing vessels maintained by FFA.

TABLE D
COMPLIANCE CONTROL AND REPORTING CONDITIONS

COASTAL COUNTRIES	*	A	B	C	D	E	F	G	H	I	J	K	L	M	N	O	P	Q	R	S	T	U	V	W	X	Y	Z
CONGO (PEOPLES' REP)	X													X													
COSTA RICA										X		X		X	X	X											X
CUBA																											
CYPRUS																											
DJIBOUTI																											
DOMINICA																											
DOMINICAN REP.																											
DENMARK		X	X												X		X	X		X	X%	X%	XO				
ECUADOR				X				X				X			X											X	X
EGYPT, ARAB REP.																											
EL SALVADOR			X	X								X		X	X											X	X
EQUATORIAL GUINEA				X										X	X	X						XO				X	
ETHIOPIA																											
EUROPEAN COMMUNITY		X	X												X		X	X		X	X%	X%	XO				
FIJI *		X		X	X	X	X		X		X	X	X	X			X24	X		X24	XD	XW	XD	X	X72		
FINLAND																											
FRANCE		X	X												X		X	X			XW	XW	X				
FRENCH DEP. TERRIT.																											

- For key to alphabetical code see page preceding this table.
- Numbers represent periodicity of reports (in days/hours) or deadlines for submission of reports; W = weekly; D = daily; M = monthly; R = on request.

% = Reports to be made daily for Spanish vessels, every 3 days for vessels from Norway, Sweden and Faroes when fishing for herring, weekly when fishing for other species.

0 = Logbook to be filled out (radio report to be made) after every fishing operation.

* = Country is a party to the South Pacific FFA arrangement that licences will not be issued to foreign fishing vessels unless those vessels are listed in good standing on the regional register of fishing vessels maintained by FFA.

TABLE D
COMPLIANCE CONTROL AND REPORTING CONDITIONS

COASTAL COUNTRIES	*	A	B	C	D	E	F	G	H	I	J	K	L	M	N	O	P	Q	R	S	T	U	V	W	X	Y	Z
-DEPT. OF GUYANA		X	X	X	X									X	X		X	X		X	X%	X%	XO			X30	
-NEW CALEDONIA			X									X					X	X		X			X				
GABON															X									X			
GAMBIA THE												X	X	X										X			
GERMAN DEM. REP.																											
GERMANY FED.REP.		X	X												X		X	X		X	X%	X%	XO				
GHANA		X												X										X			
GREECE		X	X												X		X	X		X	X%	X%	XO				
GRENADA																											
GUATEMALA								X		X				X										X			
GUINEA	X	X		X		X		X				X	X		X	X	X				XR		X	XM		X	
GUINEA-BISSAU				X										X		X								X90			
GUYANA		X												X			X	X			XD		X	X90		X	
HAITI												X		X	X	X							X	180			
HONDURAS															X												
ICELAND																					XD			X			
INDIA		X		X				X					X				X	X	X	X			XD				X
INDONESIA								X								X										X30	
IRAN																											
IRAQ																											
IRELAND		X	X												X		X	X		X	X%	X%	XO				

- For key to alphabetical code see page preceding this table.
- Numbers represent periodicity of reports (in days/hours) or deadlines for submission of reports; W = weekly; D = daily; M = monthly; R = on request.

% = Reports to be made daily for Spanish vessels, every 3 days for vessels from Norway, Sweden and Faroes when fishing for herring, weekly when fishing for other species.

0 = Logbook to be filled out (radio report to be made) after every fishing operation.

* = Country is a party to the South Pacific FFA arrangement that licences will not be issued to foreign fishing vessels unless those vessels are listed in good standing on the regional register of fishing vessels maintained by FFA.

TABLE D

COMPLIANCE CONTROL AND REPORTING CONDITIONS

COASTAL COUNTRIES	*	A	B	C	D	E	F	G	H	I	J	K	L	M	N	O	P	Q	R	S	T	U	V	W	X	Y	Z
ISRAEL																											
ITALY		X	X												X		X	X		X	X%	X%	XO				
IVORY COAST															X												
JAMAICA																											
JAPAN		X	X												X												
JORDAN																											
KAMPUCHEA																											
KENYA																											
KIRIBATI *	X	X	X	X				X					X		X		X	X			XW	XW	XD	X		X45	
KOREA, D.P.R.																											
KOREA, REP OF										X				X	X									X			
KUWAIT																											
LEBANON																											
LIBERIA		X		X										X	X									X90			
LIBYA																											
MADAGASCAR				X				X							X	X					X3	X3		XM		X	
MALAYSIA	X							X		X			X		X		X										X
MALDIVES	NO FOREIGN FISHING ALLOWED																										
MALTA														X										X			
MAURITANIA				X										X	X									X			
MAURITIUS																											
MEXICO								X		X				X	X	X								X			
MONACO																											

\- For key to alphabetical code see page preceding this table.

\- Numbers represent periodicity of reports (in days/hours) or deadlines for submission of reports; W = weekly; D = daily; M = monthly; R = on request.

% = Reports to be made daily for Spanish vessels, every 3 days for vessels from Norway, Sweden and Faroes when fishing for herring, weekly when fishing for other species.

0 = Logbook to be filled out (radio report to be made) after every fishing operation.

* = Country is a party to the South Pacific FFA arrangement that licences will not be issued to foreign fishing vessels unless those vessels are listed in good standing on the regional register of fishing vessels maintained by FFA.

TABLE D
COMPLIANCE CONTROL AND REPORTING CONDITIONS

COASTAL COUNTRIES	*	A	B	C	D	E	F	G	H	I	J	K	L	M	N	O	P	O	R	S	T	U	V	W	X	Y	Z
MOROCCO															X												
MOZAMBIQUE		X																									X
NAMIBIA																											
NAURU																											
NETHERLANDS		X	X												X		X	X		X	X%	X%	XO				
NEW ZEALAND *		X	X	X	X	X			X		X	X	X	X	X		X24	X		X24	XD	XDW	XD	X	X72		
(DEPENDENT TERRITORIES)																											
-TOKELAU *															X		X	X			XW	XW	X				
(ASSOCIATED STATES)																											
-COOK ISLANDS *		X	X	X	X	X			X		X	X	X	X			X24	X		X24	XD	XDW	XD	X	X72		
-NIUE *															X		X	X			XW	XW	X				
NICARAGUA										X				X	X												
NIGERIA	NO FOREIGN FISHING ALLOWED																										
NORWAY	X	X	X	X	X									X	X		X	X	X			XW	XD	XM			
OMAN	X												X									X	X				
PAKISTAN														X										X			
PANAMA								X							X									X			
PAPUA NEW GUINEA *		X		X				X				X	X		X		X24	X24			XW	XW	XD			X45	
PERU	X		X				X		X					X		X	X		X	XD	XD				X		
PHILIPPINES				X										X		X							XD	XM			

- For key to alphabetical code see page preceding this table.
- Numbers represent periodicity of reports (in days/hours) or deadlines for submission of reports; W = weekly; D = daily; M = monthly; R = on request.

% = Reports to be made daily for Spanish vessels, every 3 days for vessels from Norway, Sweden and Faroes when fishing for herring, weekly when fishing for other species.

0 = Logbook to be filled out (radio report to be made) after every fishing operation.

* = Country is a party to the South Pacific FFA arrangement that licences will not be issued to foreign fishing vessels unless those vessels are listed in good standing on the regional register of fishing vessels maintained by FFA.

TABLE D
COMPLIANCE CONTROL AND REPORTING CONDITIONS

COASTAL COUNTRIES	*	A	B	C	D	E	F	G	H	I	J	K	L	M	N	O	P	Q	R	S	T	U	V	W	X	Y	Z
POLAND		X																									
PORTUGAL		X													X		X	X				X	XW	X		X60	
QATAR		X												X										X			
ROMANIA																											
ST. CRISTOPHER & NEVIS	X												X														
ST. LUCIA	X												X														
ST. VINCENT																											
SAO TOME & PRINCIPE	X			X											X	X	X	X			XD	XD					
SAUDI ARABIA																								X			
SENEGAL				X						X				X	X	X									X1		
SEYCHELLES	X	X		X		X	X	X		X	*	X	X	X	X	X	X	X48		X24	X3	X3	XD	X		X30	X
SIERRA LEONE		X													X									X			
SINGAPORE																											
SOLOMON ISLANDS *	X	X	X	X				X					X		X		X24	X			XW	XW	XD			X7	
SOMALI DEM REP				X																	X					X	
SOUTH AFRICA		X																					X	X			
SPAIN																											X
SRI LANKA		X		X	X	X		X					X		X		X24	X24			X	X	XD	X		X30	
SUDAN		X												X													
SURINAME		X	X														X	X			XD		X			X	X

- For key to alphabetical code see page preceding this table.
- Numbers represent periodicity of reports (in days/hours) or deadlines for submission of reports; W = weekly; D = daily; M = monthly; R = on request.

% = Reports to be made daily for Spanish vessels, every 3 days for vessels from Norway, Sweden and Faroes when fishing for herring, weekly when fishing for other species.

0 = Logbook to be filled out (radio report to be made) after every fishing operation.

* = Country is a party to the South Pacific FFA arrangement that licences will not be issued to foreign fishing vessels unless those vessels are listed in good standing on the regional register of fishing vessels maintained by FFA.

TABLE D

COMPLIANCE CONTROL AND REPORTING CONDITIONS

COASTAL COUNTRIES	*	A	B	C	D	E	F	G	H	I	J	K	L	M	N	O	P	Q	R	S	T	U	V	W	X	Y	Z
SWEDEN		X																	X		XD	X	X				
SYRIAN ARAB REP																											
TANZANIA		X																									
THAILAND																											
TOGO																											
TONGA																											
TRINIDAD & TOBAGO															X												
TUNISIA																								X			
TURKEY																											
TUVALU *		X	X	X							X	X	X	X	X		X24	X24			XW	XW	XD			X45	
USSR			X											X													
UNITED ARAB EMIRATES				X										X										X			
UK	X	X												X		X	X		X	X%	X%	XO					
UK DEP. TERRITORIES																											
-BERMUDA		X		X		X	X	X							X	X	X	X					X			X	
-BRITISH VIRGIN ISLES																											
-CAYMAN ISLANDS																											
-PITCAIRN ISLANDS																											
-TURKS & CAICOS		X																									
USA	X	X	X			X	X	X			X			X				X				XD	X14				

- For key to alphabetical code see page preceding this table.
- Numbers represent periodicity of reports (in days/hours) or deadlines for submission of reports; W = weekly; D = daily; M = monthly; R = on request.

% = Reports to be made daily for Spanish vessels, every 3 days for vessels from Norway, Sweden and Faroes when fishing for herring, weekly when fishing for other species.

0 = Logbook to be filled out (radio report to be made) after every fishing operation.

* = Country is a party to the South Pacific FFA arrangement that licences will not be issued to foreign fishing vessels unless those vessels are listed in good standing on the regional register of fishing vessels maintained by FFA.

TABLE D
COMPLIANCE CONTROL AND REPORTING CONDITIONS

COASTAL COUNTRIES	*	A	B	C	D	E	F	G	H	I	J	K	L	M	N	O	P	Q	R	S	T	U	V	W	X	Y	Z
US DEPENDENT TERRITORIES																											
-FED STATES OF MICRONESIA *	X	X	X	X			X	X							X								XD	X		X45	
-MARSHALL ISLANDS *	X	X	X	X			X	X					X		X		X	X	X	X	X	X	XD	XW		X45	
-PALAU *	X	X	X	X			X	X							X								X	X		X45	
URUGUAY											X			X		X	X			XD	XD						
VANUATU *	X	X		X									X		X		X	X			XW	XW	XD	X		X45	
VENEZUELA														X	X												
VIET NAM													X				XW							XY		X	
WESTERN SAMOA *													X		(X)		(X)	(X)			(XW)	(XW)	(X)				
YEMEN ARAB REP		X																									
YEMEN PEOPLES D.R.				X								X		X	X	X					XD	XDW					
YUGOSLAVIA																											
ZAIRE																											

- For key to alphabetical code see page preceding this table.
- Numbers represent periodicity of reports (in days/hours) or deadlines for submission of reports; W = weekly; D = daily; M = monthly; R = on request; Y = yearly.

% = Reports to be made daily for Spanish vessels, every 3 days for vessels from Norway, Sweden and Faroes when fishing for herring, weekly when fishing for other species.

0 = Logbook to be filled out (radio report to be made) after every fishing operation.

* = Country is a party to the South Pacific FFA arrangement that licences will not be issued to foreign fishing vessels unless those vessels are listed in good standing on the regional register of fishing vessels maintained by FFA.

TABLE E
PENALTIES FOR UNAUTHORIZED FOREIGN FISHING

STATE	Fines		Imprisonment	Forfeiture		
	Local Currency	U.S.$ equivalent		Vessel	Gear	Catch
ALBANIA		N O I N F O R M A T I O N				
ALGERIA	5 000 - 50 000 DA double for second offence	US $ 1 096-10 965	15 days - 6 months for second offence	Court may order on second offence.	COURT SHALL ORDER	
ANGOLA	6 000 000 Kz + 50 000 Kz per GRT*	US $ 202 566 US $ 1 688	NO		COURT MAY ORDER	
ANTIGUA AND BARBUDA	Up to $500 000	US $ 201 410	NO	COURT MAY ORDER		COURT SHALL ORDER
ARGENTINA	Fines expressed in US $ denomination	US $ 10 000 up to US $ 1 000 000	NO	COURT MAY ORDER**	COURT MAY ORDER	COURT SHALL ORDER
AUSTRALIA	Not exceeding $ 5 000 (summary conviction***) $ 250 000 (indictment)	US $ 4 348 US $ 217 391	NO	C O U R T M A Y O R D E R		

* Fishing or preparing to fish. Fines doubled for offences in territorial sea or during closed season and for 2nd offences. Fines tripled where explosives or poisons used.
** For serious and deliberate violations of the law, taking into account repeated offences, number of vessels, methods of fishing, size of catch and the conduct of the captain at the time of detention of the vessel.
*** A$ 25 000 for offence by body corporate of having possession or charge of vessel equipped with nets etc. in proclaimed area of fishing zone without statutory defence (having licence, gear stowed etc.)

TABLE E

PENALTIES FOR UNAUTHORIZED FOREIGN FISHING

STATE	Fines		Imprisonment	Forfeiture		
	Local Currency	U.S.$ equivalent		Vessel	Gear	Catch
BAHAMAS	$ 50 000 (summary conviction) Double for second offence	US $ 50 000 (summary conviction) Double for second offence	one year Double for second offence	C O U R T	M A Y	O R D E R
BAHRAIN	300 Dinars	US$	Up to 2 years	C O U R T	M A Y	O R D E R
BANGLADESH	100 000 taka	US $ 4 120	not exceeding 3 years (rigorous)	C O U R T	S H A L L	O R D E R
BARBADOS	Up to B$ 20 000 on summary conviction. up to B$ 50 000 on indictment	US $ 10 000 US $ 25 000	up to 2 years on summary conviction up to 5 years on indictment	C O U R T	M A Y	O R D E R
BELGIUM	1 500 up to 40 000 francs	US $ 30 to 808	NO	COURT	MAY	ORDER
BELIZE	B$ 500	US $ 253	6 months	C O U R T	M A Y	O R D E R
BENIN	200 000 to 4 000 000 francs CFA	US $ 540 to US $ 10 811	10 days to 6 months	C O U R T O N	S H A L L S E C O N D	O R D E R O F F E N C E

TABLE E
PENALTIES FOR UNAUTHORIZED FOREIGN FISHING

STATE	Fines		Imprisonment	Forfeiture		
	Local Currency	U.S.$ equivalent		Vessel	Gear	Catch
BRAZIL	Criminal offence punishable under criminal legislation inforce		NO	C O U R T	M A Y	O R D E R
BULGARIA	N O	I N F O R M A T I O N				
BURMA	Unspecified		Up to 10 years	C O U R T	M A Y	O R D E R
CAMEROON	[1 000 000 up to 4 000 000 francs CFA]*	[US $ 2 703 to US $ 10 811]	[NO]	[COURT	MAY ORDER	seized and sold]
	*Note: penalties given are those in force up to 1981. Penalties under new legislation adopted 1981 not yet known.					
CANADA	Up to C $25 000 (summary conviction) up to C $100 000 (on conviction on indictment) per person	US $ 4 065 US $ 20 325	NO	C O U R T	M A Y	O R D E R
CAPE VERDE ISLANDS	Up to 20 000 escudos per G.T. for unlicensed fishing in EEZ.	Up to US $ 297 per G.T.	Imprisonment provided for on second offence only	C O U R T	M A Y	O R D E R

TABLE E
PENALTIES FOR UNAUTHORIZED FOREIGN FISHING

STATE	Fines		Imprisonment	Forfeiture		
	Local Currency	U.S.$ equivalent		Vessel	Gear	Catch
CAPE VERDE ISLANDS (Cont'd)	Up to 35 000 escudos per G.T. for illegal fishing in archipelagic waters or territorial sea or for crustaceans in EEZ.	Up to US $ 520 per G.T.				
CHILE	Up to 5 times the value of the catch		Up to 3 years	-		CATCH FORFEITED
COLOMBIA	1 000 - 100 000 pesos	US $ 13 - 1 331	NO	Not clear whether vessels are included in forfeiture clauses in Decree Law of 1978 Art.181 and 184	COURT SHALL	ORDER
COMORO ISLANDS	10 to 80 million CFA double for second offence within 5 years	US $ 27 027 to 216 216	NO	COURT SHALL ORDER	COURT SHALL	ORDER

TABLE E
PENALTIES FOR UNAUTHORIZED FOREIGN FISHING

STATE	Fines		Imprisonment	Forfeiture		
	Local Currency	U.S.$ equivalent		Vessel	Gear	Catch
CONGO	200 000 up to 2 000 000 francs CFA double for second offence	US $ 541 to US $ 5 405	15 days up to 3 months on second offence			
	50 000 to 2 000 000 francs CFA	US $ 1 351 to 5 405	10 days to 6 months			
COSTA RICA	Criminal sanction for piracy under Penal Code (Art. 256) + fine of 100 pesos per NRT	US $ 100 per n.r.t.		COURT SHALL ORDER ON SECOND OFFENCE		catch forfeited
CUBA	N O		I N F O R	M A T I O N		
CYPRUS	Up to 25 pounds	US $ 49	Up to 3 months	COURT MAY ORDER		COURT SHALL ORDER
DENMARK	Unspecified fine	-	NO	C O U R T	M A Y	O R D E R
DJIBOUTI	Fines fixed by decree		NO			
DOMINICA	Up to EC $ 96 (Note: There are no specific provisions relating to foreign fishing)	US $ 35	Up to 6 months	C O U R T	M A Y	O R D E R

TABLE E

PENALTIES FOR UNAUTHORIZED FOREIGN FISHING

STATE	Fines		Imprisonment	Forfeiture		
	Local Currency	U.S.$ equivalent		Vessel	Gear	Catch
DOMINICAN REP.	RD $ 6 - 100	US $ 6 - 100	6 days up to 3 months (2nd offence)	COURT MAY ORDER ON SECOND OFFENCE COURT SHALL ORDER		
ECUADOR	Two times cost of permit (i.e. US $ 320 per NRT) Fine doubled on second offence	US $ 320 per n.r.t.	NO			catch forfeited
EGYPT	NO INFORMATION					
EL SALVADOR	10 000 - 200 000 Colons Doubled for second offence	US $ 2 564 US $ 51 282	NO	DIRECTORATE GENERAL MAY ORDER		
	<u>For illegal fishing for tuna or other pelagic migratory species</u> 100 - 250 Colons per n.r.t. 250 colons per n.r.t. on second offence	US $ 26 - 64 US $ 64	-			<u>For illegal fishing for tuna or other pelagic migratory species</u> FORFEITED ON SECOND OFFENCE

TABLE E
PENALTIES FOR UNAUTHORIZED FOREIGN FISHING

STATE	Fines		Imprisonment	Forfeiture		
	Local Currency	U.S.$ equivalent		Vessel	Gear	Catch
EQUATORIAL GUINEA	PENALTY NOT SPECIFIED IN LEGISLATION					
ETHIOPIA				Regulations may provide for confiscation of fishing vessels. No such regulations made.		
EUROPEAN COMMUNITY	SEE ENTRIES UNDER INDIVIDUAL MEMBER STATES					
FIJI	F $ 100 000	US $ 101 215	NO	COURT	MAY	ORDER
FINLAND	NO INFORMATION					
FRANCE	50 000 up to 500 000 francs Double for second offence	US $ to US $	NO			COURT MAY ORDER
GABON	1 000 000 5 000 000 francs CFA	US $ 2 703 US $ 13 514	1 to 6 months	COURT SHALL ORDER ON SECOND OFFENCE (within 2 years)		seized and sold

TABLE E
PENALTIES FOR UNAUTHORIZED FOREIGN FISHING

STATE	Fines		Imprisonment	Forfeiture		
	Local Currency	U.S.$ equivalent		Vessel	Gear	Catch
GAMBIA	Up to 500 000 dalasis	US $ 234 741	Up to 2 years	COURT MAY ORDER COURT SHALL ORDER ON SECOND OFFENCE	COURT	SHALL ORDER
GERMAN DEM. REP.	Up to 100 000 marks	US $ 40 816	NO			
GERMANY FED.REP.			N O	I N F O R	M A T	I O N
GHANA	Up to C 50 000 (on summary conviction)	US $ 18 182	Up to 2 years	C O U R T	M A Y	O R D E R
GREECE		N O	I N F O R	M A T I O N		
GRENADA	Up to $ 20 000 (on summary conviction) Up to $ 50 000 (on indictment)	US $ 7 407 US $ 18 519	Up to 2 years Up to 5 years (on indictment)	C O U R T	M A Y	O R D E R
GUATEMALA	Q 1 to Q 10 per day for master, officers and crew Q 100 up to 5 000 (to be paid before vessel released)	US $ 1 to 10 US $ 100 to 5 000	NO (except where applied against Guatemalan nationals by law of flag state)			COURT SHALL ORDER

TABLE E
PENALTIES FOR UNAUTHORIZED FOREIGN FISHING

STATE	Fines		Imprisonment	Forfeiture		
	Local Currency	U.S.$ equivalent		Vessel	Gear	Catch
GUINEA	Sylis 2 500 000 up to Sylis 4 500 000 Double for second offence	US $ 195 - 9 730	NO	C O U R T COURT MAY ORDER	M A Y COURT SHALL	O R D E R ORDER
GUINEA BISSAU	From up to 1 000 000 pesos (vessels under 100 G.T.)	US $ 24 814	No on first offence	COURT SHALL ORDER		
	To up to 15 000 000 pesos (vessles under 1 000 G.T.)	US $ 372 208				
	Factory ships up to 24 000 000 pesos. (increased 15% for vessels under 5 years old) Fishing in territorial waters (1974)	US $ 595 533	30 days - 2 years forced labour on second offence If second offence caused or could cause grave damage to fauna or flora, captain liable to forced labour 2-6 years	COURT MAY ORDER ON SECOND OFFENCE COURT SHALL ORDER in cases of serious damage.		
	Note: New legislation under consideration					
GUYANA	G $ 200 000 (on summary conviction)	US $ 66 667	NO	COURT MAY ORDER		Forfeited on conviction

TABLE E
PENALTIES FOR UNAUTHORIZED FOREIGN FISHING

STATE	Fines		Imprisonment	Forfeiture		
	Local Currency	U.S.$ equivalent		Vessel	Gear	Catch
HAITI	According to the infraction: 1 000 up to 25 000 gourdes on second offence	US $ 200 - US $ 5 000	1 up to 3 years (cumulative with fine on second offence)	-	COURT SHALL	ORDER
HONDURAS	At least 10 000 Lempiras	US $ 5 000	NO		COURT SHALL	ORDER
ICELAND	Kr. 10 000 to Kr. 1 000 000	US $ 435 to US $ 43 478	NO			
INDIA	Up to 1 000 000 Rs (offences in EEZ) Up to 1 500 000 Rs (offences in T.Sea)	US $ 101 937 US $ 152 905	NO (offences in EEZ) up to 3 years offences in T.Sea	Confiscation in mandatory Vessel	Gear	Catch
INDONESIA	Guilders 500 (each crew member and leader of fishing operations) (illegal fishing in territorial sea) (1927)		3 months (illegal fishing in territorial sea) (1927)	C O U R T (illegal fishing in territorial sea) (1927)	M A Y	O R D E R

TABLE E
PENALTIES FOR UNAUTHORIZED FOREIGN FISHING

STATE	Fines		Imprisonment	Forfeiture		
	Local Currency	U.S.$ equivalent		Vessel	Gear	Catch
IRAN		N O	I N F O R M A T I O N			
IRAQ	Up to ID 200	US $ 645	Up to 9 months	COURT MAY ORDER ON SECOND OFFENCE		COURT SHALL ORDER
IRELAND	Up to £ 100 000	US $ 128 205	NO	COURT MAY ORDER	COURT SHALL ORDER	
ISRAEL		N O	I N F O R M A T I O N			
ITALY	Up to Lit. 1 000 000 (fishing without registration)	US $ 662	Up to 2 years		COURT SHALL ORDER	
IVORY COAST	360 000 to 3 600 000 CFA	US $ 973 US $ 9 730	No for fishing offences in the exclusive economic zone	C O U R T M A Y O R D E R C O U R T S H A L L O R D E R O N S E C O N D O F F E N C E		
JAMAICA	Up to J $ 100	US $ 38	Up to 6 months in default of payment of fine	C O U R T M A Y O R D E R		

TABLE E
PENALTIES FOR UNAUTHORIZED FOREIGN FISHING

STATE	Fines		Imprisonment	Forfeiture		
	Local Currency	U.S.$ equivalent		Vessel	Gear	Catch
JAPAN	10 000 000	US $ 42 553	NO	C O U R T	M A Y	O R D E R
JORDAN	D 10 - 50	US $ 28 - 140	-	-	-	-
KAMPUCHEA		N O	I N F O R M A T I O N			
KENYA	Up to 20 000 shillings	US $ 1 667	Up to 2 years	C O U R T	M A Y	O R D E R
KIRIBATI	Up to $100 000	US $ 86 957	NO	C O U R T	M A Y	O R D E R
KOREA DEM.DEP.		N O	I N F O R M A T I O N			
REP. OF KOREA	Within the territorial sea up to 20 000 000 won	US $ 26 247	Up to 5 years	C O U R T	M A Y	O R D E R
KUWAIT	50 - 500 Dinars	US $	NO	C O U R T	M A Y	O R D E R
LEBANON	NO	INFORMATION				

TABLE E
PENALTIES FOR UNAUTHORIZED FOREIGN FISHING

STATE	Fines		Imprisonment	Forfeiture		
	Local Currency	U.S.$ equivalent		Vessel	Gear	Catch
LIBERIA	$ 5 000 to $ 50 000	US $ 5 000 to US $ 50 000	NO			COURT SHALL ORDER
LIBYA	£ 100	US $ 338	6 months		COURT	SHALL ORDER
MADAGASCAR	250 000 to 2 500 000 CFA	US $ 676 to US $ 6 751	10 days to 6 months	COURT (ON	SHALL SECOND	ORDER OFFENCE)
MALAYSIA	1 000 000 ringgit each for owner and master 100 000 ringgit for each crew member	US $	NO	COURT	MAY	ORDER
MALDIVES ISLANDS	Up to R. 150	Up to US $ 21.43	Banishment or house arrest for up to 6 months	-	-	-
MALTA	£ 4 000	US $ 9 524	3 months on second offence	COURT	SHALL	ORDER

TABLE E
PENALTIES FOR UNAUTHORIZED FOREIGN FISHING

STATE	Fines		Imprisonment	Forfeiture		
	Local Currency	U.S.$ equivalent		Vessel	Gear	Catch
MAURITANIA	According to the gross tonnage 500 000 up to 100 000 000 ouguiya Factory ships 120 000 000 up to 150 000 000 (on second offence within two years maximum of the fine) Fines increased by 20% if the vessel is less than 3 years old	US $ 9 363 US $ 1 872 659 US $ 2 247 191 US $ 2 808 989	NO	MINISTER MAY ORDER SEIZED AND SOLD ON SECOND OFFENCE OBLIGATORY SEIZURE - MINISTER MAY ORDER CONFISCATION		
MAURITIUS	200 000 rupees (new legislation under consideration)	US $ 17 980	Up to 5 years	COURT MAY ORDER		
MEXICO	75 000 pesos up to 300 000 pesos second offence double fine	US $ 504 to US $ 2 016	NO	-	COURT SHALL ORDER	
MONACO	NO INFORMATION					

TABLE E
PENALTIES FOR UNAUTHORIZED FOREIGN FISHING

STATE	Fines		Imprisonment	Forfeiture		
	Local Currency	U.S.$ equivalent		Vessel	Gear	Catch
MOROCCO	Up to 50 GRT D 50 000 to 100 000 51 to 100 GRT D 100 000 to 250 000 101 to 200 GRT D 250 000 to 500 000 201 to 500 GRT D 500 000 to 1 500 000 More than 500 GRT D 1 500 000 to 3 000 000	US $ 9 643 to US $ 15 267 US $ 15 267 to US $ 38 168 US $ 38 168 to US $ 76 336 US $ 76 336 US $ 229 008 US $ 229 008 to US $ 458 015	1 month up to 1 year		FIRST OFFENCE COURT MAY ORDER (SECOND OFFENCE COURT SHALL ORDER)	
MOZAMBIQUE	Esc.750 000-10 000 000	US $ 19 231 - 256 410	NO	CONFISCATED IF FINES NOT PAID WITHIN 15 DAYS COURT SHALL ORDER For offences in territorial sea and second offences		
NAMIBIA						
NAURU	$10 000 - 100 000 (owner and master) $5 000 (crew member)	US$ 9 259 - 92 593 US $ 4 630	1 year (owner/master) 6 months (crew member)	COURT	SHALL	ORDER

TABLE E
PENALTIES FOR UNAUTHORIZED FOREIGN FISHING

STATE	Fines		Imprisonment	Forfeiture		
	Local Currency	U.S.$ equivalent		Vessel	Gear	Catch
NETHERLANDS	SANCTIONS ACCORDING TO CRIMINAL LEGISLATION IN FORCE					
NETHERLAND ANTILLES	NO LEGISLATION DIRECTLY APPLICABLE					
NEW ZEALAND	Up to $ 100 000 (master) Up to $ 5 000 (crew)	US $ 71 429 US $ 3 572	NO	Foreited on conviction	COURT SHALL ORDER	
NEW ZEALAND DEPENDENT TERRITORIES - Tokelau	Unlicensed fishing in territorial sea up to $ 100 000 (owner and master) up to $ 5 000 (crew members) Unlicensed fishing in exclusive economic zone may be prohibited by regulation	US $ 66 225 US $ 3 312	NO	COURT MAY ORDER		

TABLE E
PENALTIES FOR UNAUTHORIZED FOREIGN FISHING

STATE	Fines		Imprisonment	Forfeiture		
	Local Currency	U.S.$ equivalent		Vessel	Gear	Catch
NEW ZEALAND ASSOCIATED STATES - Cook Islands	Up to $ 100 000 (owner and master Up to $ 5 000 (crew members)	US $ 66 225 US $ 3 312	NO	C O U R T	S H A L L	O R D E R
- Niue	Up to $ 100 000 (owner and master) Up to $ 15 000 (crew members)	US $ 66 225 US $ 9 934	Up to 10 years (owner and master) Up to 5 years (crew members)	C O U R T	S H A L L	O R D E R
NICARAGUA	Up to 15 000 US $	US $ 15 000	NO		COURT	MAY ORDER
NIGERIA	N. 500 per day (operating un-licensed motor fishing boat in Nigeria territo-rial waters) (Sea Fisheries Decree 1971)	US $ 720	1 year	C O U R T	M A Y	O R D E R
NORWAY	Unspecified fines (1976)		NO	C O U R T	M A Y	O R D E R

TABLE E
PENALTIES FOR UNAUTHORIZED FOREIGN FISHING

STATE	Fines		Imprisonment	Forfeiture		
	Local Currency	U.S.$ equivalent		Vessel	Gear	Catch
OMAN	R. 60 (Double on second offence)	US $ 174		COURT MAY ORDER ON THIRD OFFENCE		
PAKISTAN	Unspecified fine (Territorial waters and Maritime Zones Act, 1976) Up to 5 000 rupees (Exclusive Fishery Zone) (Regulation of fishing) Act, 1975.	US $ 391	Up to 3 years, (Territorial waters and Maritime Zones Act) NONE (Exclusive Fishery Zone) (Regulation of Fishing) Act 1975			COURT MAY ORDER
PANAMA	B. 10 000 up to B. 100 000	US $ 10 000 to 100 000	NO	On second offence		catch forfeited
PAPUA NEW GUINEA	K. 1 000 (summary conviction) K. 2 000 up to 10 000 (on indictment)	US $ 1 205 US $ 2 410 US $ 12 048	6 months (summary conviction) to 1 year (on indictment)	Forfeited on conviction	COURT SHALL ORDER	
PERU	4 x total of registration fee permit fee and operating licence fee. Doubled for second offence within 4 year period.	US $ 8 000 + US $ 640 per n.r.t. + US $ 80 per g.r.t.	NO			

TABLE E
PENALTIES FOR UNAUTHORIZED FOREIGN FISHING

STATE	Fines		Imprisonment	Forfeiture		
	Local Currency	U.S.$ equivalent		Vessel	Gear	Catch
PHILIPPINES	P 2 000 to 100 000 Leg. presidential Decree No. 1599 11 June, 1978	US $ 204 to 10 204	6 months up to 10 years	SUMMARILY	CONFISCATED	ADMINISTRATIVELY
POLAND	Up to 4 500 zloty (second offence 25 000 up to 100 000) (1963 data relating to foreign fishing in territorial waters only)	US $ 51 to US $ 284 to US $ 1 136	Up to 3 months (on second offence up to 1 year)		COURT MAY ORDER	
PORTUGAL	From 3 500 000 escudos up to value of vessel including gear and equipment Fines doubled for offences in territorial sea.	US $ 21 212	NO		COURT SHALL ORDER	

TABLE E
PENALTIES FOR UNAUTHORIZED FOREIGN FISHING

STATE	Fines		Imprisonment	Forfeiture		
	Local Currency	U.S.$ equivalent		Vessel	Gear	Catch
QATAR	2 000 Riyals Double for the second offence	US $	NO	COURT MAY ORDER ON THIRD OFFENCE		
ROMANIA	NO INFORMATION					
ST. CHRISTOPHER & NEVIS	Up to $300 000	US $ 201 410	NO	COURT MAY ORDER		COURT SHALL ORDER
ST. LUCIA	Up to $500 000	US $ 201 410	NO	COURT MAY ORDER		COURT SHALL ORDER
ST. VINCENT	NEW LEGISLATION UNDER CONSIDERATION					
SAO TOME AND PRINCIPE	Db 500-1 000 (artisanal fishing) Db 50 000-100 000 (semi-industrial) Db50 000-100 000 perGT (pelagic not tuna) Db70 000-150 000 perGT (Tuna fishing) (All payable in convertible currency)	US $ 13-25 US $ 1 240-2 478 US $ US $ 14 126	NO	May be sold if fines not paid in 30 days		Seized and declared forfeit

TABLE E
PENALTIES FOR UNAUTHORIZED FOREIGN FISHING

STATE	Fines		Imprisonment	Forfeiture		
	Local Currency	U.S.$ equivalent		Vessel	Gear	Catch
SAUDI ARABIA	10 000 Riyals	US $	Up to 6 months			
SENEGAL	15 000 000 to 50 000 000 Francs CFA 1 500 000 + payment of licence fees for vessels from countries with reciprocal agreements. Fines doubled on second offence	US $ 40 541 to US $ 135 135 US $ 4 054	6 months to 2 years	COURT	MAY	ORDER
SEYCHELLES	750 000 Rs	US $ 114 155	NO	COURT MAY ORDER (ON SECOND OFFENCE COURT SHALL ORDER)		COURT SHALL ORDER
SIERRA LEONE	Up to 20 000 leones on summary conviction Up to 500 000 leones on indictment	US $ 8 000 US $ 200 000	Up to 3 years Up to 5 years		COURT MAY ORDER	
SINGAPORE	NO INFORMATION					
SOLOMON ISLANDS	$ 250 000	US $ 225 225	NO	COURT	MAY	ORDER

TABLE E
PENALTIES FOR UNAUTHORIZED FOREIGN FISHING

STATE	Fines		Imprisonment	Forfeiture		
	Local Currency	U.S.$ equivalent		Vessel	Gear	Catch
SOMALIA	5 000 to 100 000 Som. Shs.	US $ 331	NO			
	Fine doubled on second offence and captain liable for criminal offence	US $ 6 623	On second offence captain liable for criminal offence	COURT MAY ORDER ON SECOND OFFENCE		
SOUTH AFRICA	Up to 7 500 rands	US $ 6 944	Up to 5 years	COURT MAY ORDER ON SECOND OFFENCE	COURT MAY	ORDER
SPAIN	1 000 000 to 4 000 000 Pes. (Not to exceed 35% of value of boat, + gear.	US $ 7 194 US $ 28 777	NO			
SRI LANKA	Up to Rps. 1 500 000	US $ 65 502	NO	COURT	SHALL	ORDER
SUDAN	Up to LS 50	US $ 38	Up to 3 months	COURT	MAY	ORDER

TABLE E
PENALTIES FOR UNAUTHORIZED FOREIGN FISHING

STATE	Fines		Imprisonment	Forfeiture		
	Local Currency	U.S.$ equivalent		Vessel	Gear	Catch
SURINAME	Up to 500 000 guilders	US $ 282 486	Up to 6 years	COURT MAY ORDER? (Power to confiscate objects used to commit offence)	COURT	MAY ORDER
SWEDEN	N O		I N F O R M	A T I O N		
SYRIAN ARAB. REP.	Double amount of annual licence fee Double for second offence		One month for second offence			COURT SHALL ORDER
TANZANIA	Up to 10 000 sh Second offence up to 20 000 sh.	US $ 1 046 US $ 2 092	Up to 2 years Up to 5 years	C O U R T	M A Y	O R D E R
THAILAND	Up to 2 000 Baht	US $ 87	1 year	C O U R T	M A Y	O R D E R
TOGO	120 000 up to 1 200 000 francs CFA Fine doubled on second offence	US $ 324 to US $ 3 243	On second offence 15 days up to 3 months	Vessel may be seized in case of contravention within a 12 mile area	COURT SHALL	ORDER ON SECOND OFFENCE

TABLE E

PENALTIES FOR UNAUTHORIZED FOREIGN FISHING

STATE	Fines		Imprisonment	Forfeiture		
	Local Currency	U.S.$ equivalent		Vessel	Gear	Catch
TONGA	Up to T$ 100 000	US $ 90 910	Up to 5 years	C O U R T	M A Y	O R D E R
TRINIDAD AND TOBAGO	N E W L E G I S L A T I O N U N D E R C O N S I D E R A T I O N					
TUNISIA	10 000 up to 1 000 000 Francs Max. on second offence	US $	15 days up to 1 year Max on 2nd offence	C O U R T	M A Y	O R D E R.
TURKEY	Fines to be decided on by the court		2 to 4 years	S E I Z E D	S E I Z E D	S E I Z E D
TUVALU	$ 100 000	US $ 86 957	NO	C O U R T	M A Y	O R D E R
USSR	Up to 10 000 roubles (admin. procedure) Up to 100 000 roubles (judicial procedures)	US $ 13 661 US $ 136 612	NO	C O U R T	M A Y	O R D E R

TABLE E
PENALTIES FOR UNAUTHORIZED FOREIGN FISHING

STATE	Fines		Imprisonment	Forfeiture		
	Local Currency	U.S.$ equivalent		Vessel	Gear	Catch
UNITED ARAB EMIRATES	1 000 Darhams Double on second offence	US$ -	NO	COURT	MAY	ORDER ON THIRD OFFENCE
UNITED KINGDOM	Up to £ 50 000 on summary conviction	US $ 80 257	NO		COURT MAY	ORDER
U.K. DEPENDANT TERRITORIES - Bermuda	Up to US $ 50 000 (Double on second offence)	US $ 50 000	Up to 1 year (Double on second offence)	COURT MAY ORDER		
- British Virgin Islands	Up to $ 10 000 on summary conviction	US $ 10 000	Up to 1 year	COURT	MAY	ORDER
		(NEW LEGISLATION UNDER CONSIDERATION)				
- Cayman Islands	Unlicensed taking of coral, algae, sponge, turtle egg hermit crabs only an offence, up to $ 500 (new legislation under consideration)	US $ 600	Up to 6 months	COURT MAY	ORDER	

TABLE E
PENALTIES FOR UNAUTHORIZED FOREIGN FISHING

STATE	Fines		Imprisonment	Forfeiture		
	Local Currency	U.S.$ equivalent		Vessel	Gear	Catch
- Pitcairn, Henderson, Ducie and Oeno Islands	Fine up to $ 100 000		NO	C O U R T	M A Y	O R D E R
- Turks and Caicos	$ 50 000	US $ 19 231	Up to 1 year	C O U R T	M A Y ORDER	
- Montserrat	$ 100 000		NO	C O U R T	M A Y	O R D E R
USA	Criminal penalty Up to $ 100 000 Civil penalty Up to $ 25 000	US $ 100 000 US $ 25 000	None for illegal fishing; 6 months to 10 years for interfering with enforcement	C O U R T	M A Y	O R D E R
U.S. TRUST TERRITORIES - FEDERATED STATES OF MICRONESIA	Up to $50 000 (criminal penalty) Up to $75 000 (civil penalty)	US $ 50 000 US $ 75 000	NO	C O U R T	M A Y	O R D E R

TABLE E

PENALTIES FOR UNAUTHORIZED FOREIGN FISHING

STATE	Fines		Imprisonment	Forfeiture		
	Local Currency	U.S.$ equivalent		Vessel	Gear	Catch
U.S. TRUST TERRITORIES - MARSHALL ISLANDS	Up to $50 000 (criminal penalty)	US $ 50 000	NO	COURT	MAY	ORDER
- PALAU	Up to $50 000 (criminal penalty)	US $ 50 000	NO	COURT	MAY	ORDER
URUGUAY	Fine to be fixed yearly = not exceeding 50% of the value of vessel and cargo	US $ 5 000 - 100 000 (1971 data)	NO	COURT SHALL ORDER ON SECOND OFFENCE	COURT MAY ORDER ON FIRST OFFENCE	COURT MAY ORDER ON FIRST OFFENCE; COURT SHALL ORDER ON SECOND OFFENCE
VANUATU	Up to 20 000 000 Vatu	US $ 201 410	NO	COURT MAY ORDER	COURT MAY ORDER	COURT SHALL ORDER
VENEZUELA	B 50 - 10 000 (1944)	US $ 5 - 1 000	NO			
VIETNAM	Up to VN Dong 10 000 Criminal penalties for repeated offences or serious consequences	US $ 667	NO			

TABLE E
PENALTIES FOR UNAUTHORIZED FOREIGN FISHING

STATE	Fines		Imprisonment	Forfeiture		
	Local Currency	U.S.$ equivalent		Vessel	Gear	Catch
WESTERN SAMOA	Up to 100 000 tala	US $ 63 291	Up to 5 years	C O U R T	M A Y	O R D E R
	(Up to 100 000 tala - owner or master	US $ 63 291		(C O U R T	S H A L L	O R D E R)*
	Up to 5 000 tala for each crew member)*	US $ 3 165				
YEMEN ARAB REP.	Up to 1 000 rials	US $ 218	Up to 1 year	C O U R T	M A Y	O R D E R
YEMEN PEOPLES DEM. REP.	Unspecified fine	US$	Up to 3 years	C O U R T	M A Y	O R D E R
YUGOSLAVIA	100 000 - 3 000 000 Dinars	US $ 1 207 US $ 36 210	NO	C O U R T O N S E C O N D	MAY	O R D E R O F F E N C E
ZAIRE	20 000 Z	US $ 3 436	Up to one month	C O U R T Vessel	MAY Gear	O R D E R Catch

TABLE E

Penalties for unlicensed foreign fishing

References to legislative sources

Albania	-	-
Algeria	-	Ordinance N° 76-84, General Regulation of Fisheries, 23 October 1976, Art. 88-89.
Angola	-	Decree N° 12-A/80 of 6 February 1980, Art. 8.
Antigua & Barbuda	-	The Fisheries Act, 1983, SS. 8(6) 33.
Argentina	-	Act N° 17.500 on fisheries development of 25 October 1967, as amended by Act N° 20.136 of 5 February 1973, Art. 12 and Art. N° 22.018 of 21 June 1979.
Australia	-	Fisheries Act, 1952-85 S. 13 AB, B and C.
Bahamas	-	Fisheries Resources (Jurisdiction and Conservation) Act, 1977 SS. 16, 19 and 21 and 1st Schedule.
Bahrein	-	Decree Promulgating Law N° 5 of 1981 on Fishing Regulation Act 17 (B).
Bangladesh	-	Marine Fisheries Ordinance, 1983, S. 22.
Barbados	-	Marine Boundaries and Jurisdiction Act, 1978 S. 6.
Belgium	-	Act establishing a fishing zone of 10 October 1978, Art. 6.
Belize	-	Fisheries Ordinance CAP133, S. 10.
Benin	-	Ordinance N° 68-38 of 18 June 1968 (Merchant Shipping Code), Art. 288 as amended by Ordinance N° 69-39 of 9 December 1969.
Brazil	-	Decree Law N° 221 of 28 February 1967, Art. 9.
Bulgaria	-	-
Burma	-	Territorial Sea and Maritime Zones Law 1977 S. 21.
Cameroon United Rep. of	-	[Act N° 74/12 of 16 July 1974 (The Fisheries Code) Art. 31] now repealed and replaced by Law N° 81-13 of 27 November 1981 [Complete text not yet available].
Canada	-	Coastal Fisheries Protection Act (as amended 1984) SS. 6-8.
Cape Verde Islands	-	Decree Law N° 126-77 of 31 December 1977, Art. 13.

TABLE E

Penalties for unlicensed foreign fishing

References to legislative sources

Country		Reference
Chile	-	Customs Ordinance, 1953, Article 194 Note: US-NMFS-IFR-80/141 gives the penalties as US$120 per n.r.t. apparently on the basis of Decree Law N° 500 of 3 June 1974. This Decree, however, ceased to be in force on 31/12/1977.
China	-	-
Colombia	-	Decree N° 1681 of 4 August 1978, Art. 178 and 181.
Comoros Islands	-	Act. N° 82-015 of 6 and 11 May 1982, Art. 14.
Congo	-	Ordinance 22-70 of 14 July 1970, Art. 26.
Costa Rica	-	Decree N° 6267 of 1978, Art. 6.
Cuba	-	-
Cyprus	-	Fisheries Law, 1931, S. 3.
Denmark	-	Saltwater Fisheries Act, 1965. S. 33-34.
Djibouti	-	Law N° 52/AN/78 of 9 January 1979, Art. 19.
Dominica	-	The Fisheries ordinance, S. 12. (Fisheries Law).
Dominican Rep.	-	Law No. 5914 of 22 May 1962, Art. 47 and 49.
Ecuador	-	Act on Fisheries and Fisheries Development 1974, Art. 83.
Egypt	-	-
El Salvador	-	General Law on Fisheries Activities, Arts. 65 and 68; Art. 81 for tuna.
Equatorial Guinea	-	Law No. 15/1984 of 12 November on the Territorial Sea and Exclusive Economic Zone of the Republic of Equatorial Guinea. Art. 14.
Ethiopia	-	-
Fiji	-	Marine Spaces Act, 1977 SS. 14 and 16.
Finland	-	-
France	-	Law N° 85-542 of 22 May 1985, Art. 1 (Act. 10).

TABLE E

Penalties for unlicensed foreign fishing

References to legislative sources

Gabon	- Act N° 18-70 of 17 December 1970, Art. 1.
Gambia	- Fisheries Act, 1977 SS. 23 and 44.
German Dem. Republic	- Decree on Fishing in the Fisheries Zone of 13 October 1978, Art. 10.
Germany Fed. Republic	- -
Ghana	- Fisheries Decree 1979 S. 1.
Greece	- -
Grenada	- Marine Boundaries Act, 1978 S. 6-11.
Guatemala	- Decree No. 1412 of 7 December 1960 Art. 2-4.
Guinea	- Marine Fisheries Code, 1985 S. 57, 63 and 64.
Guinea Bissau	- Decree N° 24-78 of 7 August 1978, Art. 1 and 2. (New legislation under consideration).
Guyana	- Maritime Boundaries Act, 1977 SS. 25, 27, 28.
Haiti	- Decree of 27 October 1978, Art. 132.
Honduras	- Decree N° 154 of 9 June 1959, Art. 75.
Iceland	- Regulations concerning the fishery limits off Iceland and 15 July 1975, Art. 6.
India	- The Maritime Zones of India (Regulation of Fishing by Foreign Vessels) Act, 1981 S. 10 and 13.
Indonesia	- Coastal Fishery Ordinance 1927, Art. 15.
Iran	- -
Iraq	- Law N° 48 of 1976 for regulating and exploitation of Aquatic life and its protection, Art. 28.
Ireland	- Fisheries (amendment) Act, 1978 (N° 18) S. 2 and 4.
Israel	- -

TABLE E

Penalties for unlicensed foreign fishing

References to legislative sources

Italy	- Act N° 963 regulating sea fishing of 14 July 1965, Art. 25-26.
Ivory Coast	- Act N° 61-349 of 9 November 1961 (Merchant Shipping Code), Art. 218-9 as amended by Act N° 77.926 of 17 November 1976, Art. 5.
Jamaica	- The Fishing Industry Act, 1971, S. 18.
Japan	- Law on Provisional Measures relating to the Fishing Zone, Law N° 31 of 2 May 1977, S. 17.
Jordan	- Agrarian Law No. 20 of 1973, Art 186.
Kampuchea Dem.	- -
Kenya	- The Fish Industry Act 1968, S. 9 and 11.
Kiribati	- Fisheries Ordinance 1977, S. 7 and 15.
Korea (Dem. Rep.)	- -
Korea Rep. of	- The Territorial Sea Law of 31 December 1977, S. 7.
Kuwait	- Decree promulgating Law N° 46 of 1980 on Conservation of Fisheries Resources Art. 12.
Lebanon	- -
Libya	- Law N° 8 of 1962 regulating Fishing, Art. 30-31.
Liberia	- Revised Fishing Rules and Regulations 1973.
Madagascar	- Ordinance N° 60-047 of 1966, as amended (Merchant Shipping Code) S. 7.7.05 and 7.7.07.
Malaysia	- Fisheries Act, 1984 S. 25 and 34.
Maldives Islands	- Penal Code.
Malta	- Fish Industry Act, 1953-1979, S. 13.
Mauritania	- Code of Merchant Shipping, Act No. 78-043 of 28 February 1978, Art. 206 as amended.
Mauritius	- Maritime Zones Act, 1977, S. 12.

TABLE E

Penalties for unlicensed foreign fishing

References to legislative sources

Mexico	- Federal Law on Fisheries Development of 10 May 1972, Art. 93.
Monaco	- -
Morocco	- Act N° 1-73-255 of 23 November 1973, Art. 37-9 as amended by Act. N° 1-78-877 of 28 March 1979.
Mozambique	- Decree Law N° 31/76 of 19 August 1976, Art. 8 and 17.
Namibia	- -
Nauru	- Marine Resources Act, 1978, S. 11 and 14.
Netherlands	- -
Netherlands Antilles	- -
New Zealand	- Territorial Sea and Exclusive Economic Zone Act, 1977, S. 29.
New Zealand Dep. Territories	
- Tokelau	- Tokelau (Territorial Sea and Exclusive Economic Zone) Act, 1977, S. 8.
New Zealand Associated States	
- Cook Islands	- Territorial Sea and Exclusive Economic Zone Act, 1977, S. 17.
- Niue	- Territorial Sea and Exclusive Economic Zone Act, 1978, S. 17.
Nicaragua	- Special Law on Fishing Exploitation of 12 January 1961, Art. 45.
Nigeria	- Sea Fisheries Decree 1971, S. 1-10.
Norway	- Regulations relating to foreign fishing in the economic zone of Norway of 13 May 1977, S. 15.
Oman	- Sultanic Decree No. 53/81, promulgating the law on Marine Fisheries and Conservation of Living Aquatic Resources, Art. 28.

TABLE E

Penalties for unlicensed foreign fishing

References to legislative sources

Pakistan	-	Exclusive Fishery Zone (Regulation of Fishing) Act, 1975, S. 9.
Panama	-	Fiscal Code Art. 297 as amended by Decree Law N° 11 of 27 April 1967.
Papua New-Guinea	-	Fisheries Act 1974, S. 15-17 as amended by the Fisheries (Amendment) Use of Foreign Boats) Act, 1978.
Peru	-	Supreme Decree N° 077-71 PE of 1971. (Regulations for enforcement of Decree Law No. 18810), Art. 273. Supreme Decree N° 005-73-PE, Art. 1A (1).
Philippines	-	Fisheries Decree, 1975, S. 38-39.
Poland	-	Sea Fishing Act of 21 May 1963, S. 40 and 44.
Portugal	-	Decree Law N° 198/84 of 14 June 1984, Art. 4 & 5.
Qatar	-	Law N° 4 of 1983 on Exploitation and Conservation of Living Aquatic Resources in Qatar, Art. 26.
Romania	-	-
St. Christopher and Nevis	-	The Fisheries Act 1984 S. 8(6); 34.
St. Lucia	-	The Fisheries Act 1984 S. 8(6); 33.
St. Vincent & the Grenadines	-	-
Sao Tome & Principe	-	Decree Law N° 63/81 of 31 December 1981, Arts. 38, 39, 40, 41, 47, 35, 36.
Saudi Arabia	-	Fishing Regulation Exploitation and Conservation of Living Aquatic Resources Scheme. Art. 13.
Senegal	-	Act N° 76-89 of 2 July 1976 (Maritime Fisheries Code) Arts. 53, 55, 58.
Seychelles	-	Control of Foreign Fishing Vessels Decree, 1979, S. 12 and 16.

TABLE E

Penalties for unlicensed foreign fishing

References to legislative sources

Sierra Leone	- Fisheries Ordinance 1957-77 S. 3.
Singapore	- -
Solomon Islands	- Fisheries Ordinance 1972-1977, S. 7 and 16.
Somalia	- Law on the Somali Territorial Sea and Ports of 10 September 1972, Art. 5.
South Africa	- Sea Fisheries Act, 1973, S. 16-17.
Spain	- Act No. 53 of 13 July 1982, Arts. 6 and 7
Sri Lanka	- Fisheries (Regulation of Foreign Fishing Boats) Act, 1979, S. 15, 18.
Sudan	- Marine Fisheries Ordinance, S. 10.
Suriname	- Law on the extension of the territorial sea and the establishment of a contiguous economic zone 14 April 1978, Arts. 7, 8 and 15 and Decree C-14 of 31 December 1980 regulating the field of Sea Fishery Arts. 27, 28, 34.
Syrian Arab. Republic	- Legislative Decree No. 30 of 1964 on the protection of aquatic life, S. 51.
Tanzania	- Fisheries (General) Regulations, 1973, S. 43.
Thailand	- Act governing the right to fish in Thai fishery waters, 1939, S. 10 and 11.
Togo	- Act N° 64-14 of 11 July 1964, Art. 5-6.
Tonga	- Fisheries Protection Act, 1973, S. 3.
Trinidad & Tobago	- New legislation under preparation.
Tunisia	- Decree of 26 July 1951 revising the legislation on the regulation of Maritime Fisheries, Act. 37, 53 and 55.
Turkey	- -
Tuvalu	- Fisheries Ordinance, 1978, S. 5-15.

TABLE E

Penalties for unlicensed foreign fishing

References to legislative sources

USSR	- Decree of the Presidium of the Supreme Soviet of the USSR, of 10 December 1976, S. 7.
United Arab Emirates	- Federal Law of 1982 on the Exploitation and Conservation of Living Aquatic Resources, Act. 28.
United Kingdom	- Fishery Limits Act, 1976. S. 2.
U.K. Dependant Territories	
- Bermuda	- Fisheries Act 1972-1977, S. 7.
- British Virgin Islands	- The Fisheries Ordinance, 1979, S. 7.
- Cayman Islands	- The Marine Conservation Law, 1978, S. 25.
- Montserrat	- Ordinance N° 18 of 1982, Sec. 16.
- Pitcairn, Henderson, Ducie and Oeno Islands	- Fisheries Zone Ordinance, 1980, Sects. 5 and 9.
- Turk & Caicos	- -
USA	- Magnusson Fishery Conservation and Management Act of 1976, S. 308-310.
US Trust Territories	
- Federated States of Micronesia	- Trust Territory Code Title 52 Sec. 202, 203, 204.
- Marshall Islands	- Marshall Islands Marine Jurisdiction Act of 1978 Sec. 8.416, 8.417.
- Palau	- Public Law N° 6-7-14 of 1978 Sec. 16, 17.
Uruguay	- Decree N° 711/971 of 28 October 1971, Art. 42.
Vanuatu	- The Fisheries Act No. 37 of 1982 Sec. 4, 28.

TABLE E

Penalties for unlicensed foreign fishing

References to legislative sources

Venezuela	-	Fishery Act of 10 August 1944, Art. 27.
Vietnam	-	Enactment No. 30 of January 29 1980 on regimes and regulations allowing foreign ships to operate in the sea areas of the Scoailist Republic of Vietnam, Art. 24.
Western Samoa	-	Exclusive Economic Zone Act 1977, Sec. 9.
Yemen Arab. Republic	-	Fisheries Law of 1976, Art. 13.
Yemen dem. Republic	-	The Act of 1977 concerning the territorial sea exclusive economic zone, continental shelf and other marine areas, Art. 21.
Yugoslavia	-	Law of 22 May 1965 on Yugoslavian marginal seas, contiguous zone and continental shelf, Art. 51.
Zaire	-	Ordinance N° 79-244 of 16 October 1979, Art. 25.